REIMAGINING *GOD* AND *RELIGION*:
Essays for the Psychologically Minded

Jerry R. Wright, D.Min.

CHIRON PUBLICATIONS · ASHEVILLE, NORTH CAROLINA

www.ChironPublications.com
Interior and cover design by Danijela Mijailović
Printed primarily in the United States of America.

"Love After Love" from THE POETRY OF DEREK WALCOTT 1948-2013 by Derek Walcott, selected by Glyn Maxwell. Copyright © 2014 by Derek Walcott. Reprinted by permission of Farrar, Straus and Giroux.

"When Death Comes" - from *New and Selected Poems*, by Mary Oliver, Published by Beacon Press, Boston; Copyright © 1992 by Mary Oliver; Reprinted by permission of The Charlotte Sheedy Literary Agency Inc.

"Du bist die Zukunft.../You are the future...," by Rainer Maria Rilke, and "Alles wird wieder gross.../All will come again into its strength" by Rainer Maria Rilke; from *Rilke's Book of Hours* by Rainer Maria Rilke, translated by Anita Barrows and Joanna Macy, translation copyright © 1996 by Anita Barrows and Joanna Macy. Used by permission of Riverhead, an imprint of Penguin Publishing Group, a division of Penguin Random House LLC. All rights reserved.

"The Man Watching" -- from *Selected Poems of Rainer Maria Rilke*, translation by Robert Bly, copyright 1981, used by permission of HarperCollins.

"I Have Learned So Much" - From *The Gift*, by Daniel Ladinsky, copyright 1999, and used with permission.

ISBN 978-1-63051-495-2 paperback
ISBN 978-1-63051-496-9 hardcover
ISBN 978-1-63051-497-6 electronic
ISBN 978-1-63051-498-3 limited edition paperback

Library of Congress Cataloging-in-Publication Data
Names: Wright, Jerry R., author.
Title: Reimagining God and religion : essays for the psychologically minded / Jerry R. Wright, D.Min.
Description: Asheville : Chiron Publications, 2018. | Includes bibliographical references and index.
Identifiers: LCCN 2018000493| ISBN 9781630514952 (pbk. : alk. paper) | ISBN
  9781630514969 (hardcover : alk. paper)
Subjects: LCSH: Psychology, Religious. | Psychology and religion. | Jungian psychology. | God. | Religion. | Jesus Christ.
Classification: LCC BL53 .W75 2018 | DDC 200.1/9--dc23
LC record available at https://lccn.loc.gov/2018000493

Front cover photo: *Iona Sunrise*, Courtesy of Wade Sellers.
Author photo: *Cave on West Beach*, Iona, Scotland.

For my lifelong friends made on pilgrimages
To Iona, Ireland, Peru, and India
Where we learned that all places
Are *thin* and sacred
And all people are one.

Praise for
Reimagining God and Religion: Essays for the Psychologically Minded

Jerry Wright's Reimagining God and Religion is a personally honest, courageous, and insightful re-examination of our contemporary religious dilemma. He steps outside the fundamentalist's need for security and employs the insights of depth psychology to reappropriate received wisdom in forms which respect the intellectual integrity of the modern, thus rescuing the timeless insights of the tradition, thus making them available anew. One cannot read this book without learning something important, without being confronted in one's fixed positions. This book is a gift for those who care about the life of the spirit, whatever their traditions, or lack thereof, may be.

-**James Hollis**, Ph. D., Jungian Analyst and author of fifteen books, most recently *Living an Examined Life: Wisdom for the Second Half of the Journey.*

Jerry Wright invites the reader to value passion for life and compassion for all more than the literalism and fundamentalism of religious traditions. He masterfully utilizes Jungian psychology to expose the shadow side of religions that claim superiority and exclusivity bestowed by their view of God. His candid picture of the destructive energies that grow out of such attitudes is a clarion call for all to grow up spiritually!

-**Kathleen Wiley, MHDL**, Jungian Analyst, author of *New Life: Symbolic Meditations on the Promise of Easter and Spring.*

A bold invitation to faithfully imagine the Sacred at the heart of you and everything. In other words, the kingdom of god is within you.

-**John Philip Newell,** author of *The Rebirthing of God.*

By weaving together his deep grasp of psychology, theology, science, and poetry, Dr. Wright sets out to reimagine the mysteries around us, within us, and just beyond our grasp. With his open-minded voice of conviction, he challenges traditional religious dogma and certitude, concluding, "if religions are dropped down fully formed from some remote domain and deity, written in stone, unchangeable, and gifted to a very few, our future as a species will be very bleak." Plunge into this thought provoking book and devour the power and hope that Jerry Wright has reimagined.

-**Alice Smith**, poet, author of several poetry volumes, including *The Rhythm of Stillness.*

This book is a real treasure for the spiritual or psychological pilgrim searching for tools in the quest for consciousness. It is well thought out and researched both theologically and psychologically using the tools of analytical psychology. This book can be a real asset to individuation or spiritual growth. An added bonus is the writer's courage in interweaving his personal journey into the fiber of the material.

-**Ben F. Toole**, Jungian Analyst, Inter-Regional Society of Jungian Analysts, Memphis-Atlanta Jung Seminar

ACKNOWLEDGEMENTS

Birthing a book that is both personal testament and psychological commentary requires an extensive gestation period. All that I have learned and experienced, all the teachers, mentors, analysts, clients, family, friends, and colleagues who have left their indelible mark on my psyche have sat on my shoulder during the writing process. Some offered encouragement, others provided puzzled looks, still others offered advice to include this or that; some cautioned me to avoid the more controversial topics. An author must decide what is true for him or her, then engage in the laborious task of waiting for the best words or images to emerge and, finally, take responsibility for what feels like a tender, fragile child offered for public view and critique.

Among the multiple voices, the sage advice of Howard Thurman (author, philosopher, civil rights leader) continued to come to the forefront. Paraphrasing, he wrote, there are two questions that life presents to us again and again: "Where am I going? Who will go with me?" They must be asked in that order, he advised, or else one's integrity is compromised or vanishes altogether. If we alter the order, we will forever dance to the music of others or be slave to another's opinion, myth, or authority. While I have appreciated both comforters and critics, I take responsibility for the writing.

Among my traveling companions on this labyrinthine path called life, I want to acknowledge with gratitude those who have shared pilgrimages with me, those who have attended retreats and conferences, and those parishioners and analysands who have allowed me entry to their lives and souls. I have offered many words, images, and ideas, and received much more in return.

Special thanks to the professionals at Chiron Publications who helped me navigate the publication maze, and to friend Susan Smartt for her keen and kind editorial eye in the final stages of the manuscript.

To my wife, Kay, whose memory has abandoned her but whose love and devotion have never wavered over our fifty-three years, I am especially indebted and grateful. In the words of singer/songwriter Dan Tyler (dantyler@dantyler.net), *everything must change, but love remains.*

As far as we can discern,
the sole purpose of human existence
is to kindle a light
in the darkness of mere being.
(C. G. Jung)

REIMAGINING *GOD* AND *RELIGION*
Essays for the Psychologically Minded

INTRODUCTION

'Tis the season of Advent on a Tuesday before noon, and already two inner protests that will sound heretical to most Christians, and probably are, have surfaced. While sitting in the dentist's chair, one of the beloved Christmas carols of my childhood, "O Little Town of Bethlehem," came wafting through the speakers in the ceiling, a welcomed aural distraction from the oral procedure being performed. When the lovely disembodied voice got to the beginning of the second stanza, *For Christ is born of Mary*, an inner inaudible voice protested, *No, Jesus was born to Mary, not Christ! Christmas is about the birth of Jesus, not Christ!*

Driving home a short time later, a local radio preacher was complaining that the Christian greeting, *Merry Christmas*, was being replaced by the secular wish, *Happy Holidays*, and he went on to advocate that we need *to put Christ back into Christmas*, which echoed something I had preached numerous times in my former professional life as a Presbyterian minister. However, this morning that inaudible inner heretic responded, *No, we actually need to keep Christ out of Christmas so that we can celebrate the birth of Jesus!*

It is now a couple of hours later, and the sky has not yet fallen on my head, thankfully. I am also grateful that these two experiences now provide introductory sentences to this book, which may give my inner heretic a larger voice. Perhaps this inner companion will then permit me a full night's sleep; I can only hope.

A few days ago, a third experience presented itself that rounds out an introductory trinity, again perhaps to some readers an unholy triad. A very thoughtful neighbor from a nearby community dropped by to present us with a small gift, as he has done for many neighbors the last few years during Advent. I know very little about his life and story, only that he is a retired Christian missionary. After chatting amicably for a few

9

minutes, we thanked him for his gracious gift, and he turned to leave wishing us a *Merry Christmas*, which we gladly reciprocated. As he walked toward his car, he turned abruptly as if something inside compelled him to say one more thing. *Only this morning,* he added, *I was in the barbershop and someone wished me 'Happy Holidays' which gave me the opportunity to declare that I am a 'Merry Christmas' person and 'Happy Holidays' is inappropriate for the real reason for the season.* I simply nodded and grunted, drawing on my training as a psychoanalyst, and waited for what might come next. Sure enough, he had more to say. He reported that he had also been in the local post office that morning to buy stamps. To his dismay, they were selling stamps not only with the image of the Madonna and Child but stamps that celebrate the Jewish and Islamic religions and holidays, as well. His tone was one of disgust. Without further thought or analysis, I spontaneously and genuinely said, *Oh, that's a good thing!* To which he replied categorically, *No, it isn't. It's an awful thing!*

Now, we were in a conversation, if not a dialogue. I insisted, *Yes, it's a good thing to acknowledge and honor other religions.* Without remembering in the moment that he had spent his professional life as a missionary likely promoting the exclusive salvific claims of Christianity, I added, *We have to get past the notion that we Christians have an exclusive claim to God and to truth,* and to bolster my argument included, *and if we don't, we may contribute to the end of the human experiment!* His reply was equally emphatic, *But we* do *have an exclusive truth in Christ! No,* I responded, *we may have an important religious story about Jesus and a myth about Christ, but not an exclusive truth.* He began to protest, but apparently sensing that I was a hopeless case, said dismissively or sadly (I am not sure which), *Oh forget it!* And he got into his car and drove away, leaving me standing there with a belly of not-so-merry feelings, and I imagined he was feeling something of the same.

Watching him leave I felt satisfied and a bit smug that I had honored the truth as I knew it. I also felt sad that we were still at a place where such conversations were necessary; and I felt hopeless in the moment that there was any chance at interreligious dialogue and understanding when we Christians—he a former missionary, I a former Presbyterian pastor—saw the world and religions through such different lenses.

A fourth factor, forming a quaternity which we Jungians like, prompts the publication of these essays at this time: The political divide and crisis growing out of the 2016 presidential election, which has our nation and world on edge. Those of us who see President Donald J. Trump suffering from narcissistic, sociopathic illness are convinced of our diagnosis. Those who see him as the blond champion of conservative values and the savior of our nation are equally convinced. The election has already been costly with more loss likely to come. It has already cost some of us friendships that apparently were not solid enough to include real differences in values or strong enough to keep talking about what divides us. Looking more deeply through a psychological lens, however, the election has exposed the long-standing deep fissures between conscious and unconscious that Carl Jung uncovered, about which he wrote extensively and which caused him great alarm about our future. The religious, political, and cultural divides are symptomatic of the more fundamental hidden fissures. On an optimistic note, those symptoms can be understood as psyche attempting to heal itself and inviting us, nature's most creative and destructive species, to assist. That will require engaging *fresh imagination to promote consciousness in general and religious consciousness in particular.* These essays seek to promote such consciousness.

Reflective leaders of all major religions acknowledge that we are experiencing a seismic shift in religious consciousness. My desk creaks under the weight of books addressing the religious transition and the possible cultural and political implications that seem historically unique. Of course, it may be that each generation considers its predicaments and possibilities to be unique. Rumor has it that when Adam and Eve were forced to exit their mythological garden paradise, Adam said ruefully to Eve, *My dear, we are in an age of transition!*

What does seem unique about the current state of religious, political, and cultural change, however, is the rapidity of the change fueled partly by instant global communication of all aspects of life, including the preponderance of social media, which grant any person or group a voice on any subject. Gone are the days when there were a few perceived experts or authorities in any given discipline. Sorting out facts from fiction and truth from opinion on any given day and on any given subject requires a degree of discernment as never before. These facts of modern life are obvious and the topic for much commentary and speculation about their long-range effects. What those effects will be only time and reflective consciousness will reveal.

As I read and profit from the best of religious scholarship, including the important perspectives of self-proclaimed atheists, two major omissions seem apparent that this work will address. First, the contributions of the analytical psychology of Carl Gustav Jung remain neglected, especially the role of the unconscious in all aspects of life, including religion. Jung's psychology was birthed in the last one hundred years. It can be seen as a necessary compensation to the one-sided, short-sighted monotheistic religions and the cultures they have spawned. The meanings of that sentence will be thoroughly explored, especially in the Essay "**Monotheistic Madness.**"

The second topic that has received inadequate attention and reflection is the *distinction* between the historical wisdom teacher, *Jesus*, and the psychological or archetypal image of *Christ*. This neglected distinction resulted in the mistaken name, *Jesus Christ,* in the early years of Christianity and remains the most important case of mistaken identity in religious history. Directly and indirectly, consciously and unconsciously, this mistaken religious identity has shaped Western culture and its citizens, Christian or otherwise, religious or not. Until this topic receives the light of reflective consciousness, nothing of substance will likely change in the Western religious, political, or cultural psyche. The two-part Essay **"Reimagining Jesus and *Christ*"** addresses this taboo topic.

These two perceived omissions in religious academy and in the pew are intimately connected from the analytical psychological perspective. Carl Jung identified the religious nature of the unconscious and the crucial role expanding consciousness plays for individuals, cultures, and nations. Furthermore, his psychology provides the language and tools necessary to differentiate "Jesus" and "*Christ*," which could return each to its distinctive value otherwise lost. (Author's Note: *Christ* will be italicized throughout when referring to an archetypal image). Chief among these tools is *psychological projection,* the dynamics of which remain largely unknown or undervalued, and even less applied. The Essay **"Projection and Revelation"** seeks to recover its value; its profound dynamics and applications appear throughout this collection.

As acknowledged, I am writing from a particular psychological perspective, that of the analytical psychology of C. G. Jung and his many interpreters and amplifiers. His basic psychological paradigm continues to be tweaked, massaged, and expanded, which means that it remains alive and well. As he often observed, all things change and transform, or else they die, psychological and religious paradigms alike. What continues to attract me to Jung's work is his attempt to revive the old symbols and images that had become literalized and rigidified in religious dogma and doctrine, and his passion for melting them down and pouring new meanings and new passion into the old forms. In his Terry Lectures of 1937 at Yale University, he said:

> I am not ... addressing myself to the happy possessors
> of faith, but to those many people for whom the light
> has gone out, the mystery has faded, and God is dead.
> For most of them there is no going back, and one does
> not know either whether going back is always the
> better way. To gain an understanding of religious matters,
> probably all that is left us today is the psychological
> approach. That is why I take these thought-forms that
> have become historically fixed, try to melt them down
> again and pour them into moulds of immediate
> experience (Jung 1937: 89, Emphasis mine).

Given the present state of human consciousness, and the erosion of the religious imagination through centuries of literalism and excessive rationalism, Jung proposed that a *psychological approach* to religion and religious matters can speak clearly and soulfully to modern individuals and collectives. I concur; the subsequent pages will unpack the meaning of such an approach.

With the necessary demise and death of antique cosmologies and traditional religious paradigms dependent on external supernatural deities and devils, the modern religious challenge involves two simultaneous sacred endeavors: To eulogize, bury, and grieve the theistic and monotheistic god-images and the religious paradigms dependent on them; and secondly, to bring fresh imagination to the meanings of *god* and *religion* that will satisfy both the modern mind and ancient soul. The Essay "**Reimagining *God* and**

Religion" addresses these two sacred tasks as we await a new religious myth, which Jung, and now many others, sense is being birthed.

These pages emerge from my Christian heritage and history, my professional training and experience as a Christian pastor and psycho-therapist and, for the last 17 years, my analytic practice as a Jungian psychoanalyst. The work of Jung came to my attention when "midway in life's journey I found myself in a dark wood, having lost my way." Many are familiar with that wood described by Dante. The "myth of consciousness" that emerged from Jung's life and work continues to provide meaning as the Essay **"The Universe as *Mirror* and *Icon*"** validates. Jung saw himself as a "pastor of souls" and, in the imaginative words of Jungian analyst and writer Murray Stein, Jung took on his Christian tradition much like an analyst takes on his patient in an effort to facilitate the healing of its much-maligned soul (Stein and Moore 1987: 12). Without claiming a similar competency, my efforts do grow out of similar pastoral concerns, not just for Christianity and the Church, but for all modern religions and their adherents, as well as those who claim no religious affiliation.

This book is addressed to a specific audience described in the following extended summary of my current worldview, personal creed, and, for the astute reader, some of my religious prejudices and complexes:

> I am addressing those spiritual pilgrims who have left (or who would like to leave) the confines of a religious paradigm wed to an outdated, dualistic world view, who wander courageously in the archetypal wilderness awaiting the birth of a new, life-giving, soul-satisfying, religious myth; those who have grown weary of monotheistic religions that seek to divide and conquer; those who find religious absolutism and exclusivity a violation of soul; and those who find other religions equally valid, and equally partial, in approaching the ultimate. I am addressing those who value the human mind and the discoveries of modern science, including analytical psychology, as avenues of continuing revelation; those who no longer use sacred texts to stifle the imagination or to support their fears and intellectual

laziness. My audience is those who have a felt-sense that the divine encounter happens within and spreads without rather than coming from a remote, external, metaphysical deity; those who hunger and thirst for the experience of the numinous which has innumerable names, unlimited manifestations, to which all can bow and none can control or possess.

These essays are primarily personal in nature rather than academic or clinical, though much psychological theory and some clinical examples are included. They constitute my personal psychological and religious *testament,* which may or may not be compatible with the Old and New Testaments, which were the sacred texts of my religious formation and which continue to be the supporting documents of monotheistic faiths. My personal *testament* reveals the labyrinthine spiritual trek of one person combining religious experience and psychological theory. The first two Essays, "**From the Back Porch of the Church**" and "***Beyond* the Back Porch of the Church,**" chronicle some of the highlights and lowlights of that unfolding path. My experience is not meant to be copied, even if that were possible, but I trust it will prompt the reader to find the words and images to express his/her own testament; that is, to claim one's inner authority. Paraphrasing psychologist Sam Keen, the most important text one must learn to read is one's life. For me, failing to do that renders all external texts unreliable at best and dangerous at worst. Jungian analyst and author John Dourley states clearly the psychological approach to religious realities: "All those who cannot write their own sacred scripture directly out of the unconscious are doomed to submit to another's and so live another's myth" (Dourley 2010: 35).

The Essay "**Dreams: Strangers in the Night**" focuses on the relationship between conscious and unconscious, including practical ways to serve as host to the nightly visitors who cross the imaginal threshold. Drawing on imagery from Celtic spirituality, **"Thin Times and Thin Places"** provides ways to recognize and to honor unconscious contents that populate our daytime world. Whether by night or by day, the deep unconscious seems actively intent on connection with the human ego. Whatever way the ego seeks conscious response can be called a religious practice, thereby broadening and deepening the traditional meaning of religion.

In recent years as I have been pushed and pulled to my theological and psychological edges and have attempted in public to find words and images to speak about religious mysteries, the image of *Christ*, and what it means to be on a spiritual pilgrimage, I have found it necessary to offer the following disclaimers: *What I will be sharing is, from my experience, absolutely true, but none of it is absolute.* Possessing absolute truth or certainty is not a human prerogative, especially when addressing the invisible world. From an analytical psychological perspective, we do not possess pure objective truth, since a human subject or psyche is the medium doing the speaking or writing. We never "arrive at the truth" or possess it to be dispensed to others. At best we get glimpses, like the sun on a cloudy day, or the moon by night—just enough light to walk the next step or short stretch along the path. All claims to the contrary are metaphysical assertions that are not empirically verifiable. To impose those absolute assertions on another as *the* truth is abusive.

To extend this disclaimer, I think that those of us who share our ideas for public scrutiny, whether they be religious, social, or political, would do well to invoke an Eleventh Commandment: *Thou shall not consider thy truth to be absolute and final!* Of course, the first of the familiar Ten Commandments having to do with the making of idols already covers this issue. However, it is generally ignored, oddly enough most often by those who insist that all Ten Commandments should be displayed in prominent public places! I usually add humorously that if such an Eleventh Commandment were followed or enforced, the unemployment rate in Washington, D.C., would skyrocket, most sermons would be much shorter, and the interminable talk radio and television voices would go silent—and that would be especially nice! And, to be fair, this book might be much shorter.

The final disclaimer echoes an earlier admission. I do not claim that these psychological and theological perspectives are necessarily compatible with orthodox Christian or religious thought, nor are they necessarily biblically correct. We are way past the point of thinking that new knowledge, and the images by which it is conveyed, must be judged for its veracity by the light/knowledge granted to our ancestors. Those who remain committed to premodern ways of thinking—including the perspective that the Bible (or any other ancient sacred text) marked the end of revelation and constitutes the sole authority for faith and practice ...ust bear the burden of squaring those texts with new knowledge, rather than the other way around. The tables have been turned. Specifically, the Bible, the Quran, the Torah and Talmud, and all other stories created and collected by our ancestors, need to square with our current knowledge of our visible (outer) and invisible (inner) universe. We need no longer deny what analytical psychology has confirmed: *That all religious texts are human stories about "God" rather than "God's" stories about humans.* All religions and the images they employ are products of the human imagination; the images, however, emerge into consciousness from an autonomous meta-personal (not metaphysical) source. Analytical psychology calls this source the archetypal, or collective, unconscious; religions call it the spiritual domain. These perspectives will be amplified throughout this work.

Therefore, those who appreciate analytical or Jungian psychology, symbolic thinking, and the religious imagination may find stimulation herein. Those who value religious certainty, the possession of absolute truth, and religious superiority (Christian or otherwise) will be disappointed, perhaps offended, though that is not my purpose.

In keeping with the essay format of this work, some psychological theory and religious wonderings will occasionally be repeated as we circumambulate the overall theme of bringing fresh imagination to *god* and *religion*. The repeated material represents the multifaceted meanings of key concepts when viewed from different angles of vision. On another format note, Jung's *Collected Works* will be referenced by page numbers (rather than by paragraphs).

The background theme of these pages will be an invitation to the recovery and care of psyche/soul, initially imaged here as *the numinous essence at the heart of all life*, as opposed to a thing or object that must be saved for an afterlife. Woven throughout will be the soulful voices of poets who have been, and who remain, some of our most important and efficient theologians and depth psychologists. For example, the 14th-century Persian poet, Hafiz, captures in a few words the attitude that I hope this book will convey:

"I Have Learned So Much"

I
Have
Learned
So much from God
That I can no longer
Call
Myself

A Christian, a Hindu, a Muslim
A Buddhist, a Jew.
The Truth has shared so much of Itself
With me

That I can no longer call myself
A man, a woman, an angel,
Or even pure
Soul.
Love has
Befriended Hafiz so completely
It has turned to ash
And freed
Me

Of every concept and image
My mind has ever known
(Ladinsky 1999: 32).

My further hope is that this book will make a contribution to the ongoing dialogue concerning the new thing, the new myth, which struggles to be birthed in our midst, variously referred to as the **New or Emerging Paradigm**, **Progressive Christianity**, the **Emergent or Cosmic Christ**, or **Ecological or Cosmic Spirituality.** All of these are likely archetypal cousins to the familiar **Kingdom of Heaven** or the **Reign of God** that Jesus of Nazareth envisioned, the hoped-for time when the human species would be able to embrace each and all as one in cooperation with the numinous energy that courses through all life.

ESSAY NUMBER ONE

From the Back Porch of the Church

(Several years ago, I wrote and distributed an article titled, "From the Back Porch of the Church." [Atlanta Jung Society, Archives; Progressive Christianity Online] What follows is an abbreviated and slightly revised version of that article to provide a context for these essays and to provide some necessary autobiographical background. I have chosen to leave the references to *God* and *Christ* unchanged since they represented my thinking at the time, references that continue to change/transform to this day.)

After more than a half century within the walls of the institutional Church, half of those as an ordained Presbyterian minister, I now find myself on the back porch of the Church. Here I sit in my rocking chair, listening, chatting, and watching. I look out and scan the horizon for new life-giving images that the deep unconscious may be offering the growing number of people who no longer look to the Church for their primary soul sustenance.

From my back porch vantage point, I occasionally look nostalgically into her windows, and often I am invited to offer lectures and workshops by groups who meet within her hospitable walls. Occasionally, I still perform the functions of an ordained minister, which requires arduous inner work in the moment to reinterpret and reimage much of the Church's liturgy and language. For example, if I am asked to share the bread and wine of the Eucharist, it is sufficient for me to share them as symbolic of the *Life of the Christ Within and Among Us*, rather than as the body and blood of Jesus (See Essays "Reimagining Jesus and *Christ*").

As a Jungian analyst in private practice, some of the people who meet me on the porch still find life in the institutional Church vital to their soul, as it was for me well into my middle years. Others still occupy a pew but find the religious institution rather dull or irrelevant; still others are very agitated or sad and would like to leave but do not know where to find the bread for which they hunger. Still others who seek me out for analytic work have never darkened the doors of a church, and some come from other religious or spiritual traditions. I talk with those who believe in God, or not, but who have a deep longing for something more. All are welcome on the back porch, and each has a very important spiritual story, though many prefer the language of modern depth psychology to tell it.

Regarding my own story, I was reared in what Marcus Borg and others call the "earlier paradigm" as compared to the "emerging paradigm," which struggles to be birthed (Borg 2006: 16-26). I was taught that the words and stories of the Bible were literally true, and when the Bible and science were in conflict, the latter had to be set aside or explained away. I was taught that my deepest nature was opposed to God, rather than being of God, and that God was a kind of remote monarch who required the literal blood sacrifice of his Son as a payment for my sinful nature. Jesus was presented as the *only* path to God, and all other paths led to a very hot place in eternity. The Christian religion was presented as being superior to all others, and we had a divine obligation to convert (or simply ignore) all the heathens to our way of thinking and believing; that is, to embrace *our God*. Even as a little boy I knew there was something wrong with that picture, but I dared not question it, as week after week it was reinforced by my church fathers and mothers. However, when one is required to close off one's mind, it is a short distance to becoming *close-minded* and *exclusive*. Regrettably, some version of this paradigm remains the primary perspective within the walls of the Church. I imagine that most readers will recognize some version of this personal story, either in their own history or in Western cultures formed and deformed by it.

The exclusive claim to truth remains Christianity's (as well as other monotheistic religions') greatest embarrassment and illusion and, psychologically, the most glaring pathology. It grows out of fear and arrogance accompanied by the narcissistic need to be special by claiming that our tribe is superior to all other religious tribes.

From the back porch of the Church, it has become clear to me that there are no "chosen people" in the sense of having an "in" with that mystery, or mysteries, we have deemed divine. That which humans have named "God" does not have a favorite tribe, country, political party, or dating website (!), nor is God captured in any one set of doctrines or creeds. There are no sacred texts that can claim to be <u>the truth</u>, including the Bible. The Bible is the Church's story of God, not God's story of the Church as the Church has claimed from the fourth century. More provocatively from a depth psychological perspective, there is no such document as "<u>The</u> Word of God" recited weekly by both conservative and liberal religious. On the other hand, there has been, and will be, endless "words about God" as our species seeks images to express experiences deemed numinous, to employ the word created by Rudolph Otto and borrowed by C. G. Jung.

The early and later Church Fathers, consciously and unconsciously, employed a very convenient marketing device: They proposed the only solution (sacrificial blood of Jesus) to a universal problem (original sin); then added the claim that their interpretations and perspectives were divine revelation; and, finally, closed the canon of sacred texts that seemed to support their claims. This unfortunate version of the Christian story was then wed to the imperial powers committed to empire building, which resulted in enormous bloodshed in the name of God. The Church does not like to visit its shadowy past and is, therefore, bent on repeating it, albeit in more sophisticated forms. Rather than claiming exclusive truth about the invisible mystery(s) we have named "God," we need to adopt the attitude that other religious traditions and perspectives aid the Church in coming to a more complete God-image. That alone would be the Church's best contribution to peacemaking and would be far more effective than papal decrees and theological papers emanating from church assemblies.

Speaking from my religious upbringing, as long as Christianity and the Church retain the illusion of being superior, that it has some exclusive corner on the truth, or that believing in Jesus is the <u>only</u> path to God, it will contribute knowingly and unknowingly to division, hatred, violence, and terror in our world! The same needs to be said about fundamentalists of all stripes, whether Christian, Jewish, or Muslim, as well as fundamentalists in theistic religions such as Hinduism and nontheistic religions like Buddhism.

At a recent conference where we were exploring some of these perspectives, a college professor of world religions made the frightening observation that of the nine major world religions, only Christianity and

Islam actively seek to convert others to their way of believing. Both claim a divine imperative to evangelize the world, to impose their God-image on all others. Our present wars and numerous religious conflicts simmering around our small planet, as well as the bloodshed over the centuries in the name of God, underscore the power of religion and its perversity.

Currently, the back porch of the Church is a hospitable place; I like it here. At an earlier time, I might have said that this is "where God has called me." Now I am content to claim that I am here by a combination of wise and not-so-wise choices (both by me and the Church), fate, and multiple mysterious life threads that have been woven by an invisible hand. Life has become too large to reduce to simple formulas, religious clichés, or well-crafted creeds. The view from the back porch is quite different from that of pew or pulpit.

From the back porch one can see the "shadow of the Church," so to speak, more clearly. Carl Jung reminds us that the individual and collective shadow can be very destructive or, with consciousness, a potential gold mine. When the Church refuses or neglects the work of consciousness, it becomes a "sanctuary for shadow," a safe haven for intellectual laziness, and unexamined prejudices and fears. Xenophobia (fear of those who are different) and homophobia are two of the most obvious contemporary culprits. With the arduous, courageous work of consciousness, however, much treasure awaits the individual or Church.

From the shadow of the Church, one is closer to nature and to her wisdom from which the Church has been separated for centuries while promoting the split between spirit and matter. When we look closely enough, nature teaches us everything we need to know about life and death, about the relationship between a Creator and the created, and about trust. Nature is faithful to her rhythms, she is the great recycler, and she bows to her Source. We would do well to learn from her, as the poet Rilke, employing the metaphor of "Storm" for God, writes: *If only we would let ourselves be dominated / As (nature does) by some immense storm / we would become strong too.*

Nature contains all the feminine wisdom we human beings will ever need if we can give up the notion that we are superior to her and have a divine right to subdue and consume her. Unfortunately, this is one right we have practiced all too well. The Church has yet to recover from its patriarchal, hierarchical notion that we are above nature. Slowly, nature is teaching us our rightful place within and alongside her; even more accurately, as an organic part of her.

Of course, these perspectives will be considered by many to be heretical—and they are! Heresy is simply, and profoundly, one of a pair of opposite truths that was discarded by the Church Fathers in favor of the other opposite, which came to be known as orthodoxy. Heresy often contains truth that could not be metabolized by the collective religious digestive tract of an earlier time, and was suppressed and repressed, often with much violence and death to those who held such views. The blood of many so-called heretics, witches, and heathens remains under the clean carpet of the Church collective. An observation from physicist Steven Weinberg speaks a tragic truth: *With or without religion, you would have good people doing good things and evil people doing evil things. But for good people to do evil things, that takes religion*. The voices of heretics in religious/spiritual traditions are very important because they announce what is not permitted by the collective mindset. From this perspective, Jesus of Nazareth would be considered a heretic by both the religious and political establishment of his day, and speaking his truth cost him a great deal.

Fortunately, from a depth psychological perspective, when a splitting process is employed by an immature ego that requires something to be pushed out of consciousness, the repressed material does not disappear but reforms and makes another incursion into consciousness at a later time. Many so-called heresies are rearing their heads, asking to be honored, which could provide the Church with the theological balance and humility it sorely needs.

In my more creative moments on the back porch, when I can let go of my arrogant notion that I have to "save the Church" (one of my residual religious complexes), I simply wait and watch what is happening out back and in the larger world. I wait and watch with the question playing around the edges of my mind and soul, "*I wonder what the Self is up to?*" (I generally prefer the designation of the archetypal "Self," which is more difficult to literalize and domesticate, not associated with gender, not limited to any one religious tradition, and does not carry all the centuries of unconscious God-talk). I ask, "*What may be emerging from the deep unconscious that is trying to get the attention of individuals, religious groups, and nations? What new images are already emerging that may give us a clue to the tectonic shift that is taking place in the deep unconscious, a shift we feel in our bones, in our souls, in our pocketbooks, in our nation and world? And how might I/we cooperate with the new life that is trying to emerge?"* In more traditional religious language, *How might I/we move from being 'children of God,'* which keeps us dependent and little, *"to being 'adults or partners with God,'"* which requires much more responsibility, creativity, and trust?

In my more hopeful moments, I remember that we do not create the images that are the carriers of new life, though the human psyche and imagination are their conduit. Life-giving and life-sustaining images have and will continue to seek us out from the archetypal depths. They are the embedded symbols in our religious traditions and sacred texts. They reach out to us in ancient stories and myths and in the new stories that are being written. They are being projected onto the screens of our night-time dreams and our daytime fantasies, onto the events of our outer world, onto the faces of those we love and hate. New images arise spontaneously in our culture and all the cultures of the world and are articulated by our artists, authors, poets, and screenwriters. The ego does not create the images that are carriers of new life, but the receptive individual and collective ego appear to be vital vessels through which meta-personal energies desire to become incarnated.

Finally, I am a child of the Church. She birthed me and mothered me, and Father God directed my earlier paths, and I could no more deny my religious parentage than I could my biological parents. The Christian myth is in my bones and bloodstream, and my soul will always bear its stamp. The Church provided me a sense of community and belonging, taught me the stories of the Bible, and the great hymns whose tunes still resonate within my soul and lift my spirit. However, my images of God, Jesus, the Church, religion, and what it means to be a spiritual being have evolved, and I hope they will continue to do so.

Now, writing from the back porch of the Church, I have a particular audience in mind:

I am not addressing those for whom the traditional interpretations of the Christian story remain vital and life-giving. I am addressing the growing number of those for whom the old, old story has been so literalized that it has lost its power to stir and feed the soul; those for whom the creeds no longer roll easily off the tongue; those who hunger and thirst for a god-image that has innumerable names, and unlimited manifestations, a god-image to which all can bow and none can possess.

ESSAY NUMBER TWO

Beyond the Back Porch of the Church

Make your mistakes, take your chances, look silly, but keep going.
You can't go home again. (Thomas Wolfe)

Let everything happen to you; Beauty and terror.
Just keep going. No feeling is final.
Don't let yourself lose me. (Rainer Maria Rilke)

After several years of being not too close yet not too far from ecclesial life, I fell off the back porch of the Church!

It happened when the anthropological, theological, Christological, and ecclesiological underpinnings, which had been shaky for me for years, finally collapsed under the weight of common sense and new knowledge of our visible world through the hard sciences, and the invisible world through the soft science of analytical or Jungian psychology. It was a painful fall, accompanied by acute grief, and my soul will always bear the scars and the subsequent freedom to imagine fresh ways to live *as if* the universe, and my/our wee portion of it, is saturated with the sacred.

Not only did the foundations of the Church collapse for me but, deeper still, the 4,000-year-old god-image at the core of Judaism, Christianity, and Islam crumbled as well. The monotheistic god-image of a metaphysical, supernatural being, external to physical life and the life of the human psyche, a being who intervenes from time to time—that is, the God of Abraham, Father God of Mother Church, Allah the Great—lost its meaning, its vitality. That ancient theological formulation, which has shaped not only three major religions (and their offshoots) but numerous institutions and cultures as well, had to go, whatever the personal and professional costs. Drawing on the most graphic metaphor, for me the monotheistic god-image died.

The careful reader will notice that I avoid the pronouncements of the last century that "God is dead!" for several reasons. First, the distinction between god and god-image is critical. All our theological words are symbols (or their cousins: images, metaphors, analogies) and are not synonymous with that which is being symbolized. Only the discipline of depth psychology consistently makes this vital differentiation. Most theologians, even those considered liberal and progressive, continue to refer to *God* as if he (or she) is a separate being, a noun so to speak, rather than an *inner experience designated religious or spiritual.* Many of the theologians and religious writers I most admire offer compelling perspectives concerning the dangers of an anthropomorphized, personified deity only to suggest in the next paragraph that *God did or desires this or that,* or even that *God loves,* effectively reinforcing the notion of *God* as a metaphysical Being beyond or outside life. Of course, it is almost impossible to do otherwise after centuries of personification, anthropomorphism, and literalism. But try, we must; our lives may depend on doing so.

C. G. Jung made this vital distinction in his dialogues with the theologians and psychologists of his day. Noting the modern superstitious belief in the power of the word to capture or contain that which is being described, he writes, "We don't produce God by the magic word or by representing his image. The word for us is still a fetish, and we assume that it produces the thing of which it is only an image. What God is in himself nobody knows; at least I don't" (Jung 1958: 710). Jung's humility in this regard may be considered heretical to those who are certain their words and dogma provide very certain knowledge of the divine. Near the end of his voluminous writing career, he reportedly commented that he wished he could change all his references to *God* to *God-image.*

E. Forrester Church, longtime associated with the Unitarian Church of All Souls in New York City, concludes: "The power which I cannot explain or know or name I call God. God is not God's name. God is my name for the mystery that looms within and arches beyond the limits of my being" (Hiles 2008: 68). Rainer Maria Rilke was a masterful poet in addressing the divine mystery with creative images that gave expression to mystery without trying to capture or contain it:

> You are the future
> the red sky before sunrise
> over the fields of time.

> You are the cock's crow when night is done,
> you are the dew and the bells of matins,
> maiden, stranger, mother, death.

You create yourself in ever-changing shapes
that rise from the stuff of our days –
unsung, unmourned, undescribed,
like a forest we never knew.

You are the deep innerness of all things,
the last word that can never be spoken.
To each of us you reveal yourself differently:
to the ship as coastline, to the shore as a ship.
(Barrows and Macy 1996: 119).

If/when the distinction between god and god-image is embraced and takes root in the collective religious mind, the long-debated issue over the "existence of God" will be settled. The debate has centered on the word *existence,* which implies a physical or material presence or manifestation and/or theoretical abode. That debate as currently framed can never be won either for or against. First, it could be resolved if we consider that all gods and goddesses have been, and will be, creations of the human psyche and imagination; that is, real and powerful inward experiences and latent capacities seen in projected form (See Essay "Projection And Revelation").

Secondly, I avoid the "God is dead" declaration well aware that all religious statements are purely subjective. The statements emanate from one's psychological complex around those experiences humans have named "God." They reveal the state of the psyche of the one making the statements rather than providing objective knowledge about a supposed metaphysical domain or deity. Remaining clear about this vital distinction diminishes psychological and religious inflation to which I remain sus-ceptible from my fundamentalist religious upbringing. Old complexes, especially powerful ones like God complexes, do not disappear; with sufficient consciousness and courage, they can be sufficiently dissolved to give birth to a rare religious virtue—humility.

Thirdly, and the most important psychological reason to avoid the "God is dead" frame of the last century is this: When an image, symbol, or myth dies psychologically, it means that the animating, compelling energy that once gave the image life has disappeared into the unconscious. That dynamic energy does not simply evaporate but retreats into the un-conscious, where it remains alive and remobilizes for a later incursion into consciousness in another form. In the imaginative words of James Hollis, when the energy of an image disappears, the individual or collective "may cling to those image-husks with fundamentalist fervor to mask our disquietude" (Hollis 2000: 19). Sadly, such clinging seems rampant among monotheists who, from the perspective presented in these essays, refuse to recognize the demise of their myth. On the other hand, because numinous energy never disappears, we can imagine that the unconscious is actively engaged in new myth-making and inviting individuals to be co-creators.

A fourth reason to avoid the absolutist "God is dead" declaration emerges from a pastoral perspective. While the monotheistic god-image no longer speaks to me, millions of monotheistic believers remain committed to the god-image in question, some because it continues to provide meaning and others out of tradition and convention. Still others have never been challenged to consider otherwise, and many more live in desperate conditions without the privilege of deep theological and psychological reflection. The latter are occupied with survival needs rather than the finer points about the difference in god and god-image, or the future of religion. Daily bread is more important.

However, while sensitive to the varied human predicaments and honoring the many ways of being religious, as well as the various stages of religious consciousness, it is my personal psychological observation that *as long as our deities and devils are considered to be external to physical life and the life of the psyche, our species will continue to do great harm to each other and to our nest*. This subjective analysis will be repeated and amplified throughout these essays. It highlights the urgency of bringing depth psychological analysis to our natural religious urgings and their conscious, rather than unconscious, expressions.

Lastly, to speak about the demise and death of the monotheistic god-image from yet another angle, for me it is less a theological or ecclesiastical judgment and more a statement of faith. It comes from my continuing search for meaning and my obsessive wrestling match with what we humans have named divine. Along with the poet Rilke, *I circle around God, around the primordial tower / I've been circling for thousands of years / And I still don't know / Am I a falcon, a storm, or a great song*? To be clear, the declaration that the metaphysical, monotheistic god-image has died represents a statement of faith rather than a denial of, or resignation from, experiences deemed religious. I rest my case for the moment.

To propose, then, the death of the monotheistic deity means to declare that the god-image that has occupied the psyche of Jews, Christians, and Muslims, as well as the Western cultural and political psyche, is no longer viable; furthermore, to deny its demise may be the greatest obstacle for the embrace of new god-images, images that may better serve the modern mind and ancient soul.

Moving from the center of Church leadership to its metaphorical back porch after a quarter-century was a necessary move for my psychological, professional, and spiritual life. The ecclesial container had become too small, too suffocating for the life of soul. What had been a sanctuary for much of my life began to feel more like a prison. I needed more religious and intellectual space and freedom that the back porch afforded—not too far from my religious roots, yet not too close. The much-needed retreat was short-lived, however. Though freed from tending the fires of institutional maintenance and politics, as well as from the projected expectations and needs of diverse parishioners, I now had to face intense inner fires that had been smoldering for years. Serving as a professional religious (pastor, minister, priest, nun, bishop, etc.) can be hazardous to one's health. Serving and tending others, even with sincerity and compassion, can become a holy substitute for tending one's own psyche or soul. There is always one more person to visit or comfort, one more crisis to tend, one more person troubled about their faith, or lack of it—all are legitimate needs, as well as holy excuses, for neglecting one's inner parishioners crying for attention.

Though satisfying in many ways at a relational, pastoral level, my relationship with the Church had been ambivalent for years. I was consciously aware that some of the ambivalence was rooted in my rejection of its archaic, dualistic worldview, its exclusive biblical and salvific claims, even its claims related to Jesus and his divinity—no small issues. However, what I discovered on the back porch, thanks to Jungian psychology and personal analysis, was that I had been *grieving* for a long time, unconsciously so, due to the death of the god-image at my religious core. I became aware of this through an initial dream in personal Jungian analysis, the details of which are explored in the "Epilogue." Again, my grief was largely unconscious, hidden away in the depths for fear of the consequences of facing a hard, inconvenient truth, including the imagined social, relational, professional, even political, implications. There is a sadness deeper than grief: It is not knowing one is grieving. It is knowing that something is amiss, but the cause remains hidden or unconscious.

Becoming aware of these heretofore unconscious or barely conscious psychic or spiritual facts had the force of personal revelation, which was both frightening and freeing. The awareness called into question my lifelong religious identity, as well as much of what I had been taught by the Church and theological seminary, and much of what I had taught others as a religious professional. It left me without a religious home, at least until I could recover my balance and reclaim my identity as a religious pilgrim or sojourner, an identity based on one's inner authority rather than on outer authorities, institutions, or sacred texts.

It has taken me a very long time to write these words, to publicly acknowledge what I have known at some subterranean level for at least half of my 75 years. Heretofore, I had neither the language nor courage to articulate what I know to be a personal truth. Now, drawing on the insights and language of analytical psychology, I am wondering if there is a larger, though painful, truth waiting to be embraced by the monotheistic faithful. What if the god-image that lies beneath Judaism, Christianity, and Islam can no longer serve the modern mind and ancient soul? What if the image of external deities and devils can no longer be entertained, given what we know about our visible and invisible worlds? And what if, like me, the monotheistic faithful, institutions, and cultures shaped by that image are in *various stages of unconscious grief*? What then?

Short of declaring absolute truth, I suggest that such a diagnosis is worthy of further reflection. In many ways, it makes perfect *psychological* sense. Stated succinctly: *The monotheistic god-image of a metaphysical, super-natural being, external to physical life and the life of the human psyche, who intervenes from time to time—that is, the God of Abraham, Father God of Mother Church, Allah the Great—has (metaphorically) died. His many self-proclaimed favored children and the monotheistic religions, institutions, and cultures founded and perpetuated in his name are in various stages of unconscious grief.* We will begin to unpack some of the meanings of such a psychological possibility.

Grieving the death of important persons is one of the more difficult human assignments and includes a complex of emotions and stages, including the well-documented experiences of shock, denial, anger, depression, bargaining, acceptance, and, hopefully, resolution; these stages are interrelated and are rarely sequential. Even after reaching the resolution stage, it is common to revisit any of the previous stages given the right emotional conditions. Grieving the death of personified religious powers and presences and their attendant ideas, dogmas, and communities can raise the emotional and psychological stakes exponentially. Grieving is difficult, scary work. We would rather pretend all is well. We would rather believe that something is true simply because it is ancient and served our religious ancestors. We would rather look away and try to go on with business as usual. We would rather bow to an outside authority rather than risk owning and articulating our own knowing.

Yet, psychologically, the monotheistic myth and its core god-image have died. The date of death is uncertain, though likely calculated in centuries, even before Galileo, Copernicus, and Kepler provided their nails for the heavenly coffin. To extend the metaphor, the three religions have been engaged in a variety of life-support measures for their deceased deity and created various distractions from dealing with their unconscious grief. Until we can break through our death-denying, we will likely continue our death-dealing in the name of God.

I state these analyses so emphatically and starkly to break through the most pernicious stage of grief—shock and denial. I realize, of course, that my stating it will have little impact on the inner protective fortresses erected by the faithful; hopefully, it will punch another hole in my own wall of denial. I have dealt with my own denial by trying to rescue my native Christianity and the Church from their demise, by working harder to reframe and reinterpret Christian doctrines and dogma symbolically, by reading one more book and one more expert who might save me from my own knowing. I tried running away, and running faster. Nothing eased the grief, nor should I have expected it. Death has to be mourned, not managed.

It should be noted that denial can play a necessary psychological function until the ego personality, whether individual or collective, is sufficiently strong to entertain, integrate, and metabolize a new awareness. However, prolonged denial invariably promotes pathology, and religious pathology is a deadly virus infecting our world. That virus, aptly named "monotheistic madness" is the subject of the following essay. An effective antidote has yet to be found, though many charlatans have claimed otherwise. Whatever the future antidote to monotheistic madness, analytical psychology with its emphasis on human consciousness in general and religious consciousness in particular, will likely be a major ingredient.

To the psychological eye, one of the most obvious forms of denial manifests in the anti-science, anti-intellectual attitudes of many, if not the majority, of monotheistic religious minds. When the scientific discoveries of the outer, material universe are denied or ignored, often on the basis of ancient sacred texts created by people living in a three-tired, earth-centered universe, and denied with passion, one has to suspect that denial has the upper hand; or it could be ignorance disguised as faith, which is shameful at best and pathological at worst. Before his demise, the Abrahamic deity was kept alive for centuries by the insistence that he was a supernatural theistic Being living outside the physical world he had created and into which he intervened from time to time to reveal truth to a particular few, and to perform occasional miracles by setting aside the very physical laws he created. This was supposedly set in motion about 6,000 years ago, 10,000 at the extreme, or so the sacred, monotheistic texts suggest. No modern mind can entertain such ideas except, of course, through denial. However, the conscious denial is likely fueled by unconscious grief, grief involved in a death that cannot yet be acknowledged.

If the psychological analysis concerning the death of the Abrahamic god-image and the religions founded in its name has validity, it clarifies why so many of his children are so *angry*, another familiar stage in the grief process. It puts my own anger, uncovered in Jungian analysis, in a larger perspective as well. Grief invariably includes anger, especially when the deceased has served purposes of security, safety, and meaning. Even when those provisions may have been illusions and delusions, their loss is felt as real and as deprivation, giving way to blame and rage. Some of that anger is expressed in violence and acts of terror and religious conflicts and wars, all of which continue to plague the children of the God of Abraham. The promises attributed to an external deity have failed to materialize and have grown more remote over the centuries, prompting some to embrace Jihad to bolster their proposed inheritance and to hasten its receipt; others await an outside Armageddon intervention to settle the score against perceived religious enemies. Still others mask their anger with mean-spirited political rhetoric and reflexive calls for military force to solve disputes, careful, of course, to conclude with "God bless America." Homicidal anger takes many religious and political forms.

Unconscious anger also manifests in mean-spirited dogmas that divide and exclude others who are different. Anger expresses itself through inflated claims of possessing inerrant sacred texts that supposedly contained eternal truths given, of course, to one's own tribe. Finally, anger generated by the death of the monotheistic god-image takes more subtle forms such as depression and malaise, which are common to the grief process. Speaking from the Christian tradition, many pews and pulpits are likely occupied by those for whom the religious light has gone out but who stay put for reasons other than spiritual nourishment. Religious professionals are especially vulnerable to the kind of depression that accompanies decisions made for security rather than soul. And, given the paucity of available, soul-sustaining religious options at the present, staying with an institution whose myth has vanished may be necessary, as it was for me for many years.

On the other hand, staying too long in the sanctuary of the deceased or at the imagined divine gravesite may be part of the *bargaining stage* involved in severe grief. Closely related to denial, bargaining is an attempt to ward off the inevitable loss by cutting an emotional, even religious, deal. I have already alluded to my efforts to revive the ecclesial corpse by new and creative programs, new language and liturgies, and psychological interpretations of biblical texts to dilute their patriarchal and exclusive character. Like many others in recent decades, I gladly embraced more feminine god-images to dilute some of the patriarchal, hierarchal character of monotheism. Yet altering the *gender* of an external metaphysical, interventionist deity was not, is not, sufficient. Though done with utmost sincerity, I was also making an unconscious deal or bargain: *I will work hard, even faithfully hard, if I don't have to suffer the loss of the God of my childhood and early adulthood, AND endure the suffering entailed in claiming my own religious authority.* Again, no small matters. I even proposed that perhaps I could stay on the back porch of the Church, close but not too close, to what had given me identity and meaning. Bargaining. It did not keep the porch or the sanctuary from collapsing under my feet.

Acceptance of death and its resolution are the final stages of conscious grieving, though final is always qualified when dealing with important losses. No doubt many individuals have sufficiently worked through their religious grief while their religious institutions remain stuck in their grief. Resolution has taken many forms. Some have done the necessary inner work of owning their religious/spiritual authority retrieved from external religious authorities and/or external god-images, and have chosen to stay in a *conscious* relationship with their particular institution. They are no longer psychologically identified or contained within the institution or its primary myth, meaning their identity is no longer dependent on adherence to external dogma or creed. Those who have owned their religious/spiritual authority can be self-critical of their myth, as well as its sacred texts, and do not feel personally threatened when hard questions are raised. Revelation is seen as continuing rather than a one-time past event. Those who have reached a stage of resolution do not consider their religion or their religious discipline to have a monopoly on the next revealed truth. They are able to honor other religious/spiritual traditions as equal to their own, as well as equally partial. They are free to continue their spiritual journey within an institutional framework, or not, in allegiance to their experience of the sacred wherever it may be found and however it may be mediated. When external deities no longer rule the heavens, one is no longer threatened with new scientific knowledge about the outer, physical world, or the inner, psychological world. Both domains can be experienced as saturated with the sacred. Religion and science are seen as partners, each a gift to the other.

Others are resolving their grief by searching for, and finding, meaning in endeavors other than formal religion. There are many "ways on the Way" that honor the numinous essence at the heart of existence. Formal religion is but one avenue for meaning-making and for satisfying that instinct, which Jung named religious. Psychologically speaking, working through the death of former external deities may mean that *passion* for life itself in all its valances, and *compassion* for all, become the primary religious touchstones, replacing the values of perfection and doctrinal purity. An ever-expanding consciousness in general and religious consciousness in particular may become the best gifts, and the best worship, one can offer for the privilege of being alive. Whatever endeavor promotes such consciousness and compassionate incarnation could rightly be called religious.

The Abrahamic god-image has disappeared from the consciousness of many modern and postmodern people; for them it has effectively died. It has taken its place among the numerous other divine images—the gods and goddesses of antiquity who, having served their purpose in the human psyche and imagination, exited the inner stage for newer divinities; that is, for more appropriate, life-giving, life-sustaining personified presences and powers, i.e., new god-images.

As I read and profit from the sincere efforts to articulate and embrace an "emerging Christian paradigm" (which is one of the more creative alternatives before us) as contrasted with the "earlier Christian paradigm," I am regularly struck by the hesitation to address the death of the monotheistic god-image. Many of the most enlightened and progressive thinkers/writers seem able to carry the theological casket to the metaphorical gravesite but are unable to lower the deceased image, cover the grave, and move on to mourn the death consciously. I well appreciate the hesitation since to do so might call into question an entire career of teaching, preaching, and writing. Yet to avoid the burial ritual may leave to our children and grandchildren a task we were unwilling or unable to accomplish. I am no longer willing to burden them with a religious and psychological task assigned to me. Jung often warned that the greatest burden a child could carry is the unlived life of the parents! Of course, only the reflective consciousness of future generations will evaluate the truth or error of these perspectives.

This is a hard pill to swallow for most monotheists and, at this point in the collective religious consciousness, perhaps too much to ask. However, until the death is accepted and the grief worked through consciously, the children birthed and formed by that god-image will likely feel spiritually impoverished and, by necessity, seek to fill the void in other ways. As Jung noted, the void will likely be something ending with "ism," like literalism, fundamentalism, materialism, commercialism, and, yes, terrorism. The children of the God of Abraham will likely continue to vie for an imagined favored religious status, claiming that their particular god-image is the best, or the one and only. Our world will remain a religious cauldron rather than a human community. And it is unlikely that new laws, peace plans, cease-fire resolutions, and nuclear arms treaties will have any lasting effect. Even war is deemed better than facing the void created by the death of the deity. It gives the fearful and their politicians the illusion of doing something tangible and significant. The unconscious contract might be stated: Perhaps more human death will distract us from facing the death of our deity, a grief too big to face.

Of course, the death of a particular god-image, and/or a particular religion(s), does not mean the end of religion or at least the religious instinct. This is particularly true for those steeped in the analytical psychology articulated by Jung. He was the first depth psychologist to propose an innate religious instinct comparable to the inborn physical instincts. Both physical instincts and the religious instinct, neither visible under a microscope, are known by how they manifest, by their effect on the animal world and animal behavior. For the psychologically minded, humanity has outgrown its need for external deities and devils but not its need for reverence for that which is greater than the ego alone can create, command, and control. The evolution of consciousness has exceeded the slow pace of religious inquiry and religious development, the latter being hampered by god-images appropriate for an earlier stage of religious consciousness but, predictably, with a limited lifespan. As Jung repeatedly noted, "Only a thing that changes and evolves, lives, but static things mean spiritual death" (Jung 1958: 711). And further, "even revealed truth has to evolve. Everything living changes. We should not be satisfied with unchangeable traditions"; and addressing the Christian tradition, "The great battle that began with the dawn of consciousness has not reached its climax with any particular interpretation, apostolic, Catholic, Protestant, or otherwise" (Jung 1958: 731).

John Dourley describes Jung's psychology as "an appreciative under-mining" of the Christian myth, both validating its place in the evolutionary religious unfolding and shining a critical light on the dangers of any religious myth devoid of conscious reflection. Dourley concludes: "Humanity is incorrigibly religious and as such faces an ambiguous situation in which its life can be enhanced or destroyed by a religiosity it cannot escape. In this sense Jung's psychology is both the ultimate validation of humanity's religiosity and its most ardent critic" (Dourley 1992: 53, 75).

Psychologically, the religious instinct manifests in the need to make meaning of one's life and to find one's role in the larger, mysterious order. Particularly evident in the middle and later years in the modern world, this innate need can be satisfied in countless ways, including, but not limited to, participation in a religious community. Predictably, it can also be thwarted and damaged by religions that have forfeited their capacity to mediate the depths of unconscious life; or, in keeping with the theme of these pages, by allegiance to god-image(s) or religions no longer viable, no longer sufficient to satisfy the soul's passion on the one hand, or able to connect one empathically with the larger world on the other.

James Hollis begins his book *Finding Meaning in the Second Half of Life: How to Finally, Really Grow Up* with a series of questions proposed by our life as we approach those highly charged middle years. Three of those questions are particularly relevant here: *Why is the life you are living too small for the soul's desire? Whose life have you been living? What gods, what forces, what family, what social environment, has framed your reality, perhaps supported, perhaps, constricted it* (Hollis 2005: Preface)? Upon first reading Hollis' book more than 10 years ago, I made the following notes in the margins: *How do we find a worldview sufficient for soul? We keep trying to cram soul into an ego-sized container and soul feels cramped, diminished, and its primary symptom is deep longing.* While the monotheistic god-image and myth have died, soul remains alive. She longs for new expressions, new venues, whether or not they carry the traditional label *religious*.

As difficult as these perspectives are to articulate, and even more difficult to metabolize, they have provided me, paradoxically, with renewed hope not only for my personal life and religious/spiritual identity, but for our worldwide religious dis-ease and the socio-political chaos, violence, and terror that touch each of us daily and often threaten to engulf us. If, as I imagine, our suffering is symptomatic of unconscious grief following the death of the most significant god-image of the past 4,000 years, along with the religious and cultural myth(s) dependent on that image, working through that grief consciously may allow us to recognize and incarnate new life-giving, life-serving images that are (likely) on the religious horizon. I say *likely* in recognition of the psychological perspective that we do not create with our rational faculties and willful intent the images that emerge from, and then feed, soul and its expressions. We can, however, acknowledge the death of symbols that have been literalized, commercialized, rationalized, and trivialized to death; that is, the monotheistic god-image under our autopsy.

Hope springs also from a basic dynamic proposed by Jung's analytical psychology. Contents that emerge into consciousness and are then lost through repression, suppression, or neglect never totally vanish. They return to the unconscious where they re-form, re-mobilize, and re-turn to consciousness in another symbolic form. The unconscious does not have a digestive tract whereby contents are eliminated; everything gets recycled, so to speak. This psychological dynamic includes god-images. It may be that we are witnessing a return of the repressed as evidenced by the increasing disenchantment with unbelievable god-images and associated doctrines, as well as with glimmers of new god-images that may promote the peace, justice, human solidarity, and compassion that healthy religion could offer. Furthermore, it may be that the discipline of Jung's analytical psychology and the religious attitude it promotes were birthed to facilitate that transformation and transition. We can hope.

Finally, the image of being on the back porch of the Church served me well. I am grateful for its gift, and it will remain an important place in my religious/spiritual trek. However, all safe and secure places must be relinquished if we follow the soul's longing, if we attempt to walk the inner way so many others have mapped out. The poet Mary Oliver counsels: *To live in this world / you must be able to do three things / to love what is mortal / to hold it against your bones / knowing your life depends on it / and when the time comes / to let it go, to let it go* (Oliver 1992: 177).

Yes, there is always the temptation to return to the safety and familiarity of a former religious identity or institution, especially in times of stress, loneliness, and uncertainty. However, caution needs to be sounded: The turnstile at the exit of traditional monotheism and its institutions and meanings likely operates one way. There may be no way to return with integrity or without damage to soul. This may be one home to which we cannot return. Having placed one's hand on the plow, only new fields of meaning are open to cultivation.

Whether or not one can relinquish external and metaphysical deities and devils and retain identity as a Christian remains an open question, one with which my mind and soul continue to wrestle Jacob-like. Widening the lens, along with others I question whether Western Christian culture can become whole and remain Christian (Dourley 1992: 57). In the mind of the orthodox, there is likely little question. Such a probable verdict means little to me, however, compared with honoring my own experience, my own knowing, and my own authority. At this stage of my life I claim no moral purity, but religious/spiritual integrity remains a prime value.

My own experience of leave-taking from Father God and Mother Church does not feel like a personal achievement. Rather, it feels like an enactment of an archetypal pattern variously described over the centuries as a life-death-rebirth process. Nor is recounting my own experience meant to be a prescription for anyone else, though it may aid others to leave their old monotheistic identifications or to stay more consciously.

In recent years a trinity of touchstones has emerged for me in assessing the value of any religion or religious doctrine or text from an analytical psychological perspective: Whether it is *inclusive, intellectually and scientifically honest,* and *soul-satisfying.* That is, can its core worldview be universally embraced? Is it consistent with current scientific knowledge of the visible universe(s) from the physical sciences, and is it consistent with the current knowledge of the invisible universe(s) from the soft-science of analytical psychology? Does it aid individuals to address the unanswerable, yet unavoidable, existential questions about our origins, purpose, and future? Does it aid individuals to locate themselves meaningfully in the universe and in the wee bit of time and terrain we are privileged to occupy and share? A fourth touchstone, forming a quaternity, might be suggested: Is it sufficiently strong to support the present level of religious consciousness and flexible enough to give way to the ever-evolving mystery of human consciousness?

In summary, the preceding psychological analysis suggests that we are experiencing a collective PTSD (post-traumatic stress disorder) and collective grieving initiated by the death of the Abrahamic god-image and the collapse of the monotheistic myth supporting Judaism, Christianity, and Islam, and underlying Western cultures. Living on this side of Copernicus, Galileo, and Kepler, the only way a metaphysical domain and deity can be kept alive requires one or more psychological defenses, defenses that have also been identified with various stages of the grief process. Each stage may serve a necessary function on the way toward resolution, which means an acceptance of the death of the monotheistic myth and its core god-image and the capacity to move on psychologically and religiously.

This kind of analysis can neither be proven nor disproven; future generations will make that evaluation. It represents, however, an effort to make meaning of my own spiritual trek as well as to address the worldwide religious, cultural, socio-political angst in whose grip we suffer. We are caught in a perpetual cycle of division, conflicts, and wars, most of which are fueled by what can best be described psychologically as "monotheistic madness," a disorder addressed in the following essay.

ESSAY NUMBER THREE

MONOTHEISTIC MADNESS

*Our world is way too small for us to wait to see
how bad the idea of God can get.* (Sam Harris)

*As long as our deities and devils are perceived to be beyond physical life
and the life of the human psyche, our species will continue to do
great harm to each other and to our nest.* (Jerry R. Wright)

Using the vernacular to assess a religious reality, the expiration dates for the monotheistic myth and its core god-image have passed. Their shelf life has expired. The consumer labels of *Best By* or *Use By* have long faded over the centuries. The religious product created through the human mind and imagination some 4,000 years ago, as necessary as it was, is not only spoiled, it is psychologically hazardous to the health of individuals, cultures, and institutions. Given these stark realities, we are challenged to reimagine theism in general and monotheism in particular, the latter being the most familiar and influential form of theism not only for the Western psyche, but arguably the world psyche due to its cultural and political reach over the centuries.

For our purposes, theism may be described as the belief in a being (or beings as in polytheism) supernatural in power, dwelling outside or beyond the physical world, who invades the physical world periodically to accomplish its purpose (Spong 2001: 21-22). In its three major forms, monotheism is the belief in a *one* and *only* being who is supernatural in power, who resides in a metaphysical domain, and who intervenes from time to time to accomplish his divine will, including choosing a particular human tribe to carry out that will; his will is revealed in exclusive sacred texts that are applicable to all time and all people. While Judaism, Christianity, and Islam purportedly worship the same divinity, the God of Abraham, each claims to be the chosen ones—Jews the first chosen, Christians the next chosen, and Muslims the last and final chosen. All three purport that its sacred texts, which cannot be challenged, support its divinely chosen status.

The narcissistic notion of being the chosen tribe of a supernatural one and only god, along with the dualistic split between natural/supernatural, earth/heaven, physical/spiritual, constitute the core problems of monotheism that can no longer be entertained by many in the modern and post-modern world. Judaism, Christianity, and Islam—the three major theistic/monotheistic religions that have informed and deformed the Western psyche, culture, and institutions—have long claimed to be the solution to what ails the human heart. Such claims are no longer believable to a growing number of disenchanted religious.

Roman Catholic priest and Jungian psychoanalyst John Dourley writes:

> Until not long ago the religions could still present themselves as somehow saving humanity. Today a fearful and much more sober humanity asks how it can be saved from its religions (Dourley 1992: 136). ... In the face of the undeniable shadow hanging over contemporary institutionalization of religion, West and East, the civilized mind now moves to the search for salvation from religion rather than through it" (Dourley 2010: 2).

Nobel Prize physicist Stephen Weinberg offers a similar observation, that with or without religion we would have some people doing good things and some people doing evil things. But for good people to do evil things, he proposes, that takes religion! More precisely from a depth psychological perspective, it requires *unconscious religion*, the religious impulse that operates without the aid of consciousness.

Monotheism was birthed through the conflicted human psyche, as are all religions and their dogma, and has been perpetuated by the same. With claims to be the chosen one(s) of a metaphysical deity who has revealed exclusive sacred truth/texts to one's religious tribe, the three major monotheisms have promoted what can best be described as *monotheistic madness*. While not a diagnosis found in the *Diagnostic and Statistical Manual of Mental Disorders* (DSM), the religious, social, and psychological symptoms of this deadly virus are so obvious as to be overlooked for centuries. The symptoms are indeed deadly, both figuratively and literally. One needs only to look at the bloody history of Judaism, Christianity, and Islam and, even more alarming, at the present worldwide wars, conflicts, divisions, and simmering hatreds.

To be sure, political, social, and economic factors fuel the historical and present chaos, conflicts, and wars, as Karen Armstrong argues in *Fields of Blood*. She begins her book by stating her belief that "modern society has made a scapegoat of faith" and concludes, quoting others, that "terrorism is fundamentally and inherently political, even when other motives—religious, economic, or social—are involved. Terrorism is *always* about power," either acquiring it or keeping it (Armstrong 2014: 3, 343-34). However, I believe the majority of those socio-political-economic factors have a predominant monotheistic origin, foundation, and continuing influence, both conscious and unconscious. Monotheistic madness has infiltrated and contaminated all vital human endeavors and institutions by perpetuating the illusion that *my tribe*—be it religious, political, or social—is the recipient of divine favor and the attendant power, privilege, and entitlement that supposedly accompany such eternal selection.

Even more alarming, the dangerous attitudes, assumptions, and motivations underlying monotheistic madness operate largely at an *unconscious* level. The divisions, discord, and death brought on by the untreated religious illness are all around us but overlooked. Religion has been exempt from close scrutiny and common sense; there is a collective taboo against speaking critically about the deceased metaphysical god-image known as the God of Abraham. The demise, death, (or, psychologically speaking, its disappearance into the unconscious), and funeral are described in an earlier essay (See Essay "From the Back Porch of the Church").

The outbreak of monotheistic madness began more than 4,000 years ago, but has gone undiagnosed until the last century with the emergence of analytical psychology, which has also proposed a treatment leading to a possible remedy as these essays address. Again, from a depth psychological perspective, monotheism was created through the human psyche and imagination, as are all religions and their images and dogmas. Though claiming to be *revealed religions* from a supernatural metaphysical deity, the three major monotheisms actually reveal something of the state of the collective psyche of the time and/or of the individual psyche of its particular founder(s) and prophets(s). Contrary to traditional claims that revelation emanates from the metaphysical heights of heaven, depth psychology proposes that revelation involves projective processes emanating from the meta-personal depths of life. What is revealed in all stories and myths, including religious ones, are the contents, contours, and crevices of the archetypal psyche or soul waiting to be brought into consciousness and integrated into the life of the individual and/or collective. For the psychologically minded, monotheism reveals nothing about a metaphysical domain or an all-powerful, self-sufficient god, but reveals much about the human mind and imagination, which are organically linked with nature herself in her cosmic, biological, social, and psychological unfolding and history. Jung employed the metaphor of the *collective* or *archetypal unconscious,* which serves as both the repository of that history and the active agent in presenting those contents to human consciousness. He described these natural processes as the *religious instinct,* or the inherent human drive for meaning-making, of locating oneself in a purposeful way in the mysteries of life itself. Locating these mysteries within physical life of matter, rather than beyond it, marks one of the differences between the psychologically minded religious person and the theistically minded.

The vital distinction between *metaphysical* and *meta-personal,* and the profound dynamics and purposes of psychological projection, are addressed in several other essays. In order to unpack here more of the meanings of monotheistic madness, it will suffice to remind the psychological reader that god-images are birthed through the human psyche and imagination, and reflect both the creative and destructive energies and potential of psyche or soul. In the wisdom of psyche, these powerful god-like potentials *are projected* onto the outer world to be recognized, owned, and ultimately integrated by the individual personality and/or religious collective. Succinctly, projection is the purposeful process whereby heretofore unconscious contents are offered to consciousness for integration. Understood in its profundity, projection can be seen as a primary form of revelation, religious or otherwise. Contrary to popular usage, projection is not pathological; however, when projected contents are not recognized, withdrawn, or integrated into consciousness, especially after long periods of time, they invariably manifest as pathology on the part of individuals, groups, nations, and religious collectives.

Such is the case with theism and monotheism. Though the externalization both of deities and devils was necessary at one point in the unfolding of religious consciousness, failure to recognize them as products of the human mind and imagination seen in projective forms has manifested in centuries of pathology. When the human capacities for good and evil, creativity and destruction, are exported to a metaphysical domain and assigned to a supernatural deity or devil, the human shadow remains outside and unintegrated. Monotheism has provided a safe haven for the human shadow in all its valences. When deities and devils are perceived to be external to life, we are tempted to import the deified qualities as personal possessions or belonging to those of our kind while exporting the devilish qualities to neighbors near and far. The monotheistic God is perceived as a supernatural Being who intervenes here but not there, who casts "His" light and favor here but not there, on me and mine but not on those and them.

At the core of monotheism is religious *tribalism*, the attitude that one's immediate group is superior to all others and must be preserved at all costs. Generations of Jews, Christians, and Muslims have been taught, consciously and unconsciously, that their religious tribe (with its god-image and sacred texts) is superior to all others. All three tribes have been actively militant in the exercise of their supposed chosen status with supposed divine command and/or approval. "My" tribe and "my" god, or "our" tribe and "our" god, are the possessive pronouns of tribalism that fuel monotheistic madness. Emerging from a tribal mentality, monotheism has not, likely cannot, grow beyond itself to a more global mentality, since to do so would be tantamount to its death, a death that has already occurred, I propose, yet waits to be sufficiently grieved.

The preeminent biologist and naturalist Edward O. Wilson offers further wisdom about tribalism and its dangerous, deadly religious manifestations. In his chapter on "Religion" in *The Meaning of Human Existence*, Wilson begins by noting that the evidence thus far of the relatively young discipline of the neuroscience of religion strongly suggests that something akin to a religious instinct does exist, potentially validating biologically what Jung's analytical psychology has proposed for the last 100 years. As part of our evolutionary history, our species comes hardwired, so to speak, for religion; or in my view, for a need for meaning, with religion being but one avenue for the potential satisfaction of that native drive.

Wilson continues by cataloguing many of the positive roles the great religions can, and have, played throughout our relatively young history as a species. "They perform services invaluable to civilization. Their priests bring solemnity to the rites of passage through the cycle of life and death." They "comfort the afflicted, and take care of the desperately poor. … They and their ministers make more bearable tyranny, war, starvation, and the worst of natural disasters." Their sacred places often serve as places of refuge. Wilson claims that "religious faith offers enormous psychological benefit to the believers … (giving) them an explanation for their existence … (and) makes them feel loved and protected" (Wilson 2014: 150, 152).

Then, Wilson exposes the underbelly of religion: "The great religions are also, and tragically, sources of ceaseless and unnecessary suffering. They are impediments to the grasp of reality needed to solve most social problems in the real world. Their exquisitely human flaw is *tribalism*. … The true cause of hatred and violence is faith versus faith, an outward expression of the ancient instinct of tribalism. Faith is the one thing that makes otherwise good people do bad things." Continuing, he suggests that tribalism is the principal driving force of mass murders in insurgencies, civil wars, and terrorism and "the central rationale for lethal tribalism is sectarian religion—in particular, the conflict between those faithful to different myths" (Wilson 2014: 151, 154). He adds, "We are addicted to tribal conflict, which is harmless and entertaining if sublimated into team sports, but deadly when expressed as real-world ethnic, religious, and ideological struggles" (Wilson 2014: 177).

Feeling a part of one's tribe, be it religious, ethnic, or cultural, *can* promote human bonding, solidarity, and safety. Being a member of a tribe can provide a measure of identity similar to an extended primary family. On the other hand, tribalism promotes unconscious containment, which does not allow for psychological reflection nor challenge from another source. The psychological paradox is that the greater passion and zeal of the religiously faithful individual or collective, the greater the threat perceived from a differing other. Tribalism, or archetypal bonding, lowers the consciousness of those bonded in direct proportion to its bonding intensity. This psychodynamic leads to the following psychological law: "Effective social cohesion is based on archetypal energies which breed an immoral or at least amoral unconsciousness in direct proportion to the strength of the social cohesion they provide" (Dourley 2010: 137). Jung concurs, noting, "Nothing shields you better against the solitude and forlornness of the divine experience than community. It is the best and safest substitute for individual responsibility" (Jung 1958: 725). This dynamic was all-too-apparent in the recent U.S. political campaign and election, where 81 percent of evangelical voters simply overlooked their candidate's immoral and obscene behavior. The shadow side of perceiving one to be the chosen of a one and only deity is the passionate and fearful exclusion of any competing stranger or group, which by its very existence is perceived as a threat. All too often that threat results in making all competitors the source of evil to be converted or eliminated. *Monotheistic madness.*

Religious tribalism feeds off religious certitude, which is one of humanity's most lethal weapons since it assumes the voice and power of God/gods. When religious certitude is wed to political certitude, any and all weapons are deemed legitimate means to protect the faithful. However, it is a psychological law that the greater the certitude, the greater unconscious doubt has to be repressed; repressed doubt generates more anxiety on the part of the believer or the political leader. That anxiety then gets expelled onto outward others. As Thomas Moore notes in *The Soul's Religion*, "Pretending that I know more may make me feel superior, but the price is deep anxiety" (Moore 2002: 23). The central paradox, he notes, is that it takes considerable knowledge and reflective consciousness to cultivate what Nicholas of Cusa calls *educated ignorance* (Moore 2002: 24). Among those who remain enthralled by monotheistic certitude, prayers for the gift of doubt might be more genuine and more beneficial for humanity than prayers for more faith.

Monotheism, with its inherent illusion of being the favored of a one-and-only deity, breeds narcissism followed by paranoia and invariably culminating in aggression. Religious aggression over the centuries has taken active, bloody forms and continues to the present day. The passive aggression includes dismissing or devaluing all other religions as primitive or yet-to-be enlightened. When pressed by questions related to the eventual judgment of persons of another faith, most fundamentalists of all stripes resort to some version of "I am not the judge, but God will be," or "we cannot know the mind of God," all the while maintaining an attitude of superiority of those less fortunate religious who were not chosen.

In one of his poems in a collection called *Leavings*, Wendell Berry speaks to the monotheistic delusion of being the chosen ones: *If there are a "chosen few" / Then I am not one of them / If "an elect," well then / I have not been elected / I am one who is knocking at the door / I am one whose foot / Is on the bottom rung / But I know that Heaven's Bottom rung is Heaven.* Berry concludes his poem by noting that the metaphorical ladder to heaven is standing on the Earth where he works and sleeps "with my head upon a stone" (Berry 2010: 61). Such is what I call a *grounded mysticism,* which preserves the experience of the numinous that emerges from within life rather than from beyond it (See Essay "The Universe As *Mirror* and *Icon*").

Digging even deeper biologically, Edward O. Wilson suggests that "*Homo sapiens* is an innately dysfunctional species ... hampered by the Paleolithic Curse: genetic adaptations that worked very well for millions of years of hunter-gatherer existence but are increasingly a hindrance in a globally urban and techno-scientific society." He concludes by observing that "the great majority of people worldwide remain in the thrall of tribal organized religions, led by men who claim supernatural power in order to compete for the obedience and resources of the faithful" (Wilson 2014: 176-77). Expanding Wilson's observations, underneath our thin layer of apparent sophistication, we remain a dysfunctional species—fearful, protective of our toys, and biting or kicking each other when we don't get our way and our temper boils to a tantrum. At its core, the monotheistic myth has not promoted our maturation as a species from childhood toward responsible adulthood, nor is it capable of doing so. The psyche has moved beyond the religious myth that once served it and now searches the human imagination for a more comprehensive myth to be embraced and incarnated.

Perhaps the primary success of monotheism has been the communal bonding around the unquestioned belief of being the chosen of an external deity who also safeguards the chosen from an external devil in this life and promises rewards in the next one. Judged by the power of archetypal bonding, to use the psychological designation, monotheism has been a roaring success for more than 4,000 years. Success gauged by any other criteria is doubtful at best. Theistic and monotheistic collectives have seldom been on the forefront of promoting peace and justice, for example, and have been forced by secular and political movements to embrace the human values at the core of their formal religious doctrine. Neither have monotheistic collectives been champions for new knowledge. More often they have impeded advancement of knowledge of our universe while elevating ignorance and anti-science to the status of virtues. Happily, there have been heroic religious individuals who have led the way for peace, justice, and new knowledge, though often at their peril.

From the depth psychological perspective, for religions to be evaluated as authentic in the modern era, they must promote the expansion of human consciousness in general and religious consciousness in particular. This may be the most important psychological criterion of any human endeavor—the promotion of consciousness. The three major monotheisms continue to fail in this primary task, and likely never succeeded, except for those marginalized as mystics or heretics. Rather than encouraging and promoting a widening of consciousness, monotheists have all too often resisted this vital function along with resisting the embrace of new knowledge, preferring outdated cosmologies and Bronze Age literature to the ever-new discoveries of the visible and invisible universe, or universes, as the case may prove to be. When conscious contents are suppressed or repressed, they then leak out in subtle and not-so-subtle ways: fear, intolerance, prejudice, depression, violence, and war.

Monotheism is regressive. With its theological eye turned heavenward toward a nonexistent metaphysical domain and deity, and its authority vested in ancient literature, it promotes a regressive mentality. By necessity, it must deny modern science to remain legitimate in the minds and hearts of most of its constituents. *Monotheistic madness.*

Again, theism and monotheism impede the expansion of consciousness by exporting the opposites of life to a metaphysical realm, thereby robbing the human psyche of its most vital psycho-spiritual function; that is, the creation of more and more consciousness by holding in conscious tension all the opposites of life, including good and evil. Consciousness is birthed as the opposites are held internally, both given their legitimacy and value until an unforeseen third can manifest. Jung called this process the *transcendent function,* since the resolution of the inner conflict transcends either of the opposite poles. Again, Jung's psychological reference to transcendent is not equated with supernatural or metaphysical. Rather than holding the opposites in creative tension, the monotheistic myth promotes instead the splitting of opposites, which requires repression and eventual human scapegoating.

Echoing a depth psychological insight, biologist E. O. Wilson reminds us that internal conflict is not a personal irregularity, but a timeless human condition born from the competing levels of evolution. On the one hand, we are driven by individual safety and survival needs; on the other hand, by group survival needs requiring altruism. "All normal humans are ignoble and noble, often in close alteration, sometimes simultaneously," he concludes (Wilson, 179-80). This evolutionary perspective renders obsolete dogmas like *original sin* and/or *original blessing* since there was no original creation point for either 'sin' or 'blessing.' However, we do find ourselves wired with potential good and ill as a result of our evolutionary drives and needs. Rather than accepting our natural conflicted selves through honest introspection, which precedes consciousness, we have exported the conflict to external deities and devils. Until we can take full ownership and responsibility for our conflicted potentials, we will place our species in danger of extinction.

When the innate capacities of good and evil are assigned to an external deity and devil, they are not transformed within. Rather, the deified qualities are conveniently imported as personal possessions while the devilish qualities are redirected toward neighbors near and far. In the latter case, human others are then seen as enemies, devils, or collectively as the axis of evil. Psychologically, it is necessary to demonize an enemy before elimination to avoid the human and societal taboo of murder. One wonders about the unconscious guilt stored and carried by individuals and nations who designate young warriors to do its bidding; and the high cost of PTSD of warriors trained to repress the taboo, albeit for reasons like national security and freedom.

Furthermore, the dualism inherent in monotheism renders the physical world to be less valuable than the so-called spiritual world and thus an expendable resource. When the afterlife is prized more than present life and future rewards take precedence over the rewards of being responsible stewards of creation, Earth's resources are reduced to objects to be consumed. Or, as the monotheistic myth suggests, to be subdued by and for the tribe. *Monotheistic madness.*

Returning to the theme of this essay, monotheistic religions are tribalism on steroids! The monotheistic imagination created a warrior god-image to validate a tribal history and to compete with and destroy all perceived enemies in the path toward the realization of perceived divine promises of life, longevity, land, power, and influence. Tragically, that warrior-god mentality has held sway throughout our bloody history and continues to this day. The Hebrew scriptures are a biography of that imagined human/warrior-god relationship, replete with divinely initiated and divinely ordained mass murder, genocide, patricide and a host of other human horrors created by the human imagination, yet justified by attributing them to an external deity. The resulting authoritative religious texts and their interpretation, of course, are highly spiritualized and delusional. *Monotheistic madness.*

The Christian sacred texts, while blunting some of the immediate warrior mentality, claim to have the one and only divine son/messiah, thus implicitly indicting all other religions, and reserves its most devastating war for an Armageddon ending where the deity is final judge, jury, and executioner of all except the Christian faithful, plus a few others given a last chance in the final thousand years. And Islam and the Quran perpetuate similar madness, Armageddon endings, and deadly shortcuts to a supposed paradise. When the supposed promises made by a remote, all-powerful deity of land, prosperity, peace, and meaning have not been realized in this life, and hope wanes, Jihad seems like a good alternative. The warrior-mentality of Judaism, Christianity, and Islam have contributed equally to divisions, violence, and terror, and continue to do so. Of course, one's own religious tribe is exempt from such a conclusion. *Monotheistic madness.*

In his book *Not in God's Name: Confronting Religious Violence*, Rabbi Jonathon Sachs notes that tribal religions promote *pathological dualism*, a mentality that divides the world between those "who are unimpeachably good and those who are irredeemably bad." Addressing historic and current religious violence, he suggests that the pathological dualist cannot reconcile his humiliated place in the world with his own moral superiority and seeks to destroy those outside his group with apocalyptic force. Sachs calls for reinterpreting holy texts with a *theology of the Other,* which allows one to see God's face in strangers. I bow to Sachs's sentiment and wisdom; the psychological meanings of a theology of the Other are explored in the Essay "The Universe as *Mirror* and *Icon.*" However, ancient monotheistic sacred texts do not need to be reinterpreted so much as rewritten and/or replaced; at a minimum, they need to be seen as the products of the human imagination and level of consciousness of their day. The supposed religious superiority of tribe over tribe based on rival creation stories gives way to claims of cultural and political superiority, which fuels the tinderbox of international relations. Psychologically, the worship of ancient holy books remains one of the greatest hindrances to the expansion of consciousness and regularly fuels monotheistic madness.

Again, the pathology at the core of the monotheistic myth not only infects religions and the religious imagination, but, staying with the disease metaphor, it has metastasized to other human endeavors. The delusions of being the chosen of the one and only deity informs and deforms our social and political institutions and attitudes, granting supposed divine credence and approval for any and all subjective perspectives, prejudices, and whims of the day or moment. What level of religious consciousness is being exhibited when winners give thanks to the heavenly deity for aiding their victory while the losers weep? Or, more severely, to thank the heavenly watchman for saving one from danger when others were not spared? Or to declare, along with John Bradford in the 16th century as he watched wretches led to execution, "there but for the grace of God go I," which likely means "there by the grace of God goes someone else" (Hitchens 2007: 76)? Or to invoke the divinity with the mantra *God bless America* or *Allahu Akbar* (God is Great) when sending forces into battle or carrying out Jihad? Yet, Christians, Jews, and Muslims continue to send sons and daughters off to war while praying for divine blessing and safety to fight the sons and daughters of others who invoke the same external divinity, each claiming religious conviction and sincerity. When prayers are not answered and warriors are not kept safe, there is little consolation in claiming that their deaths were heroic and honorable. *Monotheistic madness.*

John Shelby Spong, perhaps the most prolific author concerning the death of theism and monotheism, notes that monotheists once thought that their God led them into battle and victory based on their faithfulness; or, if faithfulness had been compromised, allowing defeat to taste the divine wrath. However, with the advent of modern warfare, he quips, "God seems always to be on the side of the nations with the greatest arsenal" (Spong 2001: 22).

The unconscious wedding of monotheism and politics, aptly described as political monotheisms, results in special dangers given the access to power and weapons available to enforce supposed divinely ordained rights, including the seemingly benign rights of "life, liberty, and the pursuit of happiness." Political monotheisms are especially pernicious with their illusory promises of safety and security by providing more weaponry and military might. In what is likely an extension of the monotheistic attitude, it is commonly supposed that America was/is especially ordained and blessed by God, making us the last best hope for the world because of American Exceptionalism. The recent nationalist political frenzy to "Make America Great Again," with its chief strategy of America First, and the repeated invocation "God Bless America," are unconscious or barely conscious manifestations of tribalism and the religious pathology under our examination. Tribalism is another name for the populist, nationalistic waves washing upon Western shores, waters of which are attempts to dilute the emerging myth of a global, interconnected, interdependent community. Furthermore, to the nonreflective person, it all seems necessary to defeat an enemy who also justifies its existence and murderous impulses with religious conviction. *Monotheistic madness.*

We live in a terror-filled world. Some of these words were written in the days following the 2016 Paris terrorist attacks and massacre, and the terrorist attack in California and multiple attacks in London and Manchester, England, to name but a few. I listened to the 24/7 news coverage, and the raw, unedited responses from our own religious and political leaders, including the traveling circus, replete with clowns, known as the U.S. presidential campaign, election, and aftermath. I have yet to hear any significant depth psychological perspective on the global crises we face with even a hint of psychological wisdom, though we are clearly witnessing an eruption from the unconscious depths. I do hear appeals to the Bible, to evangelical voters, and appeals to an external deity to "Bless America," as well as praises to Allah before murdering innocents, all of which perpetuate *monotheistic madness.*

The unconscious power and pathology of tribalism was glaringly evident in the aforementioned political campaign. Political candidates spent months denouncing, devaluing, and in some cases demonizing rivals only to reverse their assessments later to support their political tribe. Values of consistency, honesty, and integrity were easily abandoned under the pressure of tribalism. The safety, support, and continuance of the political tribe takes precedence over all else and, alarmingly, with religious zeal and conviction inherited, I propose, from our monotheistic mindset. Faithfulness to the tribe and its hold on political power continues to trump reason and facts, and reduces the spine of most politicians of all stripes to little more than a physical entity. Perhaps more than any Western democracy, U. S. political leaders and wannabees tout their religious (predominantly Christian) identity as evidence of their capacity to lead. Paradoxically, those who are the most vocal also speak more about the constitutional separation of Church and State. Even more unconsciously, they seem quick to condemn foreign theocracies, confirming the psychological law that our species is quick to condemn that with which we are most unconsciously identified. *Monotheistic madness.*

We are reaping the harvest of 4,000 years of exporting our deities and devils to the remote regions of heaven and hell. History validates the aforementioned human tendency to import and identify with the deity and its supposed goodness and power while assigning all evil first to a personified devil, then to outer others, whether individuals or nations. Scapegoating is an unconscious attempt to rid ourselves, our religious tribe, or our nation of our own capacity for evil. Or, in the Christian myth to assign it magically to Jesus or to his mistaken name Jesus Christ, which is the topic of the two Essays, "Reimagining Jesus and *Christ*." However, the unconscious does not have a digestive tract whereby repressed contents are eliminated either through denial, Christological dogma, or uttering *Allahu Akbar*. In no case is the unconscious fooled, though the ego may well be.

Jung's views on the dangers of the unrecognized, unowned human shadow are familiar to the psychologically minded, yet no less challenging in their familiarity. Noting that Jesus did not carry his cross and suffer crucifixion so that we could escape, Jung writes, "The bill of the Christian era is presented to us: we are living in a world rent in two from top to bottom; we are confronted with the H-bomb and we have to face our own shadows. ... We are threatened with universal genocide if we cannot work out the way of salvation by a symbolic death" (Jung 1958: 734-735). In that context, then, he makes a psychological observation sure to disturb our sleep:

> The psychological rule says that when an inner situation is not made conscious, it happens outside, as fate. That is to say, when the individual ... does not become conscious of his inner opposite, the world must perforce act out the conflict and be torn into opposing halves (Jung 1959a: 71).

The psychological rule identified by Jung applies to the psyches of nations as well as to individuals: The inner opposite that is rejected, split-off, or repressed will find its battleground in the external world. The global War on Terror will eventually have to be fought on the inner, psychological battlefield where wars have always been generated by conflicted individuals and nations. So far neither Judaism, Christianity, nor Islam, nor the politics and politicians they inspire, seem capable of recognizing and changing the locus of the battle. In the wisdom of psyche, we now have before us the correct name of age-old conflicts—War on Terror—but so far we continue to fight the *right war on the wrong front*. Whether designated as *Jihad* or the *War on Terror*, the real Holy War is an internal one, a war against oneself or one's own tribe.

The oft-expressed monotheistic declaration that *with God all things are possible* is sadly and tragically true, but not in the sense usually intended. With the monotheistic God on one's side, anything has been permissible, even sanctioned: Jihad, torture, murder, genocide, genital mutilation, beheading, slavery, devaluation of women, rape, incest, witch hunts, human sacrifice, bloody crusades and inquisitions, elimination of indigenous cultures, and the gory list goes on, as do the atrocities done in God's name. Of course, none of these atrocities are mentioned when the faithful worry that with the death of religions dependent on external deities there will be no morality or compassion. It can be a hard truth for most religious to entertain that morality, kindness, and compassion are not limited to those who are religious. Those who are nonreligious or self-proclaimed atheists are equally capable of exhibiting and promoting any and all human virtues, as well as any and all vices. The human shadow is no respecter of persons but demands the respect of all. Theistic and monotheistic religions remain hiding places for the human shadow. Any behavior can be, and has been, sanctioned by imagined remote deities and ancient religious texts created by the Bronze Age male psyche. *Monotheistic madness.*

The late Christopher Hitchens, an intelligent self-proclaimed atheist, frequently asked his audiences what ethical values and behavior has religion promoted that cannot be expressed by atheists; none, of course. Atheists are just as potentially loving, creative, and compassionate, and as potentially destructive, as any religious. Hitchen's book, with the provocative title, *God Is Not Great*, subtitled *How Religion Poisons Everything*, exposes religions' shadow as few books have. For that reason, I think it should be required reading for all seminarians and those responsible for religious education of whatever monotheistic stripe. None of us can easily see our shadow, and the religious shadow is especially elusive. Atheists like Hitchens can see the religious shadow more easily. Of course, they are equally blind to their own shadow, which religion can expose. I read with great interest *God Is Not Great*. The very last page caught my Jungian eye. Hitchens acknowledges his indebtedness to the body of fiction of Ian McEwan, which "shows an extraordinary ability to elucidate the numinous without conceding anything to the supernatural. He has subtly demonstrated that the natural is wondrous enough for anyone" (Hitchens 2007: 296). The experience of the numinous is the cornerstone of Jung's psychological house, a descriptive word he borrowed from Rudolph Otto (See Essay "Reimagining *God* and *Religion*").

Compassion, generally accepted by all major religions as the highest virtue, does not spring from belief in an external benevolent, compassionate deity. It is true that kindness and generosity may be taught or generated by imitating an external example, be it a supposed external deity or a human other, and such behavior is not to be devalued. Compassion, however, cannot be so easily taught. Rather, it springs from one's intimate acquaintance with one's own suffering and one's own shadow, one's own capacity for cruelty and evil. If those potentials are denied, or magically eliminated through a substitutionary salvific formula, or assigned to an external devil, compassion may recede even though kind deeds may continue. It is no secret that gifts of money or goods, while received gladly by the recipients, can spring from guilt and expected future rewards, motivations that require no transformation of character.

The religious pathology under our examination has been perpetuated by centuries of chosen ignorance rooted in fear. There is no virtue in ignorance, especially when disguised as religious faith. In the so-called developed world, there is little excuse for ignorance except for the economically marginalized. Yet religions have too often been the state-protected nurseries of ignorance by championing anti-intellectual, anti-science agendas. To be authentic, religion must learn from science with its operative attitude "doubt seeking discovery," rather than turning a blind eye to new knowledge. Blind faith is often just that. The late Carl Sagan once noted that at the heart of theistic religion is the idea that wishing makes it so. Describing the scientific attitude, he writes, "Science thrives on errors, cutting them away one by one. ... Science gropes and staggers toward improved understanding" (Sagan 1996: 14, 20). In contrast, monotheistic religions have tended to protect their errors by claiming them sacrosanct. In doing so, religion simply staggers—and eventually dies.

We can no longer entrust the care of soul, or the care of our planet, to religious dogma and institutions devoted to gods external to material life and external to the life of the psyche. Psyche has served, and continues to serve, as the birthing canal of all divinities, devils, and religious dogma that seeks to make meaning of tribal history and tribal hope. The monotheistic god was conceived as a jealous god, a competitive god to defeat and supersede all other tribal gods. Predictably, the three religious tribes spawned by that image remain jealous as well, competing for loyalty, power, land, and resources of the faithful. Each in its own way, explicitly or implicitly, claims to be superior. Some are more politely superior than others, but superior nevertheless. None of the three religious traditions can claim exemption from promoting centuries of violence, bloodshed, and terror, except through denial and scapegoating. *Monotheistic madness.*

Articulate and self-proclaimed atheist Sam Harris regularly addresses his audiences with the ominous warning: "Our world is way too small .for us to wait to see how bad the idea of God can get!" When we add the psychology of the unconscious to the equation, it may be that we have already waited too long to avoid major catastrophes. Psychologically speaking, the underground stockpiles of nuclear weapons may well mirror the centuries of denial, repression, and scapegoating, which are residuals of a monotheistic mindset.

In light of the 4,000-year history of monotheism with its metaphysical domain, deity, and devil, one is led to the psychological conclusion: ***As long as our deities and devils are perceived to be beyond physical life and the life of the human psyche, our species will continue to do great harm to each other and to our nest.***

Echoing the concerns in the opening paragraph of this essay, this stark psychological assessment challenges us to bring fresh imagination to theism in general and monotheism in particular. This vital religious task will entail reimagining *god* and *religion* so that the archetypal or universal urgings beneath both may find expression that honors both the modern mind and ancient soul. Given the dangers posed by monotheistic madness, it could well be our most important task as a species.

Furthermore, these essays propose that the relatively young discipline of Jung's analytical psychology has already contributed significantly to this urgent task and could serve as a healing resource for the religious illness that threatens humanity. Consistent with the view of the psychic origin of all religious images, religious myths, and religious dogma, Jung proposes that the solution to our religious (and political) dilemmas will come from the same source—i.e., from psyche herself as she gives birth to more and more consciousness mediated through receptive individuals and spilling over to the various collectives. Jung framed the task clearly when he noted the historical "systematic blindness" and "prejudice that God is *outside* man," which will require that "everything of a divine or daemonic character outside us must return to the psyche, to the inside of the unknown man, whence it apparently originated" (Jung: 1939: 84–85).

For the psychologically minded, the cure for our modern religious disease will not be found in searching the heavenly heights for an interventionist deity or shunning an external devil. Neither will it require an external savior or messiah, nor an Armageddon ending, which are monotheistic delusions that have served to extend the religious illness rather than to cure or save the patient, which is humanity and its nest. Nor will it require the creation of yet another fully formed religion. The age of religions as previously conceived is likely over, though the religious instinct, or more accurately, the instinct for meaning, will persist and give birth to ever-new expressions to satisfy that need. That instinct, conceived psychologically as universal, remains alive and well, though arguably largely misdirected.

Neither will the remedy be found in interpreting and reinterpreting ancient sacred texts hoping to find the elusive magical key to unlock the metaphysical deity's nature or will or to recover a supposedly lost religious paradise. There has never been a time when religion was best or right that requires our return or recovery. Neither do we assume that Bronze Age men had a wisdom that is authoritative for all times, places, and people, though the teachings of the original monotheistic prophets—Moses, Jesus, Mohammed—might well continue to be inspiring. For the psychologically minded, there is no such document as *The Word of God*; there are unlimited *words about god* that have come through human psyches and voices over the centuries and for centuries to come, none of which can claim to be authoritative for all time and all people. The value of sacred texts created and validated by the religious imagination of ancients operating from a dualistic, three-tiered view of the universe, rests not on a one-time, for-all-time revelation from a metaphysical deity. Rather, the texts provide a glimpse into the individual and collective level of con-sciousness of the day and, more importantly, reveal the underlying archetypal urgings to which the ancients were responding and forming their images of god, religion, and dogma. The experiences of our religious ancestors can aid our recognition of the important human questions, issues, and concerns that still confront us and demand our best response. The archetypal urgings that coursed through the psyches of our former brothers and sisters, and animated their imaginations, are alive in the present day and serve as fertilizer for the modern imagination in general and the religious imagination in particular.

Carl Jung's fertile imagination, informed by his vast, unparalleled research and knowledge of world religions East and West, could serve as a rich resource for our own task to reimagine god and religion, the theme of the following essay.

ESSAY NUMBER FOUR

REIMAGINING *GOD* AND *RELIGION*

There is no god except the experience of god. (Sufi Wisdom)

Dear ones,
Beware of the tiny gods frightened men create
To bring an anesthetic relief
To their sad days. (Hafiz)

With the necessary demise and death of antique cosmologies and traditional religious paradigms dependent on external supernatural deities and devils, the modern religious challenge involves two simultaneous sacred endeavors: To eulogize, bury, and grieve the theistic and monotheistic god-images and the religious paradigms dependent on them; and secondly, to bring fresh imagination to the meanings of *god* and *religion* that will satisfy both the modern mind and ancient soul.

The necessary grieving process is addressed in an earlier Essay (See Essay "Beyond the Back Porch of the Church"). The second task has seized my imagination for the second half of my life and will likely continue for my remaining years. What follows are some of the current fruits of that labor, of imagining *god* and *religion* beyond the metaphysical, supernatural, and monotheistic categories that are no longer meaningful to me, and I imagine to a growing number of people who search for fresh religious meanings.

The Sufi imagination proposes that *there is no god except the experience of god*. Nodding affirmatively to this ancient mystical wisdom, and drawing on the dynamics of analytical or Jungian psychology, I propose further differentiation summarized here:

There is no god except powerful affective experiences beyond the creation, command, and control of the ego, experiences which humans have assigned innumerable names, and analytical psychology calls numinous.

These experiences emerge from a meta-personal (in contrast to meta-physical) source that C. G. Jung called the archetypal or collective unconscious, a metaphor for our continuing connection to all that has preceded us, cosmologically, biologically, sociologically, and psychologically.

Attending these numinous experiences in all their valences, including seeking to serve as a conscious conduit for them, constitutes a religious attitude that cultivates and promotes an expansion of consciousness in general and religious consciousness in particular, the twin goals of analytical psychology.

Living with such an attitude fuels the process of individuation by which one grows in intimate relationship with unconscious contents and empathic, compassionate connection to all.

This succinct summary contains the salient features of a religious attitude from the perspective of Jungian psychology. For me, it replaces the now extinct theistic and monotheistic paradigm(s) with their metaphysical deities and devils, and could serve as a bridge to what the deep unconscious will provide in its continuing unfolding. First articulated by C. G. Jung and continually tweaked and modified by his many interpreters, analytical psychology could be a major tool in the birthing of our religious, cultural, and political future. Whether or not that will be the case, or what the gestation period might be, we cannot yet know. Only time and reflective consciousness will tell. For the psychologically minded, I propose, it satisfies both the modern mind and ancient soul and offers hope for the future of our species and the incredible nest in which we are privileged to live and share.

As a new kid on the block, barely 100 years old, analytical or Jungian psychology has already proven to be both a hospitable refuge and challenge for those who find themselves between old religious paradigms that have lost their legitimacy and new ways of being religious, which are hopefully emerging. More and more religious are finding themselves in this in-between place, while many others have understandably abandoned religious hope altogether. Meanwhile, religious zealots of various stripes continue to monopolize the headlines, exhibiting the worst of unconscious religion, a psychopathology for which analytical psychology also provides a most accurate diagnosis and treatment.

Among the current disciplines seeking to understand our universe and our role in it, Jungian psychology seems uniquely positioned. It invites and honors the ever-new scientific discoveries of the physical world/universe in its evolutionary unfolding while simultaneously honoring religious experience as an authentic part of being human. As an integrative discipline, it honors physical and spiritual reality as two sides of the same coin. Jung once described it thus: "the spirit is the life of the body seen from within, and the body the outward manifestation of the life of the spirit— the two being really one" (Jung 1924: 94). It celebrates matter and spirit and their creative interplay without doing violence to the human intellect by perpetuating images of external, supernatural, interventionist deities or devils. Moreover, it retains the inner experience behind and beneath those obsolete images. This requires individuals and collectives to bring to bear the hard work of consciousness of, and responsibility for, the human potentials for both good and evil. In other words, the powers previously attributed to both deities and devils find expressions in and through the human psyche, which is a hard pill to swallow after centuries of exporting those potentials. The human family and our Earth home have not been well served by that exportation.

As we proceed, it should be noted that within the Jungian community there are varied perspectives on the impact of its discipline on the future of religions in general and on the future of Christianity in particular. The latter is especially considered in light of the major attention Jung granted Christian symbols and their amplification and reinterpretation. In his book, *Jung's Treatment of Christianity*, Murray Stein provides a comprehensive review of Jung's many interpreters, including their particular slant on Jung's engagement with religious themes and with Christian symbols and Christian doctrine in particular. The variety and depth of these various analyses of Jung, and what may be regarded as his healthy obsession with religion, seem to validate Jung's pivotal role in the evolution of religious thought. Stein states clearly his own perspective: "Jung's stance toward Christianity was fundamentally that of a psychotherapist, and so the goal of all his efforts with this *patient*, Christianity, was its psychotherapeutic transformation" (Stein 1985: 1-19, 18). In summary, some interpreters see

Jungian psychology as a supplement to Christian theology and its continued practice and possible transformation, while others note the inherent incompatibility of the two (Dourley 2010: 69).

After swimming in the twin waters of religion and psychology for half my life, yet claiming no prophetic gifts, my own perspective is that analytical psychology provides a necessary and timely compensation for all modern religions, and especially the theistic and monotheistic faiths whose deities and devils are perceived to be outside or beyond the physical domain. This psychological compensation could provide a necessary foundation from which a future counter myth will emerge. The future myth would replace the historical theistic and monotheistic myth(s) that have proven to be inadequate, incomplete, and largely incomprehensible to the modern mind and no longer nourish soul. Assisting psyche in her ongoing mysterious, purposeful birthing will involve a more basic, dare I say fundamental, transformation of the human conceptualizations of those experiences deemed religious and their psychological, meta-personal source, as opposed to metaphysical.

As I intend the words, *metaphysical* implies a domain beyond the physical world/universe, which necessarily perpetuates a dualism between the essence of matter and spirit, and between the realities designated physical and spiritual. Such dualism is no longer believable, or necessary, given what has been revealed about the visible physical universe by our physical sciences and the invisible/psychological universe revealed by modern depth psychology in the most recent 100 years. A metaphysical dimension, necessary as long as our gods and devils were deemed external to life itself, and necessary as long as a dualistic three-storied universe was in vogue, is necessary no more.

Meta-personal, on the other hand, proposes that there are depths and contents of the unconscious that are common to all and are more than mere forgotten products of personal history. We share a collective continuity and inheritance, not only with our human ancestors, but with all forms of biological life and, even more astounding, with the matter of the cosmos in its 13.8 billion-year unfolding. Jung used the metaphor of the collective unconscious to speak of this meta-personal dimension to which we have access and, more importantly, which seems to seek out human consciousness as its manifestation and voice. His experience of being addressed by unconscious contents prompted Jung to imagine the unconscious as a living reality as opposed to an inert collection of repressed material. He often referred to the "autonomous unconscious," the unconscious "with a life of its own," or " the reality of the psyche," which C.A. Meier, one of Jung's closest colleagues, once noted to be Jung's greatest contributions to psychology; and, I propose, a great gift to understanding the origin of religions and the god-images at their core.

As an empiricist and medical scientist, Jung was reluctant to speculate on a metaphysical dimension that can be neither proven nor disproven. As proposed in these pages, however, a hypothetical metaphysical domain is no longer believable, necessary, or advisable given the destructive delusions it has perpetuated. To state a repeated refrain, *as long as our deities and devils are perceived to be external to physical life and the life of the psyche, our species will continue to do great harm to each other and to our nest.*

From this psychological perspective, Judaism, Christianity, and Islam emerged from the same source—no, not the Middle East nor from a transcendent God—but from the depths of the human psyche and imagination. All religions and their core god-images are created or birthed through the psyche rather than dropped down from on high by a metaphysical being. More accurately, they are co-created, with the unconscious itself initiating its contents for an approach to consciousness primarily in its native language, the language of symbols. In this sense, the psychological perspective proposed here turns religion on its head, which is a much-needed turn, given its historical hierarchal and anti-intellectual character.

More poetically, the human psyche is the birthing canal and manger for all god-images, all religions, and all sacred texts. Thus, all religions and religious texts are subjective, finite, and, when alive and well, always in the process of change and transformation. This psychological perspective embraces the epistemological (theory of knowledge) premise that all human knowledge is mediated and filtered by the human psyche. While this seems self-evident, it is not easily accepted by those who deem their knowledge of the divine as an exclusive revelatory gift and consider themselves to be the possessors and dispensers of eternal truths.

When religions and their god-images are conceived as creations through the human psyche and imagination (rightly, I propose), numerous religious conflicts and pathologies are immediately eliminated. Though a difficult deflation for the collective religious ego, this means that no particular religion possesses inerrant sacred texts or supposed universal truths applicable to all for all times. It means that there are no chosen people, as traditionally formulated, which is a necessary blow to religious narcissism. Unable to claim divine favoritism and possession of exclusive truth, religions are, or could be, freed from the bloody competition known as monotheistic madness addressed in the earlier essay.

Anticipating a common objection to these psychological perspectives on religion and the theologies supporting them (objections Jung regularly fielded), they are often dismissed as *psychologizing,* of reducing the divine only to a psychological entity and religion only to psychological dynamics. Or, as Jung noted, "*It is only psychological* too often means: It is nothing" (Jung 1961: 263). On closer reflection, however, the counter view seems more accurate. That is, we tend to *theologize* psychological experiences; an experience comes first, and reflection on that experience may be deemed religious or otherwise. All human knowledge is filtered through the human psyche even if it seems revelatory or inspired, and especially then. While this appears self-evident, many religious presume they have direct access to/from the divine mind while bypassing the human mind or psyche, which is a dangerous, deadly assumption. As Jung remarked, there are those who accept this self-evident fact and those who don't. Those who do are able to talk to each other; those who don't are also able to talk to each other. But the two groups cannot talk with each other very long before the dialogue breaks down. If we want to promote a healthy, soul-satisfying religious attitude, we will be obliged to wrestle with our epistemology, with how we know what we know. That wrestling match forces one to confront magical thinking, which is too often equated with religious faith.

The familiar critique, usually offered by those who dismiss religion altogether, that *we have created God in our own image rather than being created by God in his image,* has merit. But it is not the whole story. First, that perspective fails to make the necessary distinction between god and god-image, thus perpetuating even as it dismisses the now-deceased image of the divine as a separate, supernatural, male Being. More importantly, while analytical psychology proposes that religions are human creations, both the experiences deemed religious and the images engaged to describe those experiences emerge from a source beyond the creation, command, or control of the ego. Religious experiences and religious images happen to us, so to speak, rather than being a product of pure rational thought. They come upon us unbidden, giving rise to the familiar Jungian dictum drawn from ancient sources, *called or not called the god will be present.*

Furthermore, though a rather recent discipline barely 100 years old, the subject of psychology (*psyche/soul*) actually precedes the subject of theology (*theos/god*). That is, since all knowledge is mediated through the human psyche, all knowledge—be it theology, cosmology, biology, anthropology, etc.—owes its manifestation to the human psyche and its various functions. Of course, this is not the popular, unreflective presumption. We have been conditioned to think of gods, goddesses—and, more recently, God—as metaphysical Beings, existing before and outside time and space, rather than as the name we humans assigned to our human experience(s). To say it even more provocatively, the categories of "gods," "goddesses," "spirits," and "religion," did not exist before the evolutionary gift of self-reflection, i.e., the human capacity to reflect on nature and our human nature and to symbolize those experiences with language.

As discussed elsewhere, the so-called *revealed religions* are, in fact, revelatory. Yet, what they reveal is the state of the human psyche and imagination and the level of consciousness of those who birthed the religions by naming, interpreting, and ritualizing their experiences, and, of course, dogmatizing them. Again, religions expose the human psyche rather than some imagined metaphysical domain or deity. While this perspective is problematic to theistic and monotheistic sensibilities, it is a source of good news for the psychologically minded. Because religions and their attendant god-images are products of the human psyche and imagination (again, drawing from accumulated, meta-personal wisdom), then it is possible to co-create more authentic, more humane religious categories that can serve as an antidote to the exclusive, divisive, tribal religions we have inherited. If, on the other hand, religions are dropped down fully formed from some remote domain and deity, written in stone, unchangeable, and gifted to a very few, our future as a species will be very bleak.

Our modern task entails bringing fresh imagination to the meanings of god and religion, and analytical psychology can be a rich resource for this sacred endeavor. The current psychological paradigm or myth will also give way to future possibilities birthed by psyche in her perceived movement toward wholeness and her apparent engagement of the human imagination to birth an ever-widening consciousness. Short of being a panacea or another idol, analytical psychology can direct us down a path of self-examination and expanded consciousness, which will be necessary for our salvation, whereas the theistic and monotheistic paradigms have proven to be dead-end streets. Or, switching metaphors, analytical psychology can assist in freeing us from our self-made religious prisons. We must cease to search the skies for external messiahs, saviors, or interventionist deities and search our human depths from which the old powers called gods and goddesses reared their holy heads and continue to do so.

Exercising our psychological and religious imagination, psyche seems to be demanding a universal recall of its former images of external deities and devils. Those images were once necessary but always partial and incomplete. Consciousness has evolved to a next stage and now evokes from its own unconscious origin a more whole myth, including god-images more relevant to the modern and postmodern mind, and more expressive of the ever-verdant psyche or soul.

Addressing the Western religious prejudice of God as a wholly other, self-sufficient, metaphysical Being, and noting the loss of a symbolic religious sense, Jung addressed the questions related to the status of ancient deities. What happened to all the ancient deities who ruled the outer world or the heavens? In an imaginative leap, he proposed that those personified beings once perceived as occupying an external metaphysical domain had disappeared into the unconscious. There they have "become diseases" and manifest as psychological symptoms like phobias, depressions, obsessions, etc. He concluded with an ominous observation all too relevant to the present moment: "Zeus no longer rules Olympus but rather the solar plexus, and produces curious specimens for the doctor's consulting room, or disorders the brains of politicians and journalists who unwittingly let loose psychic epidemics on the world" (Jung 1957: 37). Of course, the powers humans have named deities and devils always had their operative headquarters in the so-called inner world rather than a projected outer one. Yet it has taken humanity a very long time to recognize these psychological perspectives and to adjust its sights. In fact, most mono-theists continue to ignore what seems obvious to the psychologically minded.

The recalling of the deities to their psychogenetic origin and the responsibility of dealing with them there could be considered Jung's culminating psychological insight (Dourley 2010: 48). In the words of Murray Stein, "For Jung ... the Gods of traditional doctrine and image were dead. God had moved out of his temples, not to return, and had transmuted into an inner Presence, the Self." As Jung once put it, once the gods have left the temple, they never return (Corbett 2007: xi, 2).

Rather than proposing a new religion, as some of his most ardent critics have charged, Jung's psychology proposes a much more modest and, at the same time, more expansive possibility: *To aid in the cultivation of a religious attitude.* Such an attitude recognizes a wide range of human experiences rightly called religious or spiritual without being limited to identification with a particular religious tradition or religious doctrine. To the theologians and psychologists of his day who accused him of pro-moting another religion, Jung had various responses throughout his long and productive career. One of his most definitive responses to such charges was included in a letter to Fraulein Helene Kiener, written late in his life:

> Analytical psychology helps us to recognize our religious potentialities ... (It) only helps us to find our way to the religious experience that makes us whole. It is not the experience itself, nor does it bring it about. But we do know that analytical psychology teaches us that attitude which meets a transcendent reality halfway (Jung, 1955b: 265).

Jung generally employed the word *transcendent* to speak of a dimension of the human psyche that transcends the ego's command or control rather than a domain beyond the physical world or universe. That psychological domain is "of indefinite extent with no assignable limits"

(Jung, 1954: 258) and characterized by infinite creativity or fecundity (Dourley, 2010: 147). As stated before, I prefer the term *meta-personal* to *transcendent,* that seems more accurate given what we now know about our outer and inner universe(s). Transcendent has come to be a synonym for metaphysical or that which transcends the physical domain, a perspective no longer relevant.

Jung's emphasis on one's religious attitude or outlook is also contained in what is perhaps his most quoted observation. Speaking to the Alsatian Pastoral Conference at Strasbourg on the topic "Psycho-therapists or The Clergy," and having treated hundreds of patients by that time, he says:

> Among all my patients in the second half of life—that is to say, over thirty-five—there has not been one whose problem in the last resort was not that of finding a religious outlook on life. It is safe to say that every one of them fell ill because he had lost what the living religions of every age have given to their followers, and none of them has really been healed who did not regain his religious outlook. This of course has nothing whatever to do with a particular creed or membership of a church (Jung 1954: 334).

To speak of religion from a psychological standpoint, Jung employed a derivation of the word quite different from today's common under-standing. He notes that in antiquity the word *religion* had two etymologies from Latin: *religare* and *religere. Religare* comes from two stems, *re*, meaning "back" and *ligare,* meaning "to tie or to bind." It brings to mind our word "ligament," which ties one body part to another. From this etymology, religion means to tie or link oneself back to some prior existence or to an earlier source or state of being. This has been the preferred etymology and meaning for most monotheistic thinkers whose religious myth includes an original paradisiacal state that beckons our return.

Jung favored *religere,* which supposedly had more ancient roots, and means to take into careful account, or as we might say today, "to pay attention." Its opposite would be to neglect. Thus, when we do something religiously, we do it carefully, watchfully, thoroughly, with our best faculties or, more poetically, with all our heart. The poet Mary Oliver captures this kind of attentiveness in her poem "Mindful" — *Every day I see or hear some-thing / that more or less kills me with delight / … It was what I was born for / to look, to listen / to lose myself inside this soft world* (Oliver 2004: 58-59).

Jung's notion of *religere/*religion exhorts one, then, to pay attention. But pay attention to what in the religious sense? The one word that best encompasses the answer for Jung and for those who are psychologically minded is *numinous*. It would not be an exaggeration, in my opinion, to say that the *experience* of the numinous, or numinosum, serves as the foundation stone on which Jung built the remainder of his theoretical psychological house, including all his consideration of the interplay between psychology and religion. If one has an appreciation for, and an experiential grasp of, the numinous, then one can appreciate Jung's contribution to depth psychology, to religious experience, and to our possible religious future. Without that, his extraordinary work may well be lost or overlooked.

Jung borrowed the word numinous from Rudolph Otto, who coined the word in his book, *The Idea of the Holy*. Otto was distressed that the word *holy* had lost some of its original meaning and had come to be identified with that which was "completely good." He searched for a word that would capture that "*extra* in the meaning of *holy* above and beyond the meaning of goodness" (Otto 1923: 6). To capture this extra quality, he coined the word numinous, from the Latin *numen,* meaning a god, along with the verb *nuere,* meaning to nod or beckon, indicating divine approval. A numinous experience, then, is felt to be like a *nod from the gods*. For Otto, the presence of the numinous is the crucial element of religious experience; it is felt to be objective and to come from beyond the personal ego. While stressing the subjective "state of mind in the religious experience," Otto's emphasis is always upon the objective reference (Otto 1923: xvii). The experience of the numinous, while eliciting great feeling, is not limited to or equivalent to emotion as some critics of Otto (and Jung) have proposed. For both Otto and Jung, retaining the objective source of the subjective experience was vital. For Otto, that objective source could still be understood as a *wholly other God*. For the psychologist Jung, however, that source was *wholly immanent*, conceived as the objective psyche or the archetypal unconscious (Dourley 2010: 49). In these essays, the objective source is perceived to be meta-personal rather than metaphysical; that is, beyond the command or control of the personal ego but not beyond the physical world of matter as the theistic and monotheistic myth(s) have proposed.

While not synonymous with feeling, the numinous does announce itself by stirring strong emotions, by producing a strong affective state. Along with the strong emotions there are likely to be any number of physical manifestations, like a "shudder, or creeping flesh, the hair rising on one's neck," or a sense of something "uncanny, eerie, or weird." In the words of Frederick Buechner in *Alphabet of Grace*, "Religions start, as Frost said poems do, with a lump in the throat ... or with a bush going up in flames, the rain of flowers, the dove coming down out of the sky." One may be comforted by the presence of the numinous or terrified, gripped by a holy dread, what Otto calls the *mysterium tremendum*. Otto's own description of the experience of the visitation by the numinous Other is classic:

> The feeling of (the numinous) may at times come sweeping like a gentle tide, pervading the mind with a tranquil mood of deepest worship. It may pass over into a more set and lasting attitude of the soul, continuing, as it were, thrillingly vibrant and resonant, until at last it dies away and the soul resumes its 'profane', non-religious mood of everyday experience. It may burst in sudden eruption up from the depths of the soul with spasms and convulsions, or lead to the strangest excitements, to intoxicated frenzy, to transport, and to ecstasy. It has its wild and demonic forms and can sink to an almost grisly horror and shuddering. It has its crude, barbaric antecedents and early manifestations, and again it may be developed into something beautiful and pure and glorious. It may become the hushed, trembling, and speechless humility of the creature in the presence of –whom or what? In the presence of that which is a *mystery* inexpressible and above all creatures (Otto 1923: 12-13).

Jung latched onto this powerful word, numinous, because it described perfectly many of the experiences he had had since early childhood, experiences seldom appreciated by the adults in his Swiss Reformed setting. He had thought himself to be weird because of all the strange, uncanny, and unusual thoughts, dreams, and experiences he had as a child and adolescent. These experiences constituted the birth of Jung's own religious attitude, experiences that are well-documented in his later personal letters and in his familiar autobiography *Memories, Dreams, Reflections*, which Aniela Jaffe, who recorded and edited it, called "Jung's religious testament" (Jung 1965: x).

Jung's discovery of the word numinous not only helped to validate his childhood experiences but the experiences of his adult life, as well. He was just emerging from his deep descent into the unconscious and the powerful inner encounters that gave rise to his now-famous *The Red Book*. He knew from his personal experiences the meaning of numinous. After discovering this powerful descriptive word when he was 42, Jung would spend the remainder of his career articulating its effects and potential meanings. In his Terry Lectures at Yale University in 1937, 20 years after his important discovery, Jung spoke at length about the meaning of the word "religion," describing it as *"a careful and scrupulous observation of what Rudolph Otto aptly termed the *numinosum*"; and again, religion "designates the attitude peculiar to a consciousness which has been changed by experience of the *numinosum*" (Jung 1937: 17).

In a letter to Pastor Walter Bernet on June 13, 1955, Jung provides a lengthy discussion of the beginning of his religious attitude. He writes, "It was the tragedy of my youth to see my father cracking up before my eyes on the problem of his faith and dying an early death" (Jung 1957: 257). Edward Edinger notes that this strong statement, "the tragedy of my youth," is particularly important, not only because of the personal reference to the effects on the young child, but also because Jung was witnessing in his father's experience a collective phenomenon in the latter part of the 19th century: Western society's cracking up over the problem of its faith (Edinger 1996a: 15). The old God-image was losing its efficacy; the old religious forms were losing their symbolic power to assist people to recognize and relate to the meta-personal powers and to provide a larger meaning to secular existence. That collective phenomenon has only gotten more severe (See Essay "Beyond the Back Porch of the Church"). The

71

collective religious condition remains caught between old religious forms that are no longer vital and an enormous religious/spiritual hunger that can find no container. The poetic words of Matthew Arnold describe this in-between place for many people: *Wandering between two worlds, one dead / The other powerless to be born / With nowhere to rest my head / Like these, on earth, I wait forlorn* (Arnold 1965: 305f).

For Jung, religious dogma and creeds were of little help in his religious search since they had become solidified, stale, and lifeless. According to his father, dogma was to be accepted by faith, but the boy Jung needed to think, question, and understand dogma and creeds; he needed to understand God for himself in light of his experience(s), as opposed to blindly accepting what others had thought and taught. With his clergyman father, Jung tried to have discussions about vital religious matters, but they would come to an unsatisfactory end. His father would become irritated at his young son for his reflective questions and would say to young Carl, "You always want to think. One ought not to think, but believe." At which point young Carl would think to himself, "No, one must experience and know."

The difference between an institutional/creedal/doctrinal approach to religion and a psychological approach is magnified in this dialogue between Carl Jung and his father. In the traditional approach, the sacred texts, dogma, and creeds of the particular religion define what religious experience should be and how one might recognize an encounter with the holy. One listens to the religious authority, reads the texts, studies the creeds and doctrines, and seeks to apply these to his/her life. In other words, one becomes familiar with the codified experiences of ancient others and grants their interpretations as authoritative for all times, regardless of the worldview, knowledge, and level of consciousness of those ancestors.

From an analytical psychological perspective, however, one begins with whatever or wherever the holy, the numinous, is experienced, whether or not it is contained in an official creed or doctrine. One begins with subjective experiences of the holy, of the numinous, of the Divine, in whatever form they appear. These experiences of the numinous constitute one's religious experiences, whether or not a particular institution validates them. From a depth psychological approach, one's actual experience of religious realities is paramount. This is a critical distinction between a traditional doctrinal approach and a psychological approach, and I might add, a source of great misunderstanding and miscommunication in the dialogue between Jung and theologians, and in the ongoing dialogue between psychology and religion. It often comes down to the question, "What is one's primary sacred text? Is it one's life, one's actual experiences of the sacred, or a written document, be it Bible, Quran, Talmud or some other text describing experiences and interpretations of ancient ancestors?" For Jung it was the experience of the numinosum, regardless of how weird or unconventional the religious experience may appear from a doctrinal or institutional perspective.

Throughout the "history of God," to use Karen Armstrong's provocative book title, theologians and philosophers have attempted to identify the primary locus of divine activity along a continuum of radical transcendence and radical immanence. Generally speaking, Karl Barth's theology represents the former with his representation of God as wholly other. Paul Tillich and the image of God as the ground of being would be on the immanent side of the continuum. Jung leaned toward Tillich, which John Dourley thoroughly explores in his book *The Psyche as Sacrament*.

Until recent years, I have leaned toward the immanent side of that continuum, likely due primarily to my psychological typology and early religious training. Now, however, I have moved from radical immanence to *total immanence*. Whatever the essence, activity, and power beneath and behind all our god images, they operate within the universe, within matter, within life, within the human psyche. Summarizing Jung's perspective on the matter, John Dourley writes, "(The)… recalling of the Gods to their psychogenetic origin and the responsibility of dealing with them there is the defining characteristic and psychological culmination of Jung's psychology" (Dourley, 2010: 48). Amplifying that psychological perspective, we can imagine that psyche is demanding a universal recall of its former creations of external deities and devils, which were necessary but have proven to be incomplete. This would mean that consciousness has evolved to a next stage, evoking from its own unconscious origin a more complete myth, including god-images more relevant to the modern and postmodern mind, and better able to be a conduit for psyche herself. Practically speaking, this would mean that the divine comes to us disguised as life itself, which is the primary sacred text we must learn to read. Failing to read that sacred text would mean that all other texts are irrelevant. John Dourley is even more emphatic: "All those who cannot write their own sacred scripture directly out of the unconscious are doomed to submit to another's and to live another's myth" (Dourley 2010: 35).

Nor do I believe it helpful at this stage of religious consciousness to posit a both/and solution to this mystery, of perpetuating the notion of both immanence and transcendence, especially if transcendence is understood as metaphysical. This has been the preferred solution to this mystery over the centuries of theological debate. However, that perspective simply provides a convenient escape for the fearful ego and its desire to avoid responsibility by exporting its capacities for both good and evil, creativity and destruction. Again, as long as we cling to images of external, metaphysical deities and devils, we will likely favor both divine and human scapegoats for solutions to our very human problems. This religious outsourcing has proven to be dangerous, even homicidal and, if left unchecked, could be suicidal for our species.

In *Memories, Dreams, Reflections*, Carl Jung recalls the felt-nearness of the divine, waking and sleeping, from an early age, which planted the seeds for his psychological myth, which flowered over his lifetime. In his first remembered dream, around the age of 3 or 4, he descended stairs in a stone-lined hole in the ground until he reached at bottom a doorway with an arch, closed off by a green curtain. With great curiosity, he pushed aside the curtain and saw what he realized, many years later, was a giant, ritual phallus on a magnificent throne. He was paralyzed with terror and woke sweating and scared to death. This image of a nameless subterranean god would haunt him, especially when he would hear his father, the Jesuits, and others talk glibly and exclusively about the loving, bright, and light sight of God. In the dream, as he drew back the curtain/veil, he had a glimpse of an aspect of the holy about which he could not speak. He feared that no one would or could understand the religious nature of what he had seen and experienced (Jung 1965: 11-14). He did not speak of that dream until he was 65 years old. For the psychologically minded, the numinous other may appear in strange guise.

I am reminded of a former client, a middle-aged man, who considered himself to be a noble, good Christian, active in the church, a kindly family man, who consulted me after much hesitation. His presenting issue, revealed after numerous sessions, was a compulsive string of curses, expletives, beginning with "God damn, son of a bitch …" and continuing from there. I will spare you the images. This string of expletives had come upon him unbidden, forced its way into his consciousness. Morning after morning he would wake with them on his mind, and they would return during the day. No matter how hard he tried he could not will them away or pray them away. This was most distressing to him, as you can imagine. He asked fearfully, "What if I started saying these things in the middle of the night, or around my children?" At a timely point, many sessions into his analysis after he had some sense I was not totally kooky, and after exploring some obvious interpersonal anger issues, I asked him one day if he had ever considered the possibility that this compulsion was a religious experience and a way the divine may be trying to get his attention, the very God he was cursing and verbally persecuting. I even prescribed that he use his string of expletives as a kind of mantra and listen to it rather than trying to get rid of it. It was just enough change of attitude that allowed him to begin to wonder if he was not more than the one-sided, kindly, noble, and logical/rational man he had always considered himself to be. As he explored these new, expanded revelations about himself, his cursing compulsion dissipated. This was a religious experience for my client, where something of the depths forced itself upon him and to which he finally had to submit, something from the deep unconscious that had the force and power formerly reserved for an external deity. However, it would not likely be a religious experience he would report in his Sunday School class! He would likely be considered not only obscene and profane, but crazy! The psyche will not tolerate a one-sided, all-good view of one-self. One-sidedness could be likened to original sin from the perspective of analytical psychology!

Jung reports a similar experience about a psychiatric patient who had a compulsion to shout out the "F" word. In any company, out came the expletive. So, they brought the patient into the gathering of all the physicians and residents, and, sure enough, after a short interval, out came the "F" word. Jung observes that not one of the physicians considered the possibility that the word came from God!

75

Again, numinous experiences were formative for the whole of Jung's personal and professional life. These images, thoughts, and feelings were forced upon him, he knew, from some mysterious source his ego had not conjured, but to which his ego had to bow. This mysterious other came upon him unbidden, unannounced, unexpected, and often in unconventional ways. However they came, Jung knew that he had been visited by something/someone from a reality he did not create or control. He knew wherever these unbidden thoughts, ideas, and images came from, that it was from beyond or outside the ego, from some dimension that had its own autonomy, its own life and power that was greater than ego-consciousness. Furthermore, he was convinced that the ego was required to be respectful and responsive to these numinous encounters. This, for Jung, constituted a religious attitude.

In a 1955 letter to Piero Cogo, who inquired of Jung's religious attitude or standpoint, Jung wrote:

> From the psychological standpoint religion is a psychic phenomenon which irrationally exists, like the fact of our physiology or anatomy. If this function is lacking, man as an individual lacks balance, because religious experience is an expression of the existence and function of the unconscious. It is not true that we can manage with reason and will alone. We are on the contrary continually under the influence of disturbing forces that thwart our reason and will because they are stronger. Hence it is that highly rational people suffer most of all from the disturbances which they cannot get at either with their reason or will. From time immemorial man has called anything he feels or experiences as stronger than he is "divine" or "daemonic." God is the Stronger in him. This psychological definition of God has nothing to do with Christian dogma, but it does describe the experience of the Other, often a very uncanny opponent, which coincides in the most impressive way with the historical "experiences of God." ...The working of the Divine is always overpowering, a sort of subjugation

no matter what form it takes…We are like primitives in a dark world, at the mercy of unpredictables. Hence we need religion, which means a careful consideration of what happens and less sophistry, i.e., overvaluation of the rational intellect. (religio is derived from religere and not from religare) (Jung 1955c: 271-72).

A final reference to Jung's experience with the numinous may aid our own engagement with the theme of these essays to reimagine god and religion, which I propose to be our modern sacred task. Readers will remember the often referenced encounter the 11-year-old Jung had with the uninvited, disturbing image that seized his imagination as he passed the Basel Cathedral on his way home from school. For the next three days, the young boy was in torment as he tried to avoid thinking a thought/image he was convinced would send him straight to hell. Finally, in his own words:

I gathered all my courage, as though I were about to leap forthwith into hell-fire, and let the thought come. I saw (again) before me the cathedral, the blue sky. God sits on His golden throne, high above the world— and from under the throne an enormous turd falls upon the sparkling new roof, shatters it, and breaks the walls of the cathedral asunder. So that was it! I felt an enormous, an indescribable relief. Instead of the expected damnation, grace had come upon me, and with it an unutterable bliss such as I had never known. I wept for happiness and gratitude. The wisdom and goodness of God had been revealed to me now that I had yielded to His inexorable command. It was as if I had experienced an illumination. A great many things I had not previously understood became clear to me. … Why did God befoul His cathedral? That, for me was a terrible thought. But then came the dim under-standing that God could be something terrible. I had experienced a dark and terrible secret. It overshad-

owed my whole life, and I became deeply pensive
(Jung 1965: 39-40).

The level of philosophical and theological reflection for the 11-year-old Jung is no doubt impressive. The important consideration here was his insistence that this horrible, disgusting image was not one his ego manufactured (or one found in the canons of the Church!), but one that was forced upon him by a God who lived in the heavens high above the cathedral. This image of God's habitat was consistent, of course, with his religious family and culture even though the image of divine excrement was clearly beyond those bounds!

Borrowing Jung's unforgettable metaphor to comment on the crisis in Western Christianity, John Philip Newell writes:

> We are living in the midst of the great turd falling! It has already smashed into the spire of Western Christianity ... as long as we allow our spires to give the impression that God is primarily above and beyond the earth, in opposition to what is deepest in creation and in the body of the human mystery, then our spires are going to crumble (Newell 2011: xviii).

Jung's boyhood experience with the Basel spire gives us a glimpse into his early image of God as a heavenly being, again consistent with his family and culture, though the excrement image certainly set him apart from tradition. Now, we fast forward some 75 years near the end of his life, when Jung was asked in an interview about his idea of God. He replied:

> To this day God is the name by which I designate all things which cross my willful path violently and recklessly, all things which upset my subjective views, plans, and intentions and change the course of my life for better or worse (Edinger 1984: 68).

Such a god-image disturbs the religiously faint of heart or those who remain committed to religious orthodoxy. It is on par with the divine excrement image in terms of challenging traditional god-images. Jungian analyst and author James Hollis writes that Jung's response is "possibly the most humble, the most faithful confession ever uttered by a person in the twentieth century ... because it honors the autonomy of the gods ...

though staying open to the possibility of radical revelation in any event, any venue" (Hollis 2001: 62). Of course, Jung's experience and declaration cannot be simply copied or parroted as new theological dogma. What it can do, however, is illustrate how a god-image transforms over a lifetime and how the divine may be imagined now that the metaphysical, mono-theistic categories are no longer relevant, as these essays propose. Over the course of his lifetime and career, Jung engaged his rich imagination in service of the theme of this essay—to reimagine god and religion. In doing so, he laid a psychological foundation for a future myth that may replace the monotheistic myth that has effectively died and awaits conscious eulogizing, burial, and grieving by the monotheistic collective.

The gestation period for a new religious myth will likely be long, perhaps measured in millennia. Jung addressed this potential timetable when responding to a dream by Jungian analyst and author Max Zeller. The dream:

> A temple of vast dimensions was in the process of being built. As far as I could see ahead, behind, right and left there were incredible numbers of people building on gigantic pillars. I, too, was building on a pillar. The whole building process was in its very first beginnings, but the foundation was already there, the rest of the building was starting to go up, and I and many others were working on it.

When Jung was told this dream his remark was: "Yes, you know, that is the temple we all build on. We don't know the people because, believe me, they build in India and China and in Russia and all over the world. That is the new religion. You know how long it will take until it is built … about six hundred years" (Edinger 1984: 11; Zeller 1975: 1-3).

When I first read this dream and Jung's response years ago, my impatient response was disbelief and disappointment that the process might take so long. Though the widening of human consciousness seems like a slow slog to my/our impatience, measured against the 13.8 billion years of cosmic time, a few more generations is not that long; provided, of course, that our species can resist our destructive tendencies fueled, I propose, by the monotheistic myth. On a more hopeful note, the dream suggests that a new foundation already exists, and innumerable workers are committed to the sacred project of co-creating new images of god and religion.

Jung was one of the first notables to speak about the necessity of individuals and collectives to have a central living myth and what happens when former myths lose their meaning-making capacity. Edward Edinger describes the tragic loss that speaks clearly to our current individual, cultural, and religious predicament: "The breakdown of a central myth is like the shattering of a vessel containing a precious essence; the fluid is spilled and drains away, soaked up by the surrounding undifferentiated matter. Meaning is lost. In its place, primitive and atavistic contents are reactivated." Our poets have long recognized this apocalyptic condition, Edinger notes, and quotes W. B. Yeats' familiar poem "The Second Coming," the first part of which reads:

> Turning and turning in the widening gyre
> The falcon cannot hear the falconer;
> Things fall apart; the centre cannot hold;
> Mere anarchy is loosed upon the world.
> The blood-dimmed tide is loosed, and everywhere
> The ceremony of innocence is drowned;
> The best lack all conviction, while the worst
> Are full of passionate intensity (Edinger 1984: 9-11).

I concur with Edinger's conclusion that nothing less than a new central myth will solve our individual and collective predicament. Furthermore, Carl Jung's analytical psychology, growing out of his lifelong experience of the numinous, provides a potential foundation or framework for a future myth that could replace the 4,000-year-old monotheistic myth, which has lost its capacity to nurture the modern mind and ancient soul. Furthermore, the analytical psychological framework can be a resource for our own sacred task to reimagine god and religion.

Speaking personally, though I have fallen off the back porch of the Church and have taken leave of the monotheistic religious tribe, my obsession with locating words and images that speak to the mysterious numinous essence of life continues. Currently, that essence consists of *the animating presences and powers at the heart of all matter, and at the heart of all that does matter.* This constitutes my current god-image, the image that holds the many meanings of those indefinable, yet unavoidable, mysteries our species has variously named gods, goddesses, spirits, Maya, Brahman, God—to mention but a few. *The animating presences and powers at the heart of matter, and at the heart of all that does matter* locates the god-like powers and presences within life, within matter, rather than beyond and thus moves us beyond the dualism inherent in monotheism. The adjective *animating* honors the central place of *anima* in analytical psychology as a "personification of the unconscious" and as "a bridge to the unconscious, in other words, as a function of relationship to the unconscious" (Jung 1957: 42). And the plural *powers and presences* avoids the reductionism of the monotheistic one-and-only god which all too frequently becomes the possession of one's particular religious tribe.

Lastly, the image beckons us to return again and again to those things that really matter, inundated as we are by the superficial. *What Matters Most* by James Hollis, recognized as one of the most influential interpreters and expanders of Jung's psychology, speaks forcefully to the costs and the satisfactions of "Living a More Considered Life," the subtitle of the book. I take courage in his admonition: "We are here to be eccentric, different, perhaps strange, perhaps merely to add our small piece, our little clunky, chunky selves, to the great mosaic of being. As the gods intended, we are here to become more and more ourselves" (Hollis 2009: xiii). The late Irish poet John O'Donohue provides a beautiful blessing in the pursuit of what really matters in his exquisite book, *To Bless the Space Between Us*: *May I have the courage today / To live the life that I would love / To postpone my dream no longer / But do at last what I came here for / And waste my heart on fear no more* (O'Donohue 2008: 9).

Since these essays constitute my personal psychological and religious testament, I am well aware that these perspectives locate me well outside the walls of theistic religion, beyond the back porch of the Church, and beyond the Christian paradigm in its traditional formulations. It challenges the questions related to a Creator God and an interventionist Saving God, which are theological staples inside those walls. It also does not address the nature of the First Cause, the unanswerable question of what existed before creation or the Big Bang or the no-thing prior to some-thing. Though unanswerable, asking that question is most often used by those who need to prove the existence of a metaphysical God, usually in debates with atheists or nonbelievers. At this stage of human knowledge, however, we do not have such proof, nor is it needed from a psychological perspective. Furthermore, if such proof ever surfaces, it will most likely come from the physical sciences rather than from theological discourse or new interpretations of ancient sacred texts. More importantly from the depth psychological perspective, arguments about a metaphysical dimension are unnecessary since they inevitably result in twisted, pretzel-like speculation leading to what Jung described as sacrosanct unintelligibility (Jung 1942: 109-110). More often they serve as a defense against religious experiences themselves, experiences that have been rationalized and dogmatized, prompting Jung to observe that too often the Bible is conveniently placed between the believer and his unconscious (Jung 1961: 262).

For purposes of clarity, the psychological perspective on god and religion presented herein: (1) honors the divine or sacred within the depths of life rather than beyond; (2) moves beyond the antiquated images of metaphysical domains, deities, and devils, while preserving mystery, wonder, and awe; (3) provides a creative passage from cosmological and religious dualism toward an interconnected, interrelated worldview; (4) expands the meaning of religion and religious beyond identification with a particular religious tradition or intellectual adherence to propositional doctrines; (5) acknowledges revelation as an ongoing psychological process rather than a one-time, metaphysical intervention to/for a select few; (6) embraces and incorporates the ever-new discoveries of the visible world/universe by the physical sciences, thus putting an end to the religion/science conflict, and weds religion and science as necessary partners; (7) evaluates religions, religious ideas, and religious texts by three touchstones: whether or not they are (a) inclusive, (b) scientifically and intellectually honest, and (c) soul-satisfying. The first two touchstones are theoretically measurable; the third invites broad and multiple inter-pretations consistent with the character and essence of soul.

ESSAY NUMBER FIVE

PROJECTION AND REVELATION

Projections change the world into the replica of one's own unknown face.
(Jung)

For more than 3,000 years, monotheistic religions have perpetuated a delusion, though initially a necessary one. They have insisted that their particular religion, its core god-image, and its laws, doctrines, and dogmas were the result of direct revelations from a metaphysical deity. Compounding that core delusion, each of the major monotheistic religions has considered those revelations as proof of its chosen status by the one-and-only deity, accompanied by all the perceived status and power that such delusions engender. The resulting pathology was explored in an earlier Essay, "Monotheistic Madness."

An antidote to this rampant religious disease has been discovered in recent history, coming not from the heavenly heights as might be expected but from the psychic depths. The yet-to-be recognized antidote to monotheistic madness, as well as many other ills affecting human relationships, will be the appreciation and application of the dynamics of *psychological projection*. Though a familiar part of the modern lexicon, projection is easily misunderstood and more easily undervalued, which invites closer scrutiny by the psychologically minded religious.

While teachers of the past have employed the wisdom beneath projection (removing the log in one's own eye before extracting the speck in the eye of the other, for example), it was the pioneering work and genius of Carl Gustav Jung, and his many interpreters and amplifiers, who uncovered and articulated the profound dynamics of psychological projection.

Like many of Jung's psychological constructs that have become part of our common vocabulary (i.e., complex, archetype, psychological types, extra-version, introversion), projection is familiar to most persons and yet barely appreciated for its dynamics and depth. With this in mind, Jung observed, "Projection is so fundamental that it has taken several thousand years of civilization to detach it in some measure from its outer object" (Jung 1934a: 6). The need for that kind of detachment remains largely unrealized in ordinary human relationships and even less so in the religious/spiritual arena.

Before unpacking the dynamics of projection and exploring its multiple applications, it may be useful to rehearse a familiar critique and dismissal of these and many other psychological perspectives. Those who are either unfamiliar with analytical or Jungian psychology, or whose theology is threatened by its discoveries, resort to the dismissive phrase *psychologizing,* as in "you are reducing theology to psychology," thereby judging it to be irrelevant or unwarranted. "You are psychologizing theology or psychologizing God" was a familiar critique heard by Jung in his attempts to dialogue with theologians of his day, and it remains a familiar refrain. Actually, the opposite is true: For centuries we have *theologized* experiences that are first and foremost psychological. All experiences and the knowledge attached to them are mediated through the human psyche. This renders all knowledge subjective, limited, and terminal when new knowledge appears. This is a self-evident fact, yet regularly overlooked or ignored by those wishing to bypass the human psyche to claim direct knowledge from a metaphysical deity. When rigidly held, such claims are delusional and dangerous; evidence abounds.

Upping the ante, deities, devils, and religions have always been afterthoughts; that is, they are names and categories granted after human experience(s), experiences deemed numinous to employ the designation created by Rudolph Otto and borrowed by Jung. Again, psychological experience comes first, theological (or any other) reflection follows. Raising the theological stakes even further, prior to human self-reflection, which made possible language and symbolization, there were no categories called theology or religion, or deities, devils, and spirits. Each and all were human *inventions*—natural, necessary, partial, imperfect, and imprecise to express powerful experiences not created by the human ego or under

84

its control and possession. Yet, monotheistic religions have spent an inordinate amount of time and print attempting to understand the mind of God and precious few resources appreciating the human mind/soul through which all categories, divine or otherwise, were created. If we are to have a more complete understanding of what we have called deities and devils, it will come as we honor more thoroughly the dynamics of the human mind or its more inclusive, poetic referent—soul.

Returning to the topic at hand, psychological projection will occupy a prominent place in these vital human endeavors. It could be a key in unlocking the mysterious interplay between the categories and relationships humans have designated as divine/human, heaven/earth, and spirit/matter. Granting it even more value, psychological projection could be the one dynamic—if understood, valued, and applied—that could alter the course of human history.

In its simplest description, projection is an *unconscious* process whereby contents of one's own unconscious are perceived to be outside oneself or in others. Though usually overlooked or ignored, projection remains one of the most common psychological dynamics between humans, between humans and their environment, and between humans and their perceived deities and devils. "It is a natural and given thing for unconscious contents to be projected," writes Jung. In fact, all human relationships swarm with projections since "all the contents of our unconscious are constantly being projected into our surroundings" (Jung 1916: 264). The resulting effects and implications are startling since "projections change the world into the replica of one's unknown face," which creates an illusory state for the ego, essentially "isolating the subject from his environment" because an illusory relationship has been substituted for a real one. The more projections occupy the space between the subject and the object, the more difficult it is for the ego to see through its illusions (Jung 1948: 9). At first glance then, projection seems like a necessary evil and something we could do without. However, a closer examination reveals the genius of this natural phenomena, which is essential for the evolution of human consciousness in general and, applied to the primary theme of these essays, for the evolution of religious consciousness in particular.

Psychological projection is *natural, necessary,* and *purposeful.* Working with projections does not mean correcting a falsehood or "disabusing someone of an illusion, but as completing the process in which we find within ourselves that which corresponds to what we have perceived without" (Wink 2002: 145). When the projection is recognized, traced back to its inner source, and withdrawn from the outer object/person, real relationship becomes possible; the idealized lover becomes a flesh-and-blood person, the "mentor becomes a partner, the teacher a colleague, the parent a friend" (Wink 2002: 145).

Peering through an analytical psychological lens and granting the value it deserves, projection carries the designation of *revelation.* Psychologically, revelation is "the poetry of the soul's deepest movements" (Dourley 2010: 23). As a scientist and psychologist, Jung was more interested in revelation as an event from within the soul rather than as a transmission of knowledge about God from without:

> Revelation is an "unveiling" of the depths of the human soul first and foremost, a "laying bare;" hence it is an essentially psychological event, though this does not, of course, tell us what <u>else</u> it might be. That lies outside the province of science (Jung 1942: 74 Emphasis Jung's).

For me, this psychological meaning replaces the traditional monotheistic meanings of revealed truth from a metaphysical deity/domain that can no longer be maintained with integrity. The remainder of this essay will be an exploration of the psychological meanings of revelation.

First, to denote the process of projection as unconscious means that the initiative for the projection is the unconscious itself. This stands in sharp contrast to the popular, shallow notion that projection is a voluntary, conscious function of the ego, something *I/we* do, or something that *I/we* should not do. How often do we hear versions of "we should not project our shadow onto others," or "he projected his ideal woman onto her," or vice versa? Throughout his *Collected Works,* Jung seemed never to tire of countering and contradicting the popular, mistaken viewpoint since honoring the initiative of the unconscious grants the projective process its power and purpose. "Projection is always an unconscious mechanism, therefore consciousness or conscious realization, destroys it" (Jung 1935:

138). Again, "… it is not the conscious subject but the unconscious which does the projecting. Hence one meets with projections, one does not make them. … Projections change the world into the replica of one's unknown face" (Jung 1948: 9). Lastly, "… projection is never made; it happens, it is simply there. In the darkness of anything external to me I find, without recognizing it as such, an interior or psychic life that is my own" (Jung 1943a: 245). Relevant to the mysteries of science, art, or religion, Jung notes, "All gaps in our knowledge are still filled out with projections" (Jung 1937: 83).

The distinction between a conscious or unconscious origin of projective processes represents more than a quibble with words. It preserves both the autonomy of the archetypal unconscious and its theoretical purposeful activity. For Jung and analytical psychology, the archetypal unconscious has a life of its own. It is a *subject* rather than a collection of repressed *objects* or material. More than a mere absence of consciousness, the archetypal unconscious possesses a "creative autonomy" (Jung 1937: 84) and an apparent unlimited fecundity "for the soul is the birth-place of all action and hence everything that happens by the will of man" (Jung 1941: 94). Furthermore, also contrary to popular usage, projection is not pathological; however, when projected contents are not recognized, withdrawn, and integrated into consciousness, especially after long periods of time, they invariably manifest as pathology on the part of individuals, groups, and nations.

Considering the purposeful nature of projection, we can identify two major psychological dynamics that operate simultaneously: Projections attempt *to protect* the ego, and projections attempt *to educate* the ego. Projection protects the ego from facing directly unconscious contents or potentials that may be too powerful to metabolize or to incorporate at a particular stage of development. In this sense, projection is a necessary psychological defense that protects the ego from being overwhelmed or fragmented by the contents of the archetypal unconscious. It could be generalized that, in the wisdom of the unconscious, all projections serve this initial function for the nascent, developing personality. Some psychologies emphasize this protective function exclusively and consider projection to be a regressive force in the life of the psyche. From this perspective, projection is considered to be immature and something to grow beyond. However, analytical psychology, while acknowledging the necessary regressive aspects, emphasizes the progressive or *prospective* function of psychological projection. Alongside protecting the ego, projection seeks to educate the ego, to grant the ego glimpses, so to speak, of its unconscious potential waiting to be embraced. Looking at projective contents through a prospective lens honors the creative aspect of the archetypal unconscious as it engages the ego for its manifestation or incarnation. Paying attention to intimations of future unfolding provided by the archetypal unconscious constitutes the major part of dreamwork and in-depth psychoanalysis; and, more generally, living with a religious attitude, which means a *careful consideration* of all that happens within and without.

The educative, or prospective, dynamic of projection presents heretofore hidden aspects of the individual (or group, religion, or nation) to the attention of ego-consciousness for the purpose of recognizing, owning, and integrating those contents. Understood in its creativity and profundity, projection constitutes revelation, revealing some psychic content rightfully belonging to the individual or collective ego, something needed for the ego's health, equilibrium, and wholeness. These unconscious processes are essential for self-knowledge since often we have to see parts of ourselves in projected form before we can identify them as our own. Therefore, a major part of psychoanalytic work consists of making "conscious and dissolving the projections that falsify the patient's view of his world and impede his self-knowledge" (Jung 1963: 489). Psychological projections are treated as purposeful, revelatory mirrors reflecting one's true nature, which desires to be owned, integrated, and incarnated. For the psychologically minded, then, revelation is an ongoing dynamic of the autonomous archetypal unconscious rather than a one-time event in the ancient past initiated by a remote deity for a particular religious tribe. Revelation emerges from the depths of life rather than from the heights of heaven.

While psychological projection operates full-time in all relationships, it rarely receives reflective attention that leads to self-knowledge, since it seems clear that our neighbor exhibits all those qualities we dislike, overlook, or excuse in ourselves. "Everything that is unconscious in ourselves we discover in our neighbor," notes Jung, and what we see in him or her is usually our inferior side (Jung 1931: 65), causing us to fear, hate, or love them accordingly (Jung 1920: 308). In the projected other/object we find our intrapsychic difficulties, conflicts, and enemies, as well as what is unconsciously dear and precious to us. Jung comments sardonically: "… it is comforting to know that all evil and all good is to be found out there, in the visible object, where it can be conquered, punished, destroyed, or enjoyed" (Jung 1939: 521).

Undoubtedly the most recognizable and enjoyable (at least temporarily) aspects of projective phenomena, especially in Western cultures, are experienced in romantic relationships. The powerful experience of falling in love, often soon followed by its opposite, is now generally recognized as a projective phenomenon whereby each partner sees in the other an aspect of one's own unconscious self. Of course, this general knowledge is soon forgotten when the next romantic relationship presents itself. The archetypal images of a romantic or sexual partner are highly charged and cause even the most conscious persons to lose their heart, or head! Even here, however, it is usually presumed that the process is something initiated by the ego, by "I" as in "I projected my inner woman/man onto her/him." Even the most seasoned clinicians might offer a timely interpretation by suggesting: "You see, you projected your own beauty, or creativity, or power onto her/him," thus rendering the process under the command of the ego and failing to credit the archetypal unconscious for its purposeful, revelatory function. For projections to be sufficiently dissolved requires an integrated awareness that one was/is being addressed by a power greater than the ego is capable of creating, managing, or controlling; that is, by the contents of the archetypal unconscious that approach consciousness with powers formerly reserved for deities and devils. Such an integrated awareness constitutes a religious attitude from an analytical psychological perspective, an attitude examined in previous essays.

Jungian author Robert A. Johnson provides a beautiful metaphor for recognizing and withdrawing psychological projections. Drawing on the ancient art of alchemy, he speaks of the "innermost part of our being" (soul or Self) as our *inner gold,* which has to be discovered and owned. The primary tools for that lifelong discovery are the dynamics of projection, which govern so much of human interaction, which, expanding the metaphor, is a virtual goldmine. The exchange of inner, alchemical gold takes place almost constantly and offers us "the best chance for an advance in consciousness"; that is, if we pay careful attention to our inner responses to our outer relationships. Our hidden, unconscious gold seldom travels directly into consciousness but goes by way of an intermediary, a host so to speak, who suddenly becomes fascinating to us, even luminous, glowing in the dark (Johnson 2008: 3-4). When that happens, we can be assured that something of our inner gold is being revealed at the initiative of the archetypal unconscious with the implicit invitation to claim what is rightfully ours. "Wherever there is a numinous quality" to the relationship, there is gold, writes Johnson (Johnson 2008: 24). Of course, without knowledge of the dynamics of projection, as most often is the case, the excessive idealization of the other person continues and one's personal gold goes unclaimed, only to find another unconscious carrier. Idealization of so-called experts or gurus, hero worship, and serial romantic relation-ships are some of the outcomes when inner gold remains exported rather than withdrawn and brought into one's own psychological house.

The exchange of alchemical gold is a great mystery, full of pos-sibilities and pathos. "Gold comes in many varieties," Robert Johnson notes. "Sometimes our gold is bright, but at other times it is heavy and difficult, and seems anything but golden" (Johnson 2008: 22). As explored above, psychological projection also reveals the darker, shadowy aspects of the unconscious. However, in keeping with the educative, prospective dynamics of the unconscious, the conscious integration of the less savory parts of our unconscious are also golden opportunities for oneself and for others.

As indicated, rarely are projective phenomena given reflective consideration in human relationships. The religious and theological applications of psychological projective phenomena are rarer still. It is here that analytical psychology could extend its unique and profound con-tributions. The three major monotheisms—Judaism, Christianity, and Islam—are frequently referred to as revealed religions, meaning they owe their beginnings and authority to revelations from an external, super-natural, metaphysical deity given directly to founders and/or prophets. With these supposed direct revelations comes a sense of being the divinely chosen religious tribe with sacred texts applicable and authoritative to all for all time. As indicated in the opening sentence of this essay, this understanding of revelation began as an illusion, was perpetuated over the centuries, and grew into a great delusion under which monotheists and their cultures continue to suffer. The delusional claims to power, land, and resources based on perceived divine favoritism are no longer limited to the Middle East but extend worldwide due to the epidemic of mono-theistic madness, the theme of a previous essay. Shallow and immature understandings of divine revelation continue to fuel the religious disease that has metastasized into politics, economics, and international relations. Revelation understood as a hierarchical, metaphysical, patriarchal process has permitted any individual or religious group to validate their human agenda for better or worse; arguably, the latter has predominated.

With the advent of analytical psychology over the last century, reve-lation can now be appreciated for its deeper and more hopeful meanings. Rather than unveiling the mind of a metaphysical deity, religious ideas, dogma and god-images reveal the yet-to-be-owned aspects of the human unconscious seen in projected form(s). Revealed religions are indeed revelatory. They (necessarily) reveal the level of consciousness of their founders/prophets/adherents along with attempted validations of tribal histories, hopes, and longings. For the psychologically minded, religions and their attendant god-images, myths, and dogmas reveal the contents and dynamics of the archetypal unconscious. Or, in poetic language, the contents of the human heart.

Risking my well-earned reputation as a political and religious liberal, yet acknowledging my conservative religious heritage, I once talked publicly about falling in love with Jesus as an adolescent. He was bigger than life, my religious hero who knew all things and could do all things. I loved the stories about him and those told by him. With tongue in cheek, I mentioned that I loved the photographs of him, especially those holding little children and lambs. They made me feel safe. As a personal example of religious projection, I went on to chronicle my necessary experience of falling out of love with Jesus as a magic man in order to appreciate his humanity, teaching, and wisdom. Breaking the projective spell was also necessary to begin retrieving some of my personal gold and authority, which I had seen in projected form. My experience seemed to resonate with many others in the psychologically minded audience. Recognizing and retrieving projected contents onto cultural and religious heroes, as well as onto personified deities and devils, is natural, necessary, and purposeful; and it is an ongoing, lifelong task. Far from being unnecessary, immature, or pathological, projection provides an avenue for self-knowledge, as well as knowledge of those powers and felt-presences formerly attributed to external beings.

The metaphysical domain, an understandable image for the early stages of religious consciousness, can now be seen as a giant screen onto which were projected (at the initiative of the archetypal unconscious) unrealized human desires, hopes, and capacities for good and evil. From the psychological perspective, in the evolution of religious consciousness it was natural and necessary to see gods, goddesses, deities and devils in projected form(s)—out there in trees, rocks, water, etc., and later on Mount Olympus, Mount Sinai and up there in Heaven. As consciousness became more differentiated and gave birth to science and ever-expanding knowledge of matter and the universe, images of external deities and devils and their supposed metaphysical domains became more and more unbelievable—except, of course, through denial, wishful thinking, and the abandonment of intellectual rigor related to religious concerns. Ignorance of psychological projection, along with excessive rationalism and literalism, have contributed to the demise and metaphorical death of monotheism and its metaphysical god-image, leaving the soul, as Jung purports, abandoned and bereft. Thanks to the emergence of analytical psychology over the last century, which can be seen as a timely compensatory offering from the archetypal unconscious, a new chapter to the foregoing commentary can be written.

As the profound dynamics of psychological projection are understood, valued, and applied, we no longer need to imagine an omniscient metaphysical being who unveils his will and truth to selective individuals or religious tribes, thus perpetuating the delusions and divisions that threaten us with extinction. Rather, we are able to draw from a collective wisdom from the depths of life itself, a wisdom accumulated over eons, which, to the present moment, approaches consciousness with the force and power once attributed to external deities and devils. Jung employed the metaphor of the collective unconscious as both the container of that wisdom in the form of universal patterns of thought and behavior (archetypes) and as the creative force that offers its images to consciousness for manifestation. Unlike the dualism inherent in monotheisms that divides matter/spirit, earth/heaven, human/divine, Jung viewed the human psyche as an aspect of nature herself in her cosmic, biological, sociological, and psychological unfolding. Summarizing Jung, John Dourley writes, "Jung understood the collective unconscious to be nature itself but a nature in need of its greatest creation, the ego and its consciousness, as the only agency capable of humanely ushering the infinitely fecund unconscious into consciousness" (Dourley 2010: 12). We are no different from nature in essence; we are a particular form of nature with a particular function. We can imagine that function to be the voice of nature or, with Jung in his farthest vision, the means by which nature becomes aware of itself (See Essay "The Universe as *Mirror* and *Icon*"). This implies a mutuality in the relationship between the archetypal unconscious and consciousness, though the former (unconscious) retains its creative autonomy. Summarizing the essential gift analytical psychology can add to one's worldview, Jung concluded, "… it is the recognition that there exist certain unconscious contents which make demands that cannot be denied, or send forth influences with which the conscious mind must come to terms, whether it will or no" (Jung 1927: 370).

These revelatory projective processes, long taught by teachers of wisdom and further differentiated by analytical psychology, allow us to see aspects of our hidden, unconscious nature and potential, along with the implicit invitation to withdraw the projected content for conscious integration into the personality. At present, the psychological lens has not been sufficiently recognized or taught by religious leaders and teachers so that our perceived divinities and devils have remained external to the physical world of matter, to our collective detriment.

For example, when the forces of good and evil are considered to be external to the psyche, either as images of a good God or an evil Satan, humans tend to identify themselves with the good as a personal possession and stand ready to fight the readily identifiable humans who are incarnations of evil. Thus far, human history validates this psychological truth. The three religions of the now-deceased Abrahamic god-image have repeatedly ignored this inner, psychological law with few signs of allowing this unconscious law into consciousness. We are nature's most creative and most destructive species. We need to own those twin capacities rather than allowing external deities and devils to carry them for us. As long as our gods are worshipped in projected form and our devils dismissed likewise, humans will continue to behave badly.

An all-too-perfect example of this psychological and religious ignorance took place at the 2016 National Prayer Breakfast in Washington, D.C., as I was writing early versions of this essay. While clearly condemning the religious violence perpetuated by the Islamic State (ISIS or ISIL), President Barack Obama urged his audience, primarily members of the U.S. Congress, not to "get on our high horse, because such violence is part of our own past, as well. During the Crusades and the Inquisition, people committed terrible deeds in the name of Christ. In our own country, slavery and Jim Crow all too often was justified in the name of Christ."

This psychological honesty was too much for the religious and political conservatives who continue to attack Obama as unpatriotic, unchristian, a closet militant Muslim, and worse. Much of the outcry denied any *moral equivalency* between the past and present violence. Actually, what he was holding up as a mirror was an *immoral equivalency*, but it takes a reflective consciousness to accept that, a capacity not frequently exhibited among our political leaders or, unfortunately, the masses who vote them in office. However, President Obama might have gone further in acknowledging the human shadow and our collective national shadow, which is consistently seen in projected form on the faces of our enemies. Raising the psychological stakes, he might have asked, "Do beheaded bodies reveal more barbarism than bodies blown apart by our remote drones and long-range missiles?" Advanced weaponry and technology may keep the Western shadow out of sight, but they are no less violent and deadly, and no less a religious and psychological issue. In some ways, the Western shadow may be more dangerous because it is more hidden from view; that is, more unconscious. No individual, religion, or nation gets a free pass from taking seriously the unconscious in both its creative and destructive potential.

In fact, for a crash course on psychological projection and its dynamics, one only has to watch and listen to our political leaders, both in the months (and years) leading to a general election and in the day-by-day jockeying for power and votes. With rare exceptions, what is uttered or publicized about a political opponent or someone across the political aisle is a mirror of unconscious contents of the claimant. One might say a naked mirror since one is exposing himself or herself, at least to the psychological eye. The heated debates around the issues of passion—gun control, sexuality, national security, and, yes, religion—are generally devoid of basic psychological insight or wisdom, as if the unconscious does not exist. I worry most about our so-called normal political and religious leaders who, though perhaps well educated, exhibit shallow levels of self-awareness and consciousness. For example, of course we need to worry about keeping guns out of the hands of the mentally ill. Yet my greater concern is the great arsenals under the control of the psychologically immature who show little interest in psychological reflection. Were it not so dangerous, the political enterprise would be the best possible comedy when viewed by the psychologically minded. Our comedians, heirs to the role of the jester in the ancient royal court, do serve a vital function in exposing the human shadow. Although they provide some comic relief, what they expose is ultimately no laughing matter. They are deadly serious issues.

It also needs to be acknowledged that those of us who readily comment on our political, cultural, and religious morass, especially with passion, are in danger of the unconscious projection we so easily condemn in others. We have to find ways to critique violators of justice, equality, and compassion, as well as violators of common sense, without being self-righteous. This is no easy task. Acquaintance with the personal and collective shadow, who forever lurk, may be our only safeguard. As Jung counseled, what we reject in ourselves "is apt to turn up in the guise of a hostile neighbor, who will inevitably arouse your anger and make you aggressive. It is surely better to know that your worst enemy is right there in your own heart" (Jung 1946: 225). Or in the words of Friedrich Nietzsche, "He who fights with monsters might take care lest he thereby become a monster."

Jung warned near the end of his long career that our future hangs by a very thin thread, and that thread, he proposed, is the human psyche about which we still know very little. Such an assessment likely sends a shudder up the spine of those who have an experiential awareness of the power of the unconscious. Sounding a hopeful note, Walter Wink, a Jungian-oriented biblical scholar wrote, "Today, people in all world religions have reached the stage of individuation at which divine/human wholeness can be withdrawn from its projection onto the screen of the cosmos and discovered within persons, groups, or the created order" (Wink 2002: 145). We simply have to multiply the numbers of those individuated individuals who could serve as salt and leaven to the collective.

In conclusion, our future as a species may well require that we become more psychologically literate, beginning with the basic facts that the unconscious exists; its contents are constantly being revealed with approaches to consciousness with the force and power formerly reserved for external deities and devils. As long as revelation is reserved for the now-deceased metaphysical deities who unveiled their truth to a special religious tribe, the revelatory powers of psychological projection will likely be overlooked, although those powers will continue to operate rather continually in all our daytime interactions, as well as in our night-time dreams. Furthermore, the failure to recognize projection as a natural, necessary, and purposeful psychological dynamic has contributed to the slow decline, and I believe death, of the monotheistic myth. That failure was especially evident in the unconscious processes by which the central figure of the Christian myth, *Jesus*, became mistakenly known as *Jesus Christ*. That taboo topic is explored in the following two-part Essay, "Reimagining Jesus and *Christ*."

ESSAY NUMBER SIX

REIMAGINING JESUS and *CHRIST*
(Part I)

Christ is the image of the invisible God (St. Paul)

In an earlier Essay, "Reimagining *God* and *Religion*," two simultaneous sacred endeavors were identified as the modern religious challenge: To eulogize, bury, and grieve the theistic and monotheistic god-images and the religious paradigms dependent on them; and secondly, to bring fresh imagination to the meanings of god and religion that will satisfy both the modern mind and ancient soul.

Within that larger religious challenge to monotheistic religions and the cultures and institutions formed and deformed by the 4,000-year-old myth, Christians are presented with a further arduous challenge, and potential opportunity, as they await the emergence of a more complete religious myth. That challenge and opportunity will involve bringing fresh imagination to the central Christian figure, Jesus, as well as to the meanings of *Christ—italicized here and throughout these two essays to denote an archetypal image rather than a person*. This will involve a thorough application of the dynamics of psychological projection considered earlier, which concluded with: "… the failure to recognize projection as a natural, necessary, and purposeful psychological dynamic has contributed to the slow decline, and I believe death, of the monotheistic myth. That failure was especially evident in the unconscious processes by which the central figure of the Christian myth, *Jesus*, became mistakenly known as *Jesus Christ*" (See Essay "Projection and Revelation").

Examining Jesus and *Christ* through the lens of analytical psychology will not revitalize or resurrect the monotheistic myth, which must continue to be eulogized, buried, and mourned as proposed in the Essay "Beyond the Back Porch of the Church." However, the psychological reframing of Jesus and *Christ* could be good news to those who no longer embrace a theistic and monotheistic religious worldview but who continue to mine the wisdom of Jesus' teachings and, more importantly, still find the *Christ-image* numinous. Those many persons are particularly addressed by these two essays.

A central, recurring theme throughout this work has proposed that all religions, dogma, and god-images have a psychological genesis and are governed by psychological dynamics. Therefore, while this intense focus on Jesus and *Christ* may be of particular interest to Christians, the underlying dynamics are applicable to all religious, as well as to those who consider themselves to be nonreligious. The psychological approach to religious matters seeks to uncover what is universal rather than tribal. So, let us dive into these waters considered by many orthodox to be taboo.

In theological seminary prior to my training as a Jungian analyst, we were taught that a sermon needed to be centered on a specific text, biblical of course, which supposedly the sermon clarified or amplified and to which the expositor returned time and again. It was and remains a helpful discipline for any speaker or writer. My text for these two essays comes through the mind and soul of Carl Gustav Jung. Whether or not these words could be called a word of God depends on one's understanding of that well-worn phrase. I do propose that they are psychologically brilliant, clarifying, and inspiring. For the psychologically minded, they may well be the most important Christological formulations in the past 2,000 years!

The text inviting our circumambulation lies buried in a series of 1957 letters Jung wrote to the Rev. David Cox in response to questions Cox had raised. The Rev. Cox had inquired of Jung whether he considered *Christ* to be an external reality (historical and metaphysical) or an archetypal image or idea in the collective unconscious (Jung 1958: 730). Jung's response provides some of his clearest and most concise words about the relationship among the historical Jesus, the archetypal image of *Christ*, and the archetypal Self, Jung's psychological metaphor for the centering and reconciling energy of the psyche. It will be noted that *self* is not capitalized in this text, as often is the case when Jung and his interpreters refer to the archetype as distinct from self when referenced in other psychologies and/or philosophies. The universal, or archetypal, Self is clearly referenced here. Except when quoting others who use the lower case "s" when referring to the archetypal Self, I will use the capitalized "S" to emphasize its more encompassing, archetypal character. The emphasis in the text belongs to Jung:

> The self or Christ is present in everybody *a priori*, but as a rule in an *unconscious condition* to begin with. But it is a definite *experience* of later life, when this fact becomes *conscious*. It is not really understood by teaching or suggestion. It is only real when it *happens*, and it can happen only when you withdraw your projections from an *outward* historical or metaphysical Christ and thus *wake up* Christ within. ... The self (or Christ) cannot become conscious and real without the withdrawal of external projections. An act of *intro-jection* is needed, i.e., the realization that the self lives in you and not in an external figure separated and different from yourself. The self (or Christ) has always been, and will be, your innermost centre and periphery, your *scintilla* and *punctum solis*. It is even biologically the archetype of order and—dynamically—the source of life (Jung 1958: 725).

This brief paragraph contains the essentials of a psychological perspective on the distinction between the historical Jesus and the archetypal image of *Christ,* and the role unrealized projections have played in why and how Jesus became known, mistakenly I contend, as Jesus Christ. Furthermore, it suggests how that unfortunate merger can be addressed so that value and meaning can be returned both to the historical Jesus and the archetypal *Christ-image*. Most importantly, Jung describes the process by which the *Christ within* wakes up, so to speak, and becomes a conscious reality. For those for whom the theistic and monotheistic myths no longer provide frames for meaning-making, these psychological perspectives bring fresh imagination to the task of co-creating with the archetypal unconscious a new religious myth that will be inclusive, intellectually and scientifically honest, and soul-satisfying. As stated elsewhere, these three criteria are worthy touchstones for the validation of any religion and its dogma.

Let me state the heart of the matter under our exploration and why it deserves our careful consideration. Jesus' original disciples, the Apostle Paul, and the early Church Fathers experienced Jesus as a powerful, numinous teacher. Their experiences were not unlike what continues to happen today with charismatic leaders, teachers, and heroes as explored in the previous essay on psychological projection. During the half-century following his departure, before anything was written about him or his teachings, Jesus became a figure of mythological proportions. Over several generations, first orally and then in a few written documents, he became larger than life. He was raised to divine status and given messianic designations which, by the fourth century, were sealed in dogma and doctrine. He became known as Jesus Christ or Christ. Henceforth, this mistaken identity was reinforced by councils, creeds, and popular parlance, so much so that for most people Christ is a synonym for Jesus or simply his last name.

Referring to Jesus in these mistaken ways is so commonplace that it may be startling to allow into our consciousness the possibility that *Christ* was never meant to be a proper name for a person. Rather, *Christ* is an archetypal image, the name for an invisible mystery that courses through the universe, through all people, and seeks ever more conscious manifestation or incarnation, as it did through Jesus. *Christ* is an image for that inner, innate longing and potential to be more complete and whole, and to have the fragmented parts of our individual and collective lives united. That longing and potential are built into the fabric of life itself and into our human fabric. Humans have spoken of that longing and potential by many different symbols, one of which is *Christ.*

Again, *Christ* is an image or symbol for that which is deepest within life that strives toward completeness or fulfillment, that felt-sense that there is a *more* toward which we, and all life, moves. In other religious traditions, synonyms for *Christ* are Tao, Buddha Mind, Great Spirit, Sophia/Wisdom, Khidir, Brahman, Perusha, and countless others. The reality or dynamic to which these images speak has also been rightly described in scientific language as the evolutionary processes within nature, within matter itself. The psychologist Jung favored the archetypal image Self, noting that empirically the Self "appears synonymous with the inner Christ of the Johannine and Pauline writings" (Jung 1942: 156). With this in mind, Jung freely interchanges *Christ* and *Self*, though, as a scientist, he favored the psychological designation.

With the revelatory insights of analytical psychology, and particularly the dynamics of projection, we can now appreciate how the universal image of *Christ* was limited to Jesus in the Christian mind and why it remains largely so; and, what it will take to free the image. Without naming it as such, wisdom teachers have applied the dynamics of projection in their teaching, but it remained the task of analytical psychology to identify its subtle dynamics. Yet, these dynamics remain largely ignored, most notably in religious and political circles.

As explored in the previous Essay, "Projection and Revelation," psychological projection is a primary source of revelation, initiated by the archetypal unconscious, to bring to ego-consciousness something heretofore hidden or unknown. It is an ingenious device to mirror in the outer world something that desires to be recognized, owned, and integrated in the inner world; that is, some aspect of psychic life needed for balance and/or wholeness. Projection is not something the ego does, not something *I do*. Rather, projections happen to us and are initiated by the unconscious to promote awareness and integration of hidden aspects of our person and potential. Drawing on a familiar theological and psychological metaphor, the purpose of projection is to bring the darkness into the light. Projections are natural, necessary, and purposeful. They are neither immature nor pathological; however, failing to recognize and withdraw projections promotes pathology, and religious pathology is the most virulent kind.

Applied to the topic before us, the mystical teacher Jesus became a giant screen onto whom were projected the unconscious "hopes and fears of all the years," as the lovely Christmas carol reminds us. An apparent wise and charismatic teacher, far along the path of individuation, Jesus mirrored to his followers, then and since, something of their own longing and potential wholeness. In psychological language, he became the necessary ideal object to receive their projections and to awaken within themselves their own *Christ* nature.

Remember, at the initiative of the creative unconscious, contents are first seen in projected form to be recognized, withdrawn, and consciously owned and integrated. However, when projections are not recognized as such, their recipients remain idealized and, in the case of religious figures, often become objects of worship. This was/is the case with Jesus, and how he became the Christ in the minds of his followers, rather than one through whom the image of *Christ* was manifest or incarnated. Thus, he also became the literal one and only Incarnation, rather than one in whom is seen the kind of life that desires to be incarnated in all persons.

Through the processes of psychological projection, the human Jesus was quickly lost underneath heavy Christological expectations and hopes that were seen in him in projected form. The meaning and power of *Christ* as an archetypal image was lost, as well. More precisely, the outer historical person was mistaken for an inner, psychological reality; an outer person was tasked with meeting an inner need that, necessarily, was seen in projected form until it could be recognized as such, withdrawn, and integrated into the life of the individual or religious collective. That difficult psychological work remains largely unattended. The unfortunate consequences of its neglect are apparent, at least to the psychological eye.

As the recipient of idealized projections, Jesus became identified with one of the most familiar archetypal themes or motifs found in all religions, myths, and fairy tales—the motif of the hero. Hero worship has always been, and remains, a common occurrence, and heroes serve a necessary psychological function. They are carriers of unconscious contents of their admirers or worshippers for the purpose of mirroring to those admirers what is stirring in the unconscious desiring to be integrated into consciousness, individually and collectively. Heroes inspire and mobilize psychic energy. Their followers are energized, often highly so, as demonstrated by the emotional frenzy swirling around the latest sports personality, charismatic politician, and movie or music star. However, most of the energy in hero worship comes not from the hero but from the unconscious of those who are bowing in adulation or obeisance. Yes, the hero or heroine does possess a degree of the quality being admired, or else there would not be a sufficient hook to evoke and catch the projection. The greater volume of psychic energy, however, emanates from the unconscious depths of the followers.

For example, as a practical approach when working with analysands to identify and withdraw unconscious projections, whether they involve falling in love or being consumed with hateful distaste, I often suggest considering a *20-80 formula*. That is, 20 percent of the mobilized energy is housed in the recipient of the projection and 80 percent emanates from the analysand's own unconscious, which desires to be recognized and consciously integrated. Though highly unscientific, the exaggeration does sometimes break the illusory spell and quickens consciousness, which is the goal. It can be most revealing, therefore, to ask, "Who are your heroes? What do you admire in them? Specifically?" Those who are the carriers of highly charged projections are a mirror of who we desire to be and are capable of being manifested in our own unique form. Again, rightly understood, projection is for the purpose of promoting awareness of yet-to-be owned aspects of one's hidden personality. As such, it is an ingenious tool of the archetypal Self to promote the wholeness of personality through ever-increasing consciousness.

As indicated earlier, the hero motif is a universal theme found in the cultural and religious products of all known societies. In addition to the well-known heroes of the Judeo-Christian tradition, many of whom are chronicled in the Hebrews 11 litany, there grew in the Hebrew mind a hoped-for hero called the Messiah who would usher in an imagined religious, social, and political order. That anticipated Messiah remains in projected form to this day and will remain so until a sufficient number of Jewish faithful withdraw their projections and realize the Messiah as an inner image and possibility. Until this happens, peace in the Middle East and elsewhere will likely be an elusive dream.

In the Christian mind, Jesus was the recipient of similar messianic expectations, i.e., projections, and given the name Christ, meaning the Anointed One, or more commonly, Savior. Through that projective process, which began with the early disciples and the Apostle Paul and continued with the early Church fathers, Jesus became a mythological figure with all the attributes of the life of the archetypal hero described by Jung: "improbable origin, divine father, hazardous birth, rescue in the nick of time, precocious development, conquest of the mother and of death, miraculous deeds, a tragic, early end, symbolically significant manner of death, post-mortem effects (reappearances, signs and marvels, etc.)" (Jung

1942: 154-55). Very quickly the human Jesus became the collective figure whom the unconscious of his contemporaries expected to appear (Jung 1942: 154). Jung often referenced the archetypal antecedents to the familiar figures of the Son of Man or Christ the Redeemer (Jung 1963: 124). He reminded the Christian faithful that symbols and myths are not created consciously, nor did the image of *Christ* begin with the historical Jesus. He writes: "It was not the man Jesus who created the myth of the god-man. It existed for many centuries before his birth. He himself was seized by this symbolic idea, which, as St Mark tells us, lifted him out of the narrow life of the Nazarene carpenter" (Jung 1964: 89). In the mind of most Christians, Jesus remains the one and only external Messiah rather than one through whom the energies of the archetypal *Christ* manifested.

Commenting on this phenomenon and referring to the writings of the Apostle Paul in the New Testament, Jung remarks: "It is frankly disappointing to see how Paul hardly ever allows the real Jesus of Nazareth to get a word in. Even at this early date ... (Jesus) is completely overlaid, or rather smothered, by metaphysical conceptions: he is the ruler over all daemonic forces, the cosmic saviour, the mediating God-man" (Jung 1942: 153-54). From our available records, the Apostle Paul did not know the historical Jesus personally. His numinous encounter on the road to Damascus, which he claims to be an encounter with Jesus, was more accurately a numinous experience of the archetypal or mystical *Christ* or, psychologically, the Self. Had Paul the benefit of analytical psychology to make such a distinction, we can imagine that his theology would have taken a different turn and so might the evolution of Christianity and the Church. When Paul writes from his mystical consciousness, such as "Christ is the image of the invisible God," (Colossians 3:15) or speaking of love from his poetic heart as in I Corinthians 13, there is a ring of timeless truth. When he writes from his personal complexes and cultural biases, such as "Wives, be subject to your husbands; that is your Christian duty," (Colossians 3:18) or "I do not permit a woman to be a teacher, nor must woman domineer over man; she should be quiet," (I Timothy 2:11-12) his words have no ring of timeless truth or authority. Nor can his reference to homosexuality (Romans 1:26-27) as being a punishment for sin be anything more than expressions of cultural ignorance and/or his personal sexual complex.

Unfortunately, however, many of these passages remain favorite weapons for the literal religious mind of all-male Church hierarchies and assemblies.

Assigning to one historical person that which is a universal image and energy relieves all others from the necessity of incarnating the *Christ* within or what Jung calls the self in his letter to the Rev. Cox. *Christ* was never a proper name of a person. Rather, *Christ* was and remains one religious image/symbol among many for the deep desire in the human psyche/soul to be more complete and to have its disparate aspects reconciled and integrated into a greater, more whole personality. For 2,000 years, Christians have mistakenly treated *Christ* as the last name of one specific person rather than as an image of a psychic or spiritual reality desiring incarnation through all persons. As long as Jesus and *Christ* are unconsciously merged in the Christian mind, both the person and image will be diminished, and neither will be able to serve and transform the human psyche. The transformational wisdom of Jesus' teaching will remain lost, and the image of *Christ* as an animating, reconciling inner reality may be lost or greatly reduced.

The unconscious conflation or merger of history and myth resulted in the mistaken name Jesus Christ. The failure to distinguish the two—history and myth—often gives rise to the literalism so deadly to symbolic truth. Rather than seeing Jesus as a human icon in whom and through whom the symbolic *Christ* manifested, he was made into an object of worship and remains so. Jung was especially concerned with the destruction of symbols and the loss of symbolic thinking in the modern world. He wrote extensively about symbols that have been reduced through literalism to signs that merely point to something but are not able to connect one emotionally with that which is symbolized. In his comparative study of Jung and the theologian Paul Tillich, John Dourley explores the high regard that both had for symbols and their common concern that the loss of the symbolic leads to "the pathology of literalism" (Dourley 1981: 31). The unconscious, unreflective merger of the historical Jesus and the *Christ* symbol was a form of literalism. In Dourley's words, this has led "to a personal hero worship that misses the depth of meaning of Christ and degenerates into what Tillich calls *Jesusology*" (Dourley 1981: 29).

"There is a tendency to historize the myth, making it only about Jesus," writes William L. Dols Jr. in his article in *Jung's Challenge to*

Contemporary Religion. He notes that the historical person of Jesus is well-known in our Western culture, while the symbolic *Christ* seems like a foreigner to the Western soul. Quoting John Middleton Murray, Dols says, "Nineteen hundred years of Christianity have left Jesus … in our bones. … Our duty is to get him out of our bones and into our consciousness." For Dols, this would mean:

> To become conscious of and engaged by these same mythic motifs, i.e., virginal birthing, death/rebirth, as well as by the archetypes of the wounded healer, the messianic saving element—essentially the archetype of the Self as Christ image. The question is not whether the mythic archetypes are present and active, but whether or not we are conscious of them and how that awareness affects our choices (Dols 1987: 134-136).

When *Christ* is appreciated as an archetypal, universal image rather than the last name of Jesus, the familiar phrase, *imitation of Christ,* takes on profound significance. In *Psychology and Religion*, Jung offers the following challenge:

> We Protestants must sooner or later face this question: Are we to understand the "imitation of Christ" in the sense that we are to copy his life and, if I may use the expression, ape his stigmata; or in the deeper sense that we are to live our own proper lives as truly as he lived his in its individual uniqueness? It is no easy matter to live a life that is modeled on Jesus' but it is unspeakably harder to live one's own life as truly as Jesus lived his (Jung 1937: 340).

In the last sentence of the above quote, I have taken the liberty and responsibility to substitute Jung's designation "Christ" for the more accurate designation "Jesus" in keeping with the need to differentiate the two. I consider this consistent with Jung's overall writings on the topic before us. In any case, it is my perspective. The difference in Jesus the historical person and the *Christ* image is crucial even though it makes for awkward conversations after 2,000 years of misuse.

Without sufficient knowledge of the phenomenon of projection, and generally favoring externalized religious devotion, Christians have continued to relate to Jesus via idealized projections. In the traditional doctrine of substitutionary atonement, for example, Jesus became (and remains) for Christians primarily a scapegoat who carries both the dark and bright projected shadow. He carries their gold through the unconscious elevation of him to be the literal Christ or God. He carries the unconscious dark shadow by being the scapegoat for sins.

Unfortunately, scapegoat Christology does not eliminate the human shadow. It merely goes underground only to find enemies in the outer world, and the blood-letting continues in Jesus' name. Nor does prolonged idealization allow his followers to recognize and incarnate the qualities prized in him and his teachings. Thus, worshipping Jesus has been preferred over the risky transformational task of living "our own proper lives as truly as he lived his in its individual uniqueness," in the words of Jung, since to do so one would likely be "misjudged, derided, tortured and crucified" (Jung 1934b: 340). A *religion about Jesus* has generally been preferred over the apparent *religion of Jesus.* The dynamics and dangers of scapegoat Christology are explored further in the following essay.

From the relatively scant records available, Jesus did not encourage worship of his followers. In psychological language, he did not identify with the projections that came his way. He was consistently pointing beyond himself rather than calling attention to himself as a divine, extraordinary person. He saw himself as a conduit for a larger life rather than as a god or the God, though Christians, then and now, have thought otherwise, which attests to the illusory power of projection. When the projective processes are considered, being a follower of Jesus does not mean to worship him; rather, it is an invitation to draw from the same inner wellspring rightly called *Christ,* which bubbles from within, and, more forcefully, which demands incarnation in and through us.

On his dedicatory page of his translations of poems by Hafiz, titled *The Gift*, Daniel Ladinsky wrote: *To God's magnificent masquerade—as us!* (Ladinsky 1999: Dedicatory Page). Recently, I came across the note I made in the margin when I first read the beautiful poems. I wrote:

> That which we continue to name *God* dwells within us,
> as us. That is the meaning of incarnation which burst
> into human consciousness some two thousand years
> ago. That idea/image was so radical, so risky, and so
> intimate that very quickly we made it into a theory, a
> religious doctrine and assigned it to one man, Jesus.
> In doing so, we imagined that we could escape from
> our own call, our own task of being an incarnation of
> the divine, just as Jesus was (Author's Words).

Since that hastily scribbled entry some years ago, the mystery of incarnation has not grown less in my mind though its literal assignment to one person at one particular time has grown more preposterous. Rather than being an inflated ego notion, our call to be an incarnation of the divine evokes awe and humility when we remember that we are a conduit for both creative and destructive capacities; capacities heretofore outsourced to metaphysical deities and devils. The psychological word for *incarnation* is *individuation,* which means a lifelong process of embracing the contents of the unconscious and a simultaneous empathic, compassionate embrace of all others.

Rather than falling victim to inflation as the recipient of idealized projections, Jesus was consistently pointing beyond his personal power to a greater power. At the same time, he challenged his hearers to look within themselves for resonance, or dissonance, to his words. Like an effective teacher or analyst/therapist, he was also able to carry the projections placed upon him, positively and negatively, until such time they could be recognized as projections and withdrawn—or not, as has largely been the case thus far. Ironically, substituting an outer and visible solution for an inner and invisible longing was a typical warning in his teachings, a warning barely appreciated then or now. When an outer object becomes a substitute for an inner need, the ancient designation was idolatry. Today, it is also known as addiction and, when the outer recipient is a person, co-dependence. Whatever its name, it results in the diminishment of all involved.

Steeped as he was in the ancient wisdom tradition, as well as his own interiority, Jesus knew the subtleties of what we now call projection and its potentials and dangers. Some of his most challenging words demonstrate that acquaintance:

Why do you look at the speck of sawdust in your brother's eye, with never a thought for the great plank in your own? How can you say to your brother, "My dear brother, let me take the speck out of your eye," when you are blind to the plank in your own? You hypocrite! First take the plank out of your own eye, and then you will see clearly to take the speck out of your brother's (Luke 6:41-42 NEB).

Again, faced with the idealization of a potential follower who addressed him as *Good Master*, Jesus deflects the projection with the reply, "Why do you call me good? No one is good except God alone" (Luke 18:18 NEB). On the other hand, as the recipient of projected hatred and violence of his murderers, he could pray, "Father, forgive them; they do not know what they are doing" (Luke 23:34 NEB). When faced with the trickery of the religious professionals who brought before him a woman caught in adultery, Jesus unmasked their own unconscious, unowned projections by saying, "Let him who is without sin among you be the first to throw a stone at her" (John 8:7 RSV). To those who regarded religion as a matter of outer observances to the neglect of their inner shadow, Jesus reserved some of his harshest critique:

Alas ... you hypocrites! You are like tombs covered with whitewash; they look well from the outside, but inside they are full of dead men's bones and all kinds of filth. So it is with you: outside you look like honest men, but inside you are brim-full of hypocrisy and crime (Matthew 23:25-26 NEB).

While Jesus knew and taught the spiritual dynamics of our topic at hand, it remained for modern depth psychology to amplify the dynamics and applications of psychological projection. In my own fantasy, had Jesus written a book on the topic at hand, it would have been a major chapter since it concerns the necessity of moving from a religion that is external to a religious paradigm that addresses and transforms the inner person. Or, succinctly, the real issue is always an internal one that spills over for better or worse to the external. The poverty of modern Christianity and other monotheisms can be linked to the neglect of that fundamental psychological and spiritual law.

The conflation of Jesus and *Christ* into Jesus Christ was most unfortunate, though completely understandable given the stage of human consciousness at the time, including the available knowledge of the visible physical universe and the invisible psychological universe. We are now the recipients of greater knowledge of the outer world through the discoveries of modern science and physics, knowledge of the microscopic world through biochemistry, and knowledge of the inner world through analytical psychology. With the discoveries of the processes of psychological projection and the role they play in all relationships, including those deemed religious, a new Christian story begs to be written. These ongoing discoveries, which carry the import of revelations, could transfer into greater religious consciousness. That consciousness would likely come at a high cost to religious tribes founded and sustained by theistic and monotheistic illusions created by unresolved psychological projections.

Addressing how the historical Jesus was raised to the status of divinity in the minds of his early followers, Jung writes definitively:

> The gospel writers were as eager as St. Paul to heap miraculous qualities and spiritual significances upon that almost unknown young rabbi, who after a career lasting perhaps only one year had met with an untimely end. What they made of him we know, but we don't know to what extent this picture has anything to do with the truly historical man, smothered under an avalanche of projections. ... It makes no difference anyhow, since the image of the God-man lives in everybody and has been incarnated (i.e. projected) in the man Jesus, to make itself visible, so that people could realize him as their own interior *homo*, their self (Jung 1954b: 695).

Returning to our definitive text taken from Jung's letter to the Rev. David Cox, Jung proposes what now appears obvious to the psychologically minded: The historical person Jesus was, and remains, the recipient of vast amounts of unconscious projections. With the gift of hindsight, and now insight into the revelatory character of psychological projection, we may be able to view both Jesus and the image of *Christ* in a new light. Jung claims that the image of *Christ* is present in everyone *a priori* though largely unconscious in the beginning. It slumbers, so to speak, waiting to be awakened. In the wisdom of the psyche, that sleeping potential is first seen and experienced in projected form in the people, events, and places in the outer world that carry intense energy or numinosity. Those highly charged encounters are wake-up calls, so to speak, for yet-to-be-owned aspects of personality. As long as those vital aspects remain in projected form, i.e., thought to be housed solely in the outer recipient, they do not nourish the life of the one whose soul is being mirrored or projected. Jung insists, "The self (or Christ) cannot become conscious and real without the withdrawal of external projections." The withdrawal involves an "act of *introjection*," meaning "the realization that the self lives in you and not in an external figure separated and different from yourself" (Jung 1958: 725). Breaking through 2,000 years of Christian haze to wake up the Christ within requires, first of all, the differentiation between Jesus the person and *Christ* the image; and secondly, it requires the withdrawal of projections from an outward historical or metaphysical Christ.

Jung was especially concerned about the general Western religious attitude that tends to emphasize the outward aspects of religion to the detriment, and sometimes exclusion, of the inner. Elsewhere he writes, the Western attitude "tends to fix the ideal—Christ—in its outward aspect and thus to rob it of its mysterious relation to the inner man." It was this prejudice that impelled the Protestant scholars of the Bible to interpret the Kingdom of God as "among you" instead of "within you" (Jung 1943b: 8). "Christian civilization has proven hollow to a terrifying degree," he notes; "it is all veneer, but the inner man has remained untouched and therefore unchanged. ... His soul is out of key with his external beliefs." Elaborating his critique, he writes:

> Too few people have experienced the divine image as the innermost possession of their own souls. Christ only meets them from without, never from within the soul; that is why dark paganism still reigns there, a paganism which ... is swamping the world of so-called Christian civilization. ... So long as religion is only faith and outward form, and the religious function is not experienced in our own souls, nothing of any importance has happened (Jung 1943b: 12-13).

In his letter to the Rev. Cox, Jung freely interchanges self and *Christ,* though as a scientist he clearly preferred the psychological designation since it was more inclusive. As already noted, I, too, generally prefer the term Self (capitalized) because of its universal application and because it is more difficult to literalize, anthropomorphize, or assign gender. Its biggest drawback, of course, is its confusion with the lower-case *self,* which generally refers to the ego in most other psychologies. "I actually prefer the term self," Jung says, "because I am talking to Hindus as well as Christians, and I do not want to divide but to unite" (Jung 1958: 737). Jung's use of self is more inclusive in another important sense. In his definitive work on the relationship between the archetypal Self and the image of *Christ* contained in *Aion,* Volume 9ii of his *Collected Works,* Jung concludes that "*Christ* exemplifies the archetype of the self" (Jung 1959a: 37). This means that *Christ* is but one symbol of self, albeit the most important one for Christianity, of the more encompassing archetype. Other symbolic religious figures like Buddha, Purusha, Tao, Khidr, or Tifereth "are recognizable formulations of what I call the self." Jung concludes, "Moreover I dislike the insistence upon a special name, since my human brethren are as good and valid as I am. Why should their name-giving be less valid than mine?" (Jung 1958: 738)

The relationship between the psychological Self and the archetypal *Christ* had engaged Jung's imagination long before the letter he wrote to Cox. He had written extensively on the subject at the request of his readers "to discuss the relations between the traditional Christ-figure and the natural symbols of wholeness, the self" (Jung 1959b: x). He was well aware of the difficulties of the undertaking and the risk of being accused, as he often was, of psychologizing, of reducing the key Christian figure to *nothing but* a psychological image. To this charge, he writes:

> My reader should never forget, however, that I am not making a confession of faith or writing a tendentious tract, but am simply considering how certain things could be understood from the standpoint of our modern consciousness—things which I deem it valuable to understand ... things, finally, whose understanding would do much to remedy our philosophic disorientation by shedding light on the psychic back-

ground and the secret chambers of the soul (Jung 1959b: x).

As indicated, Jung states one of his most important psychological conclusions early on in *Aion*: *Christ exemplifies the archetype of the self* (Jung 1959a: 37). Edward Edinger considers this "a revolutionary statement which amounts to the announcement of a whole new world view." Edinger continues:

> That is a simple statement, but it is a blockbuster once it is understood in its full reality … It is the first clear announcement that Western man's experience of the Self has shifted from religious projection, into the human psyche, and that man, at least one man, Jung, is conscious of that fact. *Human consciousness has discovered the religion-creating archetype, of which the figure of Christ is just one expression, though the relevant one for our particular culture.* We can now see what is prior to, or behind, the metaphysical projection which is personified by Christ. What is prior to it is what goes by the name of the Self (Edinger 1996b: 44 Emphasis mine).

The psychological Self, then, is the more encompassing reality of which the image of *Christ* is the most important expression for Christian culture. The image of *Christ* is but one expression of the more encompassing archetype of the Self; *Christ* is the foreground of a much larger background. Or, the image of *Christ* is but one imprint of the unknown, unknowable imprinter. Conceived theoretically as the center and circumference of the psyche with indefinable limits, the Self is the psychological equivalent of what humans have experienced and named gods and goddesses and more recently, God. *Christ* is the most important symbol for the Self among Christians. As traditionally understood, however, the symbol is incomplete since it does not contain the opposites like the more inclusive archetype of the Self. The Self is "a union of opposites, *par excellence*, and this is where it differs from the Christ-symbol," since the traditional interpretation of the latter represents good only (Jung 1943b: 19).

Jung's crisp conclusion, *Christ exemplifies the archetype of the Self*, and Edinger's elaboration, call attention to the priority of the psychological perspective, the role of projection beneath the misnomer Jesus Christ, and the necessity of our immediate task to differentiate the human Jesus from the image of *Christ*. To amplify, we are psychological beings before we are religious ones; religions are human creations, albeit absolutely essential and initiated by an ego-transcending, meta-personal energy in the psyche, which Edinger refers to as the *religion-creating archetype;* i.e., the Self. Dismissive charges of psychologizing, therefore, are easily met with a counter perspective that more often we tend to theologize psychological experiences in order to make absolute and exclusive claims, often to compete with other religions and their claims. This was the case in raising the human teacher, Jesus, to divine status, though it was initially done largely unconsciously.

Jung concluded that the experience of Self and *Christ* cannot be effectively distinguished. Though representing two different disciplines, psychology and theology, they are functionally analogous; that is, they cannot be distinguished at the empirical level. Both constructs are symbols or images of an innate psychological reality or energy that, experientially and functionally, play an ordering, centering, reconciling role in the human psyche and personality; as far as we can discern both play a similar role in all creation. As noted before, in his volume on *Psychology and Religion*, he says that empirically the Self "appears synonymous with the inner Christ of the Johannine and Pauline writings" (Jung 1942: 156). With this in mind, Jung freely interchanges *Christ* and Self in the key passage before us. Elaborating on the dynamic relationship of the two, he writes:

> It was this archetype of the self in the soul of every man that responded to the Christian message, with the result that the concrete Rabbi Jesus was rapidly assimilated by the constellated archetype (Jung 1942: 156) … the image of the God-man lives in everybody and has been incarnated (i.e., projected) in the man Jesus, to make itself visible, so that people could realize him as their own interior *homo*, their self (Jung 1954b: 695).

The discoveries and framework of analytical psychology offer a way to think about Jesus and *Christ* that satisfies both the modern mind and ancient soul. Jung provides a fresh look at the old-old story, which has lost its vitality through a combination of literalism and rationalistic materialism. For the psychologically minded, this approach to Jesus and the image of *Christ* is no less mysterious or miraculous than the traditional paradigm, and far more believable. Being a Christian believer does not mean sacrificing the intellect or common sense, nor does it require pretending that the Bible is some kind of magic book that always trumps science. Analytical psychology prizes all the ways of knowing while relativizing the capacity of the ego and its rational functions to grasp, control, and market the ineffable. It is far more respectful of mystery than the literalized theological and Christological formulations that pass for traditional or popular Christianity.

However, this new way to approach Jesus and *Christ* is fraught with great difficulty because of 2,000 years of Christian doctrine. It is easier to give verbal assent to *Jesus as the only way to God,* than in Jung's words, *to live our own lives as truly as Jesus lived his in all its implications.* Then, Jung adds, "Anyone who did this would run counter to the forces of the past … and would be misjudged, derided, tortured and crucified" (Jung 1955d: 236). This ominous warning did not keep Carl Jung from pushing ahead with naming what he had discovered in the depths of his own psyche/soul, as well as those with whom he worked. It is well-documented that he is not well-received by the guardians of religious orthodoxy, then or now!

Questioning the divinity of Jesus is, indeed, a taboo topic for most Christians. Yet as Jungian analyst Elizabeth Boyden Howes writes, "There is a taboo which has to be broken in order for consciousness to be achieved. The forbidden somehow becomes the saving element … and most mysteriously and most paradoxically, the gods seem to be behind both the taboo and the thrust out of the taboo into the new pattern" (Howes 1971: 125). Speaking to the same issue, Jung declared that we should not be satisfied with unchangeable traditions since "even revealed truth has to evolve. Everything living changes. The great battle that began with the dawn of consciousness has not reached its climax with any particular interpretation, apostolic, Catholic, Protestant, or otherwise" (Jung 1958: 731).

Carl Jung's understanding of the psyche and of the archetypal Self challenges any religious orientation which claims exclusive or final revelation of truth. Jungian analyst, author, and professor of religion Ann Ulanov, in her book *The Feminine in Jungian Psychology and in Christian Theology*, interprets Jung's thought in this regard as follows:

> While treating Christianity with the utmost serious-
> ness, Jung does not accept its claim to be the final
> revelation and the only way to God. Although in
> psychological terms Christ offers one of the fullest
> disclosures of the self, and although Jung's psychology
> insists that Western man (sic), rooted psychologically
> in Christian soil, must come to terms with this re-
> velation, for Jung Christ is still but one of many
> manifestations of the Spirit. Jung cautions against
> the destructive megalomania that can result from
> thinking "that Christianity is the only truth, and the
> white Christ the only Redeemer" (Ulanov 1971: 107-08).

This psychological approach might be seen as throwing the baby out with the bathwater. The intent, however, is just the opposite. It is an effort to recover both Jesus and the *Christ* image from being submerged and lost in the waters of the unconscious. It is an effort to save both from centuries of dogmatic literalism and from being mascots to sports teams, co-pilots in our cars, gaudy signs along the highway, WWJD bracelets, and so-called Christian dating services promising to find God's match for you! Or, even more sinister, helping to win wars and political contests. Both Jesus and the *Christ* image deserve better, and so do we.

Jung's psychology provides a necessary correction to the dualistic mindset that fueled the dogmatic Christological formulations that continue to operate unconsciously in the modern religious mind. Without devaluing the human and humane gains in consciousness and culture inspired and promoted by a one-sided spiritualized Christianity, Jung saw the necessity for the reintegration of that which had been neglected and relegated to the unconscious, namely the instinctual, the feminine, and an appreciation of evil as being more than a mere absence of the good (Sanford 1981: 136ff). Commenting on the old idea of an antithesis between spirit and matter that has dogged Christianity for centuries, Jung writes, "The spirit is the life of the body seen from within, and the body the outward manifestation of the life of the spirit—the two being really one …." (Jung 1924: 94).

Jung understood the split between matter and spirit, or body and soul, as symptomatic of a deeper split between conscious and unconscious, the healing of which analytical psychology seeks to facilitate. It is the perspective of this book that a literal understanding of Jesus as the one and only Christ, promoted by the misnomer Jesus Christ, accentuates the split rather than promotes its healing. On the one hand, it promotes spirit as being ultimately more valuable than matter regardless of carefully worded dogmatic efforts to assure otherwise; on the other hand, it makes the resources symbolized by the image of *Christ* functionally unavailable to any other human.

As long as the image of *Christ* is limited to one historical person, or is the exclusive possession of one religious tradition, Christian dualism will remain intact, and Christianity will continue its decline into irrelevancy because it does not sufficiently touch the inner person. Speaking of his own well-founded ambivalence toward Christianity and the Church a year before his death, Jung notes in a letter to a Christian pastor:

> To be exact, I must say that, although I profess myself a Christian, I am at the same time convinced that the chaotic contemporary situation shows that the present-day Christianity is not the final truth. As I see it, the contributions of the psychology of the unconscious should be taken into account (Jung 1960: 575). Christianity has shown us the way, but as the facts bear witness, it has not penetrated deeply enough below the surface (Jung 1945a: 254).

In hindsight and with psychological insight, the archetypal *Christ* was hijacked by a fearful and possessive form of Christianity as it competed for a foothold among its religious competitors. That competition resulted in a literalistic interpretation of Jesus as the Messiah, an interpretation perpetuated by the misnomers Jesus Christ or Christ. With the advent of the deep spiritual perspective of analytical psychology in the last century, we have been able to recognize that hijacking, how and why it happened, and to identify the task of *saving Jesus* and *freeing the image of Christ* from its Christian imprisonment. As difficult as it is to entertain, and perhaps impossible at this stage of collective Christian consciousness, Christians do not possess *Christ*, as the name Christian may suggest. If Christians could get beyond that false notion and possessive instinct, it could open their eyes to the archetypal *Christ* in all religions and religious claimants, and nonreligious as well. This would have the dramatic effect of lowering the hostility within the Christian community and between Christianity and other major religions. It would reverse the missionary efforts from taking Christ to others to recognizing and celebrating the image and energy of *Christ* already present, though called by many other names. Freeing the *Christ*-image from the fearful and possessive clutches of Christians could open the way to genuine interfaith dialogue that will otherwise remain stymied. When Christianity gets to this place in its development and maturity, its message really will be Good News!

Father Raymond Pannikar, Christian scholar noted for his devotion to interreligious dialogue with Hinduism and Buddhism, and author of *The Unknown Christ of Hinduism*, stressed that no religion has a monopoly on *Christ*. He writes, "To the third Christian millennium is reserved the task of overcoming a tribal Christology by a Christophany that allows Christians to see the work of Christ everywhere, without assuming that they have a better grasp or monopoly of that mystery" (Panniker 2010: 10). The depth psychological perspective proposed by Carl Jung both validates that perspective and shows how it is empirically possible by proposing *Christ* as an archetypal image inherent in the psyche rather than an external figure sent by an external deity.

The traditional, unreflective references to Jesus as Jesus Christ or Christ may not be possible to alter at this stage of history and collective Christian consciousness. Or, if in doing so, Christianity may not survive. At this point, the religious corporation it has spawned may be too big to fail or to admit its failure. Likewise, the articles of incorporation of the Christian corporation may be too fixed in our minds and memory to permit new ways of imaging Jesus and *Christ*. For example, the Nicene Creed is clearly the product of a dualistic view of the universe the modern mind can no longer entertain, though it is recited and affirmed week after week. The creed may contain beautiful symbolic expressions of the archetypal *Christ* but erroneously limits them to the historical Jesus, thus perpetuating the unfortunate merger, Jesus Christ, which leaves many scratching their heads about the creed's relevancy. It may be that centuries of repetition have worn theological and Christological ruts too deep from which Christians are able to extricate themselves. In that case, Christians will continue an unconscious bailout of the monotheistic myth by trying to prop up a literalized and romanticized story that has lost its power to persuade, inspire, and transform. They will continue to do cosmetic interventions like creating new programs and new strategies for church growth, or using the latest technology to provide religious entertainment, which fuels much of the megachurch phenomenon, none of which addresses the core issue of our unconscious projections. In doing so, they may fail to tap the creative unconscious resources that beg for embrace and incarnation. Furthermore, if the underlying psychological dynamics that gave birth to the Christian movement continue to be ignored, Christianity will have little to offer the more inclusive religious myth that struggles to be born.

In summary, it was necessary to idealize Jesus at a certain stage in the unfolding of Christian consciousness by granting him projected divine and messianic status; the task now is to withdraw those *Christ* projections from Jesus *to wake up the Christ within*. For Christianity to evolve and mature as a life-giving, soul-satisfying religion, it will require saving Jesus from carrying unconscious projections, in both their positive and negative valences, and freeing the archetypal image of *Christ* from its 2,000 years of literalistic and ecclesial imprisonment. However, this difficult psycho-spiritual work must be done not for the purpose of setting aside those projected contents as unreal or unimportant, but to reclaim their value. Projected contents are of ultimate importance because they permit us to identify contents of the human soul still longing for incarnation. Again, unconscious contents are first seen in projected form so they can be recognized, withdrawn, and consciously owned. The purposeful nature of projection cannot be repeated too often.

Until these psychological insights are integrated into the religious bloodstream of its leaders and teachers, Christianity will likely remain in an adolescent stage of development incapable of promoting and nurturing a mature spirituality. It will continue to promote an external religion that avoids the inner, transformational task taught and lived by Jesus. Furthermore, it will also continue to contribute to the religious pathology that threatens our world through explicit and implicit claims to be a superior religion, to possess absolute truth, and to be the favored children of God. The other two major monotheisms, Judaism and Islam, are equally indicted since they also perpetuate idealized projections onto their religious heroes and teachers.

Any religion that claims divine favor or possession of absolute truth in its sacred texts is the victim of a psychological inflation and/or religious delusion. Unable or unwilling at the present time to face these inner, psychological realities, the three major monotheisms—Christianity, Judaism, and Islam—represent the greatest down-drag on the evolution of religious consciousness and, therefore, pose the greatest threat to our world. Psychologically, the refusal to become conscious is humanity's original and greatest sin. However, as Jung observed, that refusal "is indulged in with the greatest piety, even among those who should serve mankind as teachers and examples" (Jung 1945a: 253).

If the human Jesus and the archetypal *Christ* are unconsciously merged as this essay proposes, then the religious task will involve the laborious effort to separate them. Bringing consciousness to this long-darkened issue could return value both to Jesus and to the archetypal *Christ* and reclaim the sacredness of psyche/soul as the divine/human meeting place, a precinct abandoned early in Christianity's evolution. Consciousness could allow more of the archetypal *Christ* that flowed through Jesus to manifest in us and in our world. To paraphrase Jung: *We must withdraw our projections from Jesus in order for the archetypal Christ to incarnate more fully in and through us, as it did in and through Jesus.* The following essay continues the theme "Reimagining Jesus and *Christ*" with specific implications for traditional theological and Christological for-mulations.

ESSAY NUMBER SEVEN

REIMAGINING JESUS AND *CHRIST*
(Part II)

*The Self (or Christ) cannot become conscious and real
without the withdrawal of external projections.* (Jung)

The previous essay explored the dynamics of psychological projection underlying how and why the religious teacher, Jesus, was granted the name Jesus Christ; and, secondly, the necessity of separating the proposed unconscious merger that resulted in that familiar Christological designation and personal name. Drawing on the insights of analytical psychology, we noted the distinction between history and myth and, paraphrasing Jung, *the necessity of withdrawing projections from the historical or metaphysical Jesus in order for the archetypal <u>Christ</u> to incarnate more fully in and through us, as it did in and through Jesus.* This vital necessity was placed under the larger umbrella of promoting more consciousness in general and religious consciousness in particular. The urgent call for an expansion of consciousness extends not only to Christians but to all religious who remain in the grip of the monotheistic myth, which, I propose, has lost its capacity to nurture the modern mind and ancient soul.

What follows is a beginning attempt to differentiate the historical person, Jesus, and the archetypal image, *Christ,* and to express some of the immediate implications of such when viewed through an analytical or Jungian psychological lens. The imaginative effort, far from definitive, academic, or doctrinal, will hopefully stir the imagination of the reader as part of the larger task proposed in these Essays to "Reimagine *God* and *Religion*." As proposed, the monotheistic myth—replete with an external, supernatural, interventionist deity favoring a specific religious tribe with authoritative sacred texts applicable to all for all times—has lost its capacity to nurture both mind and soul for more and more spiritual seekers. This means that most of the traditional theological and Christological meanings and interpretations of Jesus and *Christ* are no longer relevant. When considered psychologically, however, many discover a wealth of meanings that may sustain in this *thin place* (See Essay "Thin Places and Thin Times") between the death of the old myth(s) and the hopeful birth of the new. These essays are intended to fertilize the imagination both to receive and to create food for soul in these perilous times.

Rather than trying to reform, revive, or revitalize Christianity and the Church, and the monotheistic myth on which they rest, my primary interest involves identifying the psychological or archetypal dynamics at play with the most revered religious personage in Western religious history and arguably one of the three or four in all religious history. This analysis of Jesus and *Christ* could provide essential psychological wisdom needed for the future religious myth that will be co-created by the archetypal unconscious and the human imagination. Specifically, attention is drawn to the mysterious processes of psychological projection, which play a hidden role in the emergence and formation of all religions, past and future (See Essay "Projection and Revelation").

The bullet-point format is chosen for conciseness and clarity around some of the most familiar and important traditional theological and Christological formulations. Both **Jesus** and ***Christ*** are highlighted for comparison, with ***Christ*** italicized to denote an image rather than a person. Various versions of the Jungian imperative concerning withdrawing psychological projections are repeated for emphasis:

- Beginning with the most fundamental differentiation and distinction, **Jesus** was a human being, a person just like us, who lived in the visible world. ***Christ*** is an archetypal image; an image denoting an invisible mystery that courses through the universe and through all people and that seems to desire ever more conscious manifestation or incarnation, as it did through Jesus. Succinctly, **Jesus** is a noun; ***Christ*** is an archetypal image that manifests as a verb "coursing through history as an archetypal energy driving toward wholeness ..." (Hollis 2009: 110).

- *We must withdraw our projections from **Jesus** in order to wake up **Christ** within; that is, to open ourselves to the same archetypal reality and potential.*

- **Christ** is one name among many that we humans have assigned to that innate, inner longing and potential to be more complete and whole, and to have the disparate parts of our individual and collective lives united. Modern science has identified those evolutionary dynamics that have moved the cosmos and nature toward greater differentiation and unity at the same time. As a part of nature, we share those hidden processes that manifest as human longing and hope for the more, and the more authentic. That longing and potential come with our psychic wiring, so to speak, rather than being an add-on from the outside. In the Hebrew/Jewish tradition, that deep longing was seen in projected form in a hoped-for outer figure, the Messiah or Anointed One, who would set things right and restore an outward land and a just societal order. For Christians that deep longing was projected onto **Jesus,** where it still largely remains and from whom it needs to be withdrawn.

- *Projections onto **Jesus** must be withdrawn in order to "wake up the **Christ** within!"*

- **Jesus** was neither omnipotent nor omniscient, being a limited human being like us and contained in the available three-tiered cosmology of his day. However, he, like us had access to the collective mystical wisdom and vision that enabled him to see beneath the surface of things and to imagine a more whole, more compassionate, and more peaceful way of being in this life rather than simply preparing for a later one. He spent his relatively brief adult life and career trying to awaken the imagination of others to the same possibilities. He challenged the people of his day to free themselves from the narrow religious, social, and political attitudes that kept their minds shallow and their embrace small. He mirrored the same potential wisdom and compassion in others, a perspective that was preserved in the extracanonical text, *The Secret Gospel of John*, where **Jesus** says, "I am a mirror, look into me and see yourself." Peering beneath the projections that obscured his humanity, we discover that **Jesus**, in the words of Walter Wink, was "not the omnipotent God in a man-suit, but someone like we, who looked for God at the center of his life and called the world to join him" (Wink 2002: 11).

- Again, **Jesus** was the name of a wisdom teacher from Nazareth who was rooted in the ancient mystical or wisdom tradition. **Christ** is the name for the wisdom built into the fabric of life itself, as well as the wisdom accrued over the span of human history, both of which are preserved in the metaphorical collective unconscious and available for conscious integration. Rooted in a stream of living wisdom that had been flowing for thousands of years, **Jesus** was primarily a teacher of a path of inner transformation. The wisdom tradition, sometimes known as *sophia perennis,* was the headwaters of all the great religious traditions of today (Bourgeault 2008: 4-5). Richard Rohr, a leading author addressing the emergence of a new paradigm, refers to the wisdom tradition as "The Perennial Tradition," saying it "is not just a metaphysic, but it's a psychology that finds in the soul something similar to, or even identical with, that Divine Reality"(Rohr, From a nonpublished talk at Conference in Assisi, Italy, May, 2012). That psychological perspective was first elaborated in depth by Jung, yet still largely ignored by religious scholars and writers. Western Christianity for the most part has also ignored the wisdom tradition of **Jesus**, favoring instead casting **Jesus** as Savior. As Cynthia Bourgeault notes, in the original Aramaic of **Jesus** and his followers, there was no word for salvation. "Salvation was understood as a bestowal of life, and to be saved was *to be made alive"* (Bourgeault 2008: 21).

- *Projections onto **Jesus** must be withdrawn in order to access and claim the wisdom of the **Christ** within.*

- At Christmas, Christians celebrate the birth of the human **Jesus**, not **Christ.** The reality behind the image of **Christ,** like the psyche itself, is of indeterminate age, existing "before the foundations of the world" to use a familiar phrase describing the infinite. **Christ** did not enter the world at a particular time from some metaphysical domain. Again, **Christ** is a symbol for that which is deepest within life that moves toward completeness and fullness, toward ever more variety and unity. This inherent dynamic has also been rightly described in scientific language as the evolutionary processes within natural life.

- Again, Jesus Christ did not enter the world on Christmas. **Jesus** did. This distinction between the person **Jesus** and the archetypal **Christ** prompted one of my good friends to quip, "We have to get *Christ* out of Christmas!" And he is absolutely right. So, all those sermons I used to preach about *putting Christ back into Christmas* (which were never heeded either by me or my congregations) were ill-formed ideas in the first place! I am not sure we can even get **Jesus** back into Christmas since the holiday season is little more than cultural permission to feed the addiction to consumption and to help the ailing economy, thinly disguised as gifting others.

- *The projections onto **Jesus** must be withdrawn in order to embrace the inner archetypal redeemer whom Christians call **Christ** and other religions identify by numerous other names.*

- **Jesus,** son of Mary and Joseph, was given a common human name. ***Christ,*** on the other hand, is one name among many for those experiences humans have named experiences of God, or *numinous* experiences. The transmitters or carriers of those experiences are the images that emerge from the collective unconscious and are mediated in and through the human imagination. Those images populate both our daytime interactions and our nighttime dreams via projection.

- **Jesus** was neither a god nor the God. He was a person through whom godlike energies apparently flowed. When people experienced those energies, then and now, their own archetypal potentials were and are stirred and awakened and beg to be brought into fuller manifestation or incarnation. As indicated in the previous essay, retrieving the divine status assigned to **Jesus** by removing the Christological crust that was projected onto him might be seen as throwing the baby out with the bathwater. The opposite is the case. It is an effort to recover both **Jesus** and the ***Christ*** image from being submerged and lost in the waters of the unconscious. The purpose would be to save both from centuries of dogmatic literalism and to reimagine both, which does not do violence to common sense and modern science. Equally important, the mysteries inherent in both are preserved.

- *Projections onto **Jesus** must be withdrawn in order to return sacred value both to **Jesus** and the **Christ** within.*

- Seen in projected form, **Jesus** was considered to be the salvation desired, the outer remedy for a deeply felt longing and need. While he lived, and in the decades following his death, he grew to godlike proportions, fed by projection and mythologizing, both of which are natural and necessary processes to express and feed the human religious instinct and hunger. That hunger goes unfed or unmet, however, if the *bread and water and light of life* are limited to one person, back there, rather than rightly conceived as symbols for what is always available in an inner way. For 2,000 years, **Jesus** of Nazareth has been larger than life, not because he was literally the only begotten Son of God, but because of the centuries of unconscious human longing projected onto him.

- *We must withdraw our projections from **Jesus** or a metaphysical Christ to wake up the **Christ** within.*

- When **Jesus** was elevated to God-status by unconscious projections and misnamed Jesus Christ, the result was a spiritualized being. Jung argues that this emphasis on spirit was developmentally necessary for Christianity as a compensation for the unbridled instincts that ruled the day. He writes, "We can hardly realize the whirlwinds of brutality and unchained libido that roared through the streets of Imperial Rome" (Jung 1956: 104). In a footnote, however, Jung notes that because of the subsequent one-sided emphasis on spirit and the repression of the physical and instinctual side of our wholeness, "we have experienced abominations of desolation of which Rome never dreamed" (Jung: 1956: 105). He was referring to the two world wars, which he had witnessed, the atrocities of the Holocaust, and the further threats posed by nuclear weapons. The demand of the psyche now, according to Jung, is to compensate the one-sidedness of the original Christian compensation (Dourley 1985: 29) that necessitates this depth psychological approach to **Jesus** and the image of **Christ.**

- Although a necessary stage in the evolution of Christianity and religious consciousness in general, the unresolved projection of **Jesus** as divine has had disastrous human consequences. Given the stage of conscious-ness at the time and the dualistic mindset that has characterized Christian development, the spiritualization of its central figure propelled early Christianity down a slippery slope of literalism from which it has yet to recover. Because of the dualistic mindset of the day, it was then necessary to declare **Jesus** (and later his human mother) sinless and sexless. The result has been a spirituality of perfectionism on the one hand and, on the other hand, the conclusion (consciously and unconsciously) that the human body, flesh, sex and matter are inherently evil. The misery and suffering that these unconscious dogmatic formulations have produced pour out daily in the offices of therapists, analysts, spiritual directors, pastors and priests.

- *Projections onto **Jesus** must be withdrawn in order to recover the glory of his—and our—humanity!*

- **Jesus** was not *a* redeemer, or *the* redeemer. He was a *revealer* in the sense that he reveals what it can mean to access the inner depths (what we now call the Collective Unconscious) where the resources of the archetypal redeemer are metaphorically stored. **Jesus** was apparently a remarkably individuated person who had the capacity to set aside his personal ego and power needs for the sake of others and for the sake of that invisible source he called Abba. **Christ** is the image or name of the meta-personal or archetypal power that enabled him to do that.

- *Projections onto **Jesus** must be withdrawn in order to wake up and access the same power within us.*

- When viewed through the lens of analytical psychology, **Jesus** was neither the Redeemer nor the Savior of the world. As harsh as it sounds to evangelical ears and born-again sensibilities, **Jesus** never saved anyone, either then or now. **Jesus** was not a scapegoat for our sins, for our dark shadow, though many would prefer that easy way out**.** The ritual of projecting individual and collective sins onto a goat or lamb, and either sacrificing it or sending it out into the wilderness as an antidote for sins, was carried over from the Hebrew tradition. Through projection and literalism, **Jesus** became the unblemished lamb onto whom one's sins are placed and the blood of whom supposedly appeases a remote deity. That literalistic interpretation of **Jesus'** life and death, and the outdated cosmology that supports it, continue to permeate and infantilize the Christian mind. The doctrine of substitutionary blood atonement, along with its ugly cousin, the doctrine of original sin, have bedeviled Christianity since Augustine's anthropology won out over that of the Celtic theologian Pelagius at the Synod of Whitby in 664. Leading Celtic Christianity scholar and author John Philip Newell chronicles the tragic loss for Western Christianity with the defeat of Pelagius' views and his subsequent condemnation as a heretic and his official excommunication from the Church. Newell's *Listening for the Heartbeat of God* and *Christ of the Celts* provide thorough and soulful accounts of the issues involved in the Augustine/Pelagius controversy. Concerning the doctrine of original sin, he writes:

> It is a doctrine that has wreaked untold havoc in the lives and relationships of countless men and women in the Western world, including the self-perceptions of generation after generation of children. It has distanced Christ from the heart of the human soul. And it continues to undermine the way we relate, or choose to relate, to the people and wisdoms of other cultures and communities (Newell 2008: 19-20).

- Augustine's unfortunate victory left a stain on the Christian and Western religious psyche; not the stain of a supposedly original sin, but the doctrine that was given credence by Augustine, which was likely fueled by his personal and sexual complexes. Remembering the religious diet of his own youth, Jung writes, "The killing of a human victim to placate the senseless wrath of a God who had created imperfect beings unable to fulfill his expectations poisoned my whole religion" (Jung 1958: 728). New Testament scholar Walter Wink observes that **Jesus** condemned all forms of domination, including the entire sacrificial system with its belief in "sacral violence" (Wink 2002: 14). Yet Jesus Christ as the sacrificial blood atonement for sins remains the primary mantra for the majority of Christian teaching and preaching.
- *We must withdraw the projections onto* **Jesus** *as the scapegoat for our sins to avoid making others our scapegoat for what we refuse to face within.*
- Happily, wiser religious voices in recent time, like Newell, Matthew Fox, John Shelby Spong, Richard Rohr, Marcus Borg, and many others, have begun to remedy that degraded view of the human soul by emphasizing the *original blessing* that accompanies our birth and the birth of the cosmos. Furthermore, the psychological view presented here envisions a hopeful next stage in understanding the human condition, including both its liabilities and potentials, i.e., its anthropology. While

original blessing is a necessary antidote to healing old wounds administered by the doctrine of original sin, it may not take seriously enough the human capacity for evil and destruction, which remains all too evident. Jung's psychology proposes that human nature, being part of nature itself, has the potential for both *creativity* and *destruction*; again like nature herself. The key to which potential finds greater human expression is the gift of a reflective consciousness; that is, the human capacity to reflect on the nature of our nature. This rather recent acquisition in the evolutionary process provides the human ego some measure of choice between the twin inherent possibilities, albeit never the illusion of absolute control. The unconscious is all too autonomous and tricky to permit the latter hubristic notion. The acceptance of the human potential for both creativity and destruction, for both extraordinary acts of sacrificial love and of unspeakable evil, avoids the psychological either/or splitting that has characterized the one-sided Christian myth and begs to be altered.

- Withdrawing projections onto **Jesus** means that sins—the destructive shadow—have to be faced within, in the inner wilderness where we (like Jesus) are tempted by devilish ego-centric power and fame, where we wrestle (like Jesus) with the inherent powers of destruction and creativity, which compete for consciousness. We must endure our own Gethsemanes; we must carry our own crosses, which includes coming to conscious terms with all the opposite forces that course through us and through our world. Taking responsibility is the more difficult way, however, and why the scapegoat solution remains preferred by the majority of Christians. Or, more generously, the scapegoat solution remains preferable because it has been the only one suggested by Christian teachers who inherited from their teachers the same unexamined tradition. At present, the dogma of substitutionary atonement remains a convenient substitute for the risky, meaningful, and salvific spiritual path **Jesus** walked and taught and mapped out for would-be followers.

- Only as we relieve **Jesus** from being the Christ can the inner ***Christ*** image serve the psychological and symbolic function of reconciling the disparate parts of our personality. Saving **Jesus** means lifting from his shoulders what is necessary for us to carry within. The greater danger in promoting **Jesus** as the external savior who takes on one's sins as a scapegoat is that it invariably promotes the scapegoating of human others. As Jung says, "casting one's sins on Christ" is to evade one's deepest responsibility which, ironically, is contrary to the spirit of Christianity" (Jung 1943b: 8).

- *Again, Christians must withdraw their projections onto **Jesus** as their scapegoat and face the inner and innate destructive, life-diminishing power personified as Satan or the Devil. Otherwise, enemies will be found in the outer world who have to be dismissed, converted, or eliminated.*

- Simply repeating that "**Jesus** is my personal Lord and Savior," or declaring that "**Jesus** died for my sins" or "**Jesus** paid it all," does not dilute the dark shadow. All too often it does the opposite by giving one the illusion of being whiter than snow, thus pushing the shadow deeper into the unconscious, where it then reappears in fears, prejudices, and attitudes of superiority. In the same way, repeating *Allahu Akbar* (God is great), or meticulously observing the Mosaic Law does not make the shadow go away. How else can we explain that after 4,000 years of Judaism, 2,000 of Christianity, and 1,300 years of Islam, we are no closer to the peace for which we long, while we teeter on the brink of destroying ourselves and our Earth home?

- *Projections onto an outer, metaphysical God—or the human **Jesus**—must be withdrawn in order to access and manifest the archetypal redeemer who is available equally to the consciousness of all religions and all people.*

- When Jung proposed that "neurosis is always a substitute for legitimate suffering" (Jung 1937: 75), he cast further light on the desire for **Jesus** to carry our sins and to be a proxy for our suffering, which is an attempt to avoid legitimate suffering. The notion that **Jesus** "paid it all by suffering for our sins" is a form of denial and unconscious splitting. It relieves us from nothing. It means that our suffering and guilt will surface elsewhere, always. The unconscious does not have a digestive tract that eliminates legitimate suffering and legitimate guilt, even if we have supposedly magically given it over to **Jesus** to carry for us. Too often the most vocal and rigid substitutionary atonement advocate unwittingly visits suffering on those around him or her. All too frequently the victims are the less powerful, like women, homosexuals, and ethnic minorities, as well as those of other religious persuasions who *need to be saved.* From this perspective, the doctrine of substitutionary atonement promotes religious pathology rather than salvation or healing.

- No one, including **Jesus**, can save us from the contingencies of human existence, though each of us would like to be relieved of such. Life includes suffering; we have no choice in the matter. We do have a choice, however, to suffer consciously or unconsciously, and if it is the latter, it can be hellish for us and for those around us. No religion or theory of atonement will relieve us of the wonderfully awful burden of being human or grant us the meaning that comes from consciously living "our one wild and precious life" (Oliver 1992: 94). Sufficient is the comfort that someone understands our suffering and stands beside or with us without attempting to take away our experience. What we know of **Jesus'** death illustrates the redemptive possibilities of conscious suffering, rather than magically relieving us from the same.

- **Jesus** is not the only Way to God, nor a ticket to Heaven, but he does reveal what manifesting the archetypal redeemer/**Christ**/Self looks like: The passion and compassion which result, the cost of doing so, and the ultimate meaning it may provide.

- **Jesus** lived at a time and place in history, not unlike our own, when the unconscious hopes and fears of all the years were especially intense and people needed to have an outer person (or cause or plan) onto whom their deepest longings for a redeemer could be projected and seen. Those projections were made, at the purposeful initiative of the archetypal unconscious, and continue to be made, and need to be consciously withdrawn and owned so that we, too, can move the human experiment along through our expanded consciousness. **Jesus** was a man who lived his destiny, who taught his truth, who disturbed the status quo, and who challenged the outdated social and religious prejudices of his day, so much so that he had to be silenced. He was neither omniscient nor omnipotent, being a limited human being like we are, and contained in the available cosmology of his day. However, he had access to the collective mystical wisdom and vision that enabled him to see beneath the surface of things and to imagine a more whole, more loving, and more peaceful way of being in *this* world. He spent his teaching career trying to awaken the imagination of others to the same possibilities. He challenged the people of his day, and our day, to free themselves from the narrow religious, social, and political attitudes that kept their minds shallow and their embrace small.

- *Projections onto* **Jesus** *must be withdrawn so that the universal and compassionate archetypal* **Christ** *can enrich our minds and widen our embrace.*
- **Jesus** died and did not literally rise from the dead. **Christ** is the name that captures the experience we all have of being resurrected again and again after the many deaths we experience along the way to our final one.
- **Jesus** lived and died, and he is not coming back a second time. The Second Coming of **Christ** happens every time we withdraw more of our projections onto **Jesus** and access more of the archetypal **Christ,** which is always and forever available.
- Nor is **Jesus** returning to save humanity from its own possible destruction with some kind of Armageddon coup. That, too, clearly is a projection; again not *just* a projection, but a *mirror* reflecting inner conflicts. Many would like it to be the case: A final rescue from outside that would save those of our tribe plus some Jewish converts who finally get it in the last thousand years! The Armageddon battle is going on already, in every soul, in every group and religion, and in every political party and nation, where the unconscious destructive and creative powers struggle for dominance. Currently, it is a toss-up as to which of the powers is winning the battle, and monotheistic religions are not helping the cause. The power and choice for our destruction is now in our hands; it is within our own capacity, as is the capacity to be a part of joining creation to continue her mysterious and beautiful unfolding.
- *To participate in the continuing creation, and avoid our own destruction, will require the hard work of consciousness.*
- Whether or not there is life after this one, there is no way to know, and no one does know. What we do know is that this life is so precious— largely because we experience it as limited and finite human beings (like **Jesus**) — that we are impelled to live it with as much consciousness, passion, and compassion as we possibly can. If we do that, we will have been good and faithful servants to the mysteries behind, beneath, and within reality itself, and we can entrust our dying selves, like **Jesus**, to invisible personified hands.

- *Projections onto **Jesus** as a ticket to eternity must be withdrawn in order to participate in the salvific nature of conscious living and dying.*
- Taken as a whole in terms of content and spirit or feeling-tone, what remains of **Jesus'** teachings reveals the difficult inner work required for a radical transformation of consciousness. The fruits of such a transformation are *passion* for life itself in all its valences and *compassion* for all, the two being the twin touchstones of an authentic spiritual life. Analytical Psychology uncovers and names the archetypal processes lived by **Jesus**, as well as other notable religious heroes, which are the same processes we are asked to engage consciously. Again, it seems safer to stand at a distance and allow another to live the life and to confront the necessary deaths that are ours alone to embrace.
- *We must withdraw projections from **Jesus** so that both his teachings and the **Christ** within can bring to completion their transformational work in us and the world.*
- In her poem "When Death Comes," Mary Oliver expresses the attitude worth maintaining while living, and exiting, this life:

> When death comes
> like the hungry bear in autumn;
> when death comes and take all the bright coins from his purse
>
> to buy me, and snaps the purse shut;
> when death comes
> like the measle-pox;
>
> when death comes
> like an iceberg between the shoulder blades,
>
> I want to step through the door full of curiosity, wondering:
> what is it going to be like, that cottage of darkness?
>
> And therefore I look upon everything
> as a brotherhood and a sisterhood,
> and I look upon time as no more than an idea,
> and I consider eternity as another possibility,
>
> and I think of each life as a flower, as common
> as a field daisy, and as singular,

and each name a comfortable music in the mouth,
tending, as all music does, toward silence,

and each body a lion of courage, and something
precious to the earth.

When it's over, I want to say: all my life
I was a bride married to amazement.
I was the bridegroom, taking the world into my arms.

When it's over, I don't want to wonder
if I have made of my life something particular, and real.
I don't want to find myself sighing and frightened,
or full of argument.

I don't want to end up simply having visited this world.
(Oliver 1992: 10)

- Near the end of his own life, Carl Jung included a chapter "On Life After Death" in his autobiographical work, *Memories, Dreams, Reflections*. His reflections on death remain a classical depth psychological treatise on the subject and the possibilities of an authentic life preceding it. Stressing the relationship with that meta-personal dimension imaged by the Self or **Christ**, he concludes:

  > The decisive question for (humankind) is: Is he related to something infinite or not? That is the telling question of his life. ... If we understand and feel that here in this life we already have a link with the infinite, desires and attitudes change. In the final analysis, we count for something only because of the essential we embody, and if we do not embody that, life is wasted. In our relationships to other (people), too, the crucial question is whether an element of boundlessness is expressed in the relationship. ... As far as we can discern, the sole purpose of human existence is to kindle a light in the darkness of mere being. It may even be assumed that just as the unconscious affects us, so the increase in

our consciousness affects the unconscious (Jung 1965: 326).

- *We must withdraw our projections from **Jesus** as the Light of the World to kindle the light of our consciousness, which is our unique offering to the world.*

- *Saving **Jesus*** by releasing him from being the Christ or our Christ may require sacrificing a necessary 2,000-year security for a yet unknown, but potentially more whole, myth by which to live. Might we then be closer to the deeper meaning of *incarnation,* whereby we participate more fully in the redemptive process that has always been at work in the depths of psyche/soul? In saving **Jesus** by giving up the hubristic notion that our religious hero is God and, therefore, that Christianity is superior to all other religions, might it be the redemptive sacrifice required to save ourselves and our Earth? Such a sacrifice would be beyond the power of the ego to accomplish on its own. Over time, however, the increase in consciousness of a sufficient number of individuals could be the conduit for the archetypal ***Christ*** to bring to completion what was mirrored in **Jesus.**

- Ironically, saving **Jesus** might mean the further dismantling or dissolution of the very religion perpetuated in his name. If that allowed for a more life-giving, soul-satisfying myth or paradigm to emerge, it could speak more deeply to the redemptive quality of **Jesus'** life and ours. The irony would be that in giving up the Jesus Christ of the traditional paradigm, we would find a deeper appreciation of **Jesus** and a deeper experience of ***Christ.*** Or, in more familiar words, in losing our religious life, we may indeed discover it.

These, then, are some psychological perspectives on traditional theological and Christological themes when the (necessary, I propose) differentiation between **Jesus** and the archetypal ***Christ*** is considered. For the psychologically minded, this angle of vision preserves the humanity of **Jesus**, as well as our own, while acknowledging a *meta-personal* reality to which he, and we, must respond. These psychological perspectives avoid the dualistic split between matter and spirit that has plagued monotheistic religions. It renders the dangerous notion of being the chosen tribe of a one-and-only deity no more than a narcissistic delusion.

Finally, the psychological myth preserves the possibility that any individual can contribute to the continuing creation through the hard, sacred work of consciousness, which requires continuing ownership of the human capacity for both creativity and destruction. Individual efforts toward greater and wider consciousness are akin to placing an infinitesimal grain of sand on the scale of humanity's soul that begs to be tipped toward the life **Jesus** and other wisdom teachers have envisioned. That is the same life we so sorely desire and the life that the archetypal **Christ** can empower us to incarnate. With the differentiation proposed herein, *incarnation* ceases to be a one-time-only doctrine related to **Jesus**; rather, it is a task for each person to realize. The psychological counterpart is *individuation* as opposed to *individualism*. Individuation, if authentic, "does not shut one out from the world, but gathers the world to oneself" (Jung 1946b: 226). Understood as a universal image and inner potential, **Christ** is available to all equally and fully and defies a possessive spirit that shrinks mind and soul and results in an attitude of us versus them. The latter continues to dominate monotheisms and, in turn, feeds and poisons our social and political fabric.

These two essays have circled around a selection from Carl Jung's correspondence with the Rev. David Cox some 60 years ago. We conclude with a paraphrase of another part of those letters, Jung's challenge to any and all, religious or not. I have employed the name "Jesus" rather than "Christ," which honors the differentiated meanings in this essay:

> We must now find ways and means to unite the divine opposites in ourselves. We are summoned and can no longer leave our sorrows to somebody else, not even to Jesus because it was Jesus who left us with the almost impossible task of the cross. Jesus has shown how everybody will be crucified upon his/her destiny, as he was. He did not carry his cross and suffer crucifixion so that we could escape. The bill of the Christian era is presented to us: we are living in a world rent in two from top to bottom; we are confronted with a nuclear holocaust and we have to face our shadows. Obviously God does not want us to remain little children looking out for a parent who will do our job for us (Jung 1958: 1661, Paraphrase).

ESSAY NUMBER EIGHT

THIN PLACES AND THIN TIMES

*The difference between most people and myself is that for me
the <u>dividing walls</u> are transparent. This is my peculiarity* (Jung).

(This article was originally published in Spring 79: Irish Culture and Depth Psychology (2008) by Spring Journal Books. Reprinted with permission from Spring Journal Books. www.springjournalandbooks.com)

ONCE UPON A TIME … according to Irish and Celtic storytellers, the visible and invisible worlds were one. Matter and spirit were intertwined, and human beings and gods and goddesses cavorted together. However, this commingling was confusing to mortals who needed separation to know what was *real* and *unreal*. Out of compassion for the human dilemma, the creative Powers hung a great curtain between the visible and invisible worlds (Estes, Audiotape). Furthermore, to encourage the continuing dialogue and relationship between the parties, there were certain places where the curtain remained very thin and certain times when the traffic through the curtain was especially heavy. These highly charged places and times came to be known as *thin places* and *thin times*.

The experience of the world as thin—where the visible and invisible tumble into each other and where a visitor from the otherworld may appear at any ordinary place or moment—has shaped Irish mythology, literature, and culture, and continues to fertilize the Irish imagination. From this perspective, the Irish landscape and soul are very thin, which may account in large measure for the enduring fascination and love affair with all things Irish. In a similar vein, as this essay will explore, the soul of analytical psychology can be imaged as thin, since its theory and clinical practice honor the continuous interplay between the visible and invisible, conscious and unconscious. Seen through the lens of this archetypal image, Jungian analysis involves the careful attention to the experiences of thin places/times within and between client and analyst, which facilitates the processes of transformation and individuation. Learning to move back and forth through the imaginal curtain between conscious and unconscious, thereby honoring the seamless connection between matter and spirit, constitutes a primary task of being a Jungian analyst. Widening the lens, it also describes the task of the modern religious person.

THIN PLACES/TIMES IN IRISH AND CELTIC LORE

Other Irish myths chronicle with greater detail how Ireland came to be regarded as thin. One account tells how the Tuatha De Danann, the original mythological inhabitants of Ireland, took up residence in the otherworld, that invisible domain that runs close to, and contiguous with, the visible. After an extended battle with the invading Milesians, who were Celts, a compromise was reached. It was decided that the Celts would rule the visible parts of Ireland while the Dananns would take possession of the invisible regions, sometimes imaged as being just below ground and other times just beyond the seas (Fleming 1996: 28, 55). Contrary to the modern dualistic worldview, which separates matter/spirit and physical/spiritual, however, the two domains were of one fabric. Their distinction had to do with what was seen or unseen.

The invisible otherworld was accessible through thin places in the natural landscape such as unusual stone formations, special trees, caves, wells, springs, and other portals such as the *sidhe*, or fairy-mounds, the countless prehistoric burial mounds dotting the Irish landscape. Other places of human construction such as Stonehenge and the tomb at Newgrange were portals to and from the otherworld, as well. Scattered throughout Ireland and the British Isles, these were places where one experienced "a very thin divide between past, present, and future," and encountered an ancient reality in the present moment (Sellner 1993: 25).

Not only did the Celts experience contact with the otherworld in highly charged places, they were attuned to thin times, which were special seasons, festivals, and life events like birth and death, when the curtain between the two domains seemed especially transparent. Most notable was the festival of Samhain, the Celtic New Year (November 1), when the usually thin curtain all but disappeared, resulting in an environment that was both festive and dangerous. The eve of Samhain was an in-between time, neither summer nor winter, neither light nor dark, and in this borderland time the supernatural had the greatest power to influence the lives of mortals (Rabey 1998: 68). Since the boundaries were lifted, Samhain was thought to be the occasion for divination to discover who might die in the coming year, or marry, and who might be one's bride or groom (Cowan 1993: 55). It was the night when the fairy-mounds opened and spirits appeared, often in disguise. This Celtic celebration survives to the present day as Halloween, the night when spooks and goblins roam around, and treats are given to appease the visitors from the otherworld who might otherwise provide an unsavory trick. The modern tradition of wearing masks or disguises (*guizing*) at Halloween is rooted in this ancient thin-time festival (Clark 1996: 119).

On a recent pilgrimage to Ireland that included several days on the Aran Islands off the rugged western coast, our group was intrigued listening to the locals talk about the continuing celebration of Samhain. All the homes and dwellings are opened that night, and the islanders, disguised, are free to roam through the homes of their neighbors, usually without speaking. To us Americans who vigilantly guard our homes and belongings, and dismiss Halloween goblins at the door with treats of candy, hearing how our Aran hosts celebrate Samhain was spooky indeed!

The Tuatha De Danann carried on their lives of feasting and merriment just out of sight of Celtic life but were always at liberty to interfere in human affairs if they so desired. They were thought to possess superior intelligence in certain arenas and had power over the fertility of the land. They were, therefore, in a position to make life easy or difficult for mere mortals. This gave rise to a plethora of rituals to honor or placate the invisible ones such as the "trick or treat" transaction mentioned above. In addition, the Celts regularly left offerings and sacrifices at thin places such as crossroads and holy wells and springs. To the present day, the trees and shrubs around Irish holy wells and springs are bedecked with colorful offerings of string, ribbon, and other gifts left by faithful pilgrims to honor the ancient spirits who continue to inhabit the sacred sites. Another interesting placatory ritual involved milking the first couple of strokes from the cow onto the ground rather than into the bucket as an offering to the fairies (Fleming 1996: 29).

It should be noted that the occupants of the otherworld in Irish lore have numerous designations in addition to the Tuatha De Danann. In his masterful *Irish Fairy and Folk Tales*, William Butler Yeats notes that they are sometimes called banshees, the gentry, the gods of pagan Ireland, or "fallen angels who were not good enough to be saved, nor bad enough to be lost!" Do not think the fairies are always little, he cautions, for they seem to take whatever size or shape pleases them. Their chief occupations are feasting, fighting, and making love, and playing the most beautiful music." Yeats concludes, "They have only one industrious person among them, the *leprechaun*—the shoemaker. Perhaps they wear their shoes out with the dancing! Near the village of Ballisodare is a little woman who lived among them for seven years. When she came home she had no toes—she had danced them off" (Yeats 2003: 4).

The inhabitants of the otherworld were also believed to have certain paths in the visible world along which they walked. Often referred to as fairy paths, or *trods,* they were barely visible to mortals, sometimes a deeper shade of green or circular or labyrinthine. People seeking relief from particular ailments could walk these thin places but were warned to avoid them at times when the otherworldly beings were using them. Should a Celt meet a procession of fairies on the path, and not move aside, it could prove fatal. Likewise, to build a dwelling on one on the paths could prove disastrous (Pennick 1996: 132-33). On the aforementioned pilgrimage to Ireland, we read with interest the newspaper account of a major squabble between a housing developer and local residents. At issue was a huge boulder long held to be a fairy dwelling, or thin place, a portal to the otherworld. The locals won the fight, and the new homes left the boulder undisturbed!

Modern Irish storytelling abounds with ordinary people who hear songs of merriment of the fairy folk and are taken into or slip into the twilight of the otherworld. In *The Celtic Twilight*, Yeats recalls such an encounter as he walked along the seashore, a notable thin place, with a young girl. She heard laughing, singing, and fairy music and saw the "good people" dancing at the mouth of a cave. Yeats and the young girl fell into a "kind of trance, in which what we call the unreal had begun to take upon itself a masterful reality" (Yeats 1990: 30). While walking along on an ordinary day, both had found a threshold to the otherworld.

Living with a finely tuned thin place/time attitude, the Celts had a particular fondness for places and conditions that were betwixt and between, such as twilight, dawn and dusk, mist, fogs and bogs. Crossroads, borderlands, and places or conditions marked by ambiguity, paradox, or fluidity, where the imaginal curtain was deemed particularly threadbare, were especially highly charged. This preference for threshold conscious-ness reveals itself in the love story of Diarmaid and Grainne. Diarmaid tells his bride-to-be that he will not accept her unless she comes to him under certain, nearly impossible, conditions. One version of his requirements was "I will not take you either by day or by night, clothed or unclothed, on foot or on horseback, neither within nor without." Grainne seeks help from a fairy woman who gives the young girl clothing made from mountain flowers. She appears to her potential groom, then, at dusk riding a goat. When she is in the doorway, she announces herself, "I am not without nor within; I am not on foot nor horseback; I am not clothed nor unclothed; it is neither day nor night." She had answered the riddle and won her husband (Cowan 1993: 52, 100).

Finally, the experiences surrounding death, wakes, and funerals were considered to be especially thin times. On the occasion of death, not only did the deceased move through the curtain, but the spirits of deceased ancestors were free to revisit their old homesteads. Furthermore, the living and the dead could communicate at burial places, and the deceased could intervene on behalf of the living, which later became part of the meaning of the communion of saints. In preparation for their final crossover at death, many Celts sought out thin places they designated as a *place of resurrection,* which they discerned to be a particular portal back through the curtain through which they had been birthed years before (Joyce 1998: 29).

Thus, the circle of life and death was seamless, which preserved the perspective of the world as a unified whole with no distinction between matter and spirit, or between physical and spiritual, except for what was seen and unseen. Margo Adler, in *Drawing Down the Moon*, summarizes the Celtic perspective: "The world is holy. Nature is holy. The body is holy. Sexuality is holy. The mind is holy. The imagination is holy. You are holy. Divinity is imminent in all nature. It is as much within you as without" (Adler 1979: ix).

THIN EXPERIENCES IN ANALYTICAL PSYCHOLOGY

In his writings, Carl Jung made frequent allusions to the archetypal image of the thin place/time. Describing himself, Jung said, "The difference between most people and myself is that for me the *dividing walls* are transparent. This is my peculiarity" (Jung 1965: 355 Emphasis Jung's). Referring to his near-fatal illness when he was in his late 60s, Jung claims in one of his letters that it provided him with the inestimable opportunity of a glimpse behind the veil. Again, referring to the protective walls the modern ego erects out of fear of mystical experiences, he notes that the walls prove to be very thin against the energies of the deep unconscious. (Jung 1942: 184).

Echoing the Celtic concern to honor the inhabitants of the other-world and the potential consequences of neglecting them, Jung reminds us that when the unconscious powers are no longer mediated because of neglect or repression, they form an ever-present and destructive shadow. Using a companion metaphor, he notes that when the powers are ne-glected, "the gates of the psychic underworld are thrown open," resulting in all forms of dis-ease, personal neurosis, or collective disorientation, dissociation, violence, and war (Jung 1961: 254).

Furthermore, Jung built his theoretical psychological house on the foundation of thin experiences called numinous, a descriptive word coined by Rudolph Otto in his book, *The Idea of the Holy*. From the Latin words *numen* (a god) and *neure* (to nod), a numinous experience is likened to "a nod from the gods," which is reminiscent of the encounters with the otherworld spoken of thus far. Otto's description of the *mysterium tremendum*, and the holy dread that often accompanies numinous experiences (Otto 1923: 12ff), provided Jung with a way to make meaning of his experiences of the otherworld, which, of course, he called the unconscious. In *Memories, Dreams, Reflections*, Jung describes in great detail his strange and uncanny experiences throughout his childhood, as well as during his descent into the unconscious following his break with Freud. His discovery of Otto's work was, therefore, especially significant.

The experience of the numinous, or numinosum, became the foundation on which Jung built his psychological house, including his consideration of the interplay between psychology and religion, and his concern for loss of soul and its recovery. With an experiential grasp for the numinous, one can appreciate Jung's unique contribution to depth psychology and to religious experience. Without that, the uniqueness of his work may very well be lost.

In his Terry Lectures at Yale University in 1937, Jung spoke at length about the meaning of the word "religion," describing it as "a careful and scrupulous observation of what Rudolph Otto aptly termed the *numinosum*"; and religion "designates the attitude peculiar to a consciousness which has been changed by experience of the *numinosum*" (Jung 1937: 7-8). Giving even a greater nod to the centrality of numinous experiences, in his 1945 letter to P. W. Martin, Jung wrote:

> You are quite right, the main interest of my work is not concerned with the treatment of neurosis but rather with the approach to the numinous. But the fact is that the approach to the numinous is the real therapy and inasmuch as you attain to the numinous experiences you are released from the curse of pathology (Jung 1945b: 376).

Underlying Jung's psychological reflections was what he referred to as a *religious outlook* or *attitude*. In his now-famous observation about patients in the second half of life, he identified the loss of a religious outlook as a key component of their illness and then declared that "none of them has really been healed who did not regain his religious outlook" (Jung 1934b: 334). Jung's own religious attitude grew out of his encounters with the numinous in the form of images, thoughts, and feelings that he felt were forced upon him by some mysterious other that his ego had not conjured, but to which his ego had to bow. The powerful experiences of the other came upon him unbidden, unexpected, unannounced, and often in unconventional ways. However they appeared, Jung knew that these encounters came from some source beyond or outside the ego, from some invisible dimension that had its own life, power, and autonomy. Recognizing, engaging, and honoring these encounters constituted Jung's religious attitude, an "attitude which meets a transcendent reality halfway" (Jung 1955d: 265). That same attitude could be called a thin place/time attitude.

Numerous other thin place/time analogs are apparent in analytical psychology. Most obvious is the imaginal space between conscious and unconscious, that delightful and dangerous threshold that is so heavily traveled day and night. In his essay on synchronicity, Jung describes the archetypal affective conditions that produce a partial *abaissement du niveau mental*, a lowering of the threshold of consciousness. This in turn "gives the unconscious a favourable opportunity to slip into the *space vacated*" (Jung 1952a: 436, Emphasis mine). In the language of this essay, the space vacated is the psychological thin place where the numinous contents from the unconscious make their appearance. The *abaissement* produces an opening in the curtain that normally separates conscious and unconscious contents. In this imaginal space "unexpected or otherwise inhibited unconscious contents break though and find expression in the affect" (Jung 1952a: 436-437). This dynamic is reminiscent of Samhain, when the doors between the visible and invisible were opened wide, and spirits and mortals intermingled.

One of the most powerful thin places in clinical practice is, of course, the interpersonal space between analyst and analysand, which, again, can be delightful and/or dangerous. Into this space pour the energies of the unconscious, personal and archetypal, in all their guises and valences, and each, like the inhabitants of the Celtic otherworld, require attention and honor lest they provide an unsavory trick. In the transference and counter-transference relationship, both analysand and analyst are affectively involved and, therefore, both are potentially transformed by the analytic thin place/time.

Jung addressed this powerful interpersonal, interactive field in *The Psychology of the Transference*. Furthermore, at times he imagined psyche to be in the intermediate zone between analyst and analysand. For example, in replying to a letter from a colleague who asked why dreams of a certain patient seemed to be referring to the analyst, Jung replied, "In the deepest sense we all dream not *out of ourselves* but out of what lies *between us and the other"* (Jung 1934c: 172, Emphasis Jung's).

Other depth psychologists and analysts have written extensively about the powerful encounters and psychological dynamics that occur at the imaginal threshold, including Donald Kalsched, James Hollis, Murray Stein, and D. W. Winnicott. The soulful writings of John O'Donohue and Philip Newell, both authorities on Celtic spirituality, also honor the transformative encounters at the threshold that connects the visible and invisible.

A final consideration of thin places/times in analytical psychology and its clinical practice concerns the necessity of honoring these sacred encounters. Drawing from the wisdom of our Irish and Celtic ancestors, it is imperative that the invisible powers receive some kind of ritual acknowledgement or offering. Otherwise, we open ourselves to the possibility of a psychological inflation or deflation. While there are countless ways to acknowledge the numinous encounters at thin places/times, they may be summarized with one metaphor, the metaphor of *bowing*. Furthermore, this ritual posture is implied in the meaning of the word "numinous," which we noted means "a nod from the gods." The appropriate human response seems to be a reciprocal nod or bow.

Bowing of this kind is first and foremost an inner nod, an attitude, whatever outward manifestation of word, gesture, or creative product may accompany the attitude. This is consistent with how Jung described the religious attitude, which he described as "the allegiance, surrender, or submission to a supraordinate factor or to a 'convincing' (overpowering) principle" (Jung 1959: 483-84). In terms of actual behavior, to bow may mean to submit, or to move away from, or to engage the energies of the unconscious. In all cases, it means to respect/reverence the numinosity of the archetype.

When one encounters the numinous, whether uplifting or disturbing, bowing is the best insulation from suffering a psychological inflation or deflation. The ego is inclined to think too highly of its value or too little. When encountering the benevolent gods who come through the curtain, the ego may be tempted to identify with them or possess their energy rather than relating to them. When this happens, one becomes subject to inflation. If the encounter carries the more destructive side of the archetypal energies, the ego may be more susceptible to a deflation or depression. In either instance, bowing brings one back to Earth, or to sea level, neither too high nor too low. Bowing promotes the dialectical relationship between conscious and unconscious so that the ego does not suffer too much *identification* with the Self or too much *alienation* from the Self (Kalsched 1996: 144).

THIN PLACES/TIMES IN THE EVERYDAY

In *Teaching a Stone to Talk*, Pulitzer Prize-winning author Annie Dillard tells about a neighbor, Larry, who spends time each day teaching a stone to talk. He keeps the stone, a palm-sized oval beach cobble, on a shelf, and several times a day he and the stone go through their rituals. Dillard reflects deeply on this peculiar scene, but not so much on what some might consider the strange behavior of her neighbor, Larry, because she respects the meaning of his efforts. She reflects more on the modern experience of the silence of the stone, and the silence of the mountains, trees, and streams — and on the silence of God. It was not always so, she observes. Once, for example, the nomadic Israelites requested through their leader, Moses, that God address them in their wilderness wandering. God did, "and all the people saw the thundering and the lightning, and the noise of the trumpet, and the mountain smoking." It scared them witless, Dillard writes, and they asked Moses to beg God, please, never to speak to them directly again, "lest we die" (Exodus 20:18-19). Reflecting on the Israelites' experiences, and on Larry's mute stone, Dillard writes, "God used to rage at the Israelites for frequenting sacred groves. I wish I could find one. … It is difficult to undo our damage, and to recall to our presence that which we have asked to leave. It is hard to desecrate a grove and change your mind. … We doused the burning bush and cannot rekindle it; we are lighting matches in vain under every green tree. … What have we been doing all these centuries but trying to call God back to the mountain or, failing that, raise a peep out of anything that isn't us?"

Annie Dillard concludes her mediation on our relationship with the natural world by saying: "We are here to witness. … Until Larry teaches his stone to talk, until God changes his mind, or until the pagan gods slip back to the hilltop groves, all we can do with the whole inhuman array is watch it. … That is why I take walks: to keep an eye on things" (Dillard 1982: 67-73).

Our task is to keep an eye on things, to watch carefully, to create more consciousness, and to respectfully bow. To do so cultivates an attitude toward our life and work that Jung named *religious*, and which our Irish ancestors called *thin*. It is an attitude that expects and honors the holy in the midst of the ordinary; an attitude that the invisible is as real as the visible, and often so much more powerful; an attitude that our highest human achievement is not reason, but reverence; an attitude that allows us to deepen the relationship between conscious and unconscious, seen and unseen.

The value of looking to our Irish ancestors or considering psychological theory will be measured by how it helps us to hone our attention to the "mystery in the mundane," to those experiences that remind us that the curtain is, indeed, very thin, so much so that in the poetic words of Annie Dillard, "in any instant the sacred may wipe you with its finger." Experiences like:

- ❖ Visiting that favorite place where one is refreshed, renewed, restored, where something from the invisible world is experienced with the senses and with the soul.
- ❖ Being surprised by natural beauty, perhaps a glorious sunrise or sunset, which prompts us to stop, and inwardly bow.
- ❖ Feeling a sudden rush of tears, origin or reason unknown, announcing the nearness of an invisible other.
- ❖ Hearing a piece of music or encountering an exquisite work of art and our whiskers begin to quiver, the hair rises on our neck, and goose bumps cover our skin, as if angels have brushed by ever so slightly.
- ❖ Becoming aware that two events, one inner and the other outer, having no discernible relationship, unexplainably converge.
- ❖ Being visited in a nighttime dream and we wake scared out of our wits knowing that something or someone came through the curtain while our conscious guard was down.
- ❖ Feeling the movement of the yet-to-be-born child, who still resides in the otherworld, who announces with a sharp kick to the underside

of the ribcage that he/she is ready to come through the curtain and take up residence here, and you, the mother, are suddenly aware that your body is the link between the seen and unseen.

❖ Experiencing an uninvited depression, as if Hades has reached through an invisible portal and dragged us down to the dark, possibly transforming, inner depths.

❖ Or, finally, sitting week after week, analyst and analysand, covering familiar psychological terrain, but today, suddenly, there is a palpable third presence in the space between. And we remember why we engage in this sacred work.

Finally, I will mention a very meaningful and practical psychological or spiritual discipline that has emerged with my engagement with this core image over the years. It is an exercise I have recommended to individuals and groups in lectures, workshops and on pilgrimages to sacred sites in Ireland and Scotland, as well as Peru and India. I like to imagine that we are given seven opportunities each day to bow to the numinosum. If we are paying attention, that is, if we are being religious, we will become aware that we are in the presence of some larger other, a greater power, or the mysteries that have a thousand names. The encounter may be one of supreme joy or pathos; it may be solitary or in interaction with a human other; it may be a sudden mood or insight; we may feel very empowered or impotent, but in every instance, we have a certain knowing that we have been visited, that the curtain is thin, and the commerce between the visible and invisible is taking place. Try it. Watch for these sacred encounters and, most importantly, bow, literally or figuratively.

ESSAY NUMBER NINE

DREAMS: STRANGERS IN THE NIGHT

The dream understands us more deeply than we understand ourselves.
(James Hillman)

Since these essays constitute my personal psychological and religious *testament*, I begin with some personal reflections about my experience with those mysterious strangers who visit us in the night. I began attending my dreams a half-lifetime ago when "midway in life's journey, I found myself in a dark wood, having lost my way." That archetypal wood described by Dante is well-populated, as many readers will likely attest. At age 38, I was right on time for my midlife crisis, which sent me in desperate search for help. Already having a reading acquaintance with Jungian psychology, I found a Jungian analyst to help me navigate outer personal and professional conflicts and the inevitable inner conflicts at their core. I began taking dreams seriously—recording them, working with their images, making associations and amplifications, and seeking to apply their nighttime insights into daytime relationships. Years later after training as a Jungian analyst, I began assisting others to attend their dreams, as well as offering lectures and workshops on the subject.

Now, a confession: I have never been very skilled at *interpreting* dreams, either my own or those of others. One might think that after so much personal experience and professional training, my assessment would be different. Although a Jungian analyst, I don't place much value on analyzing dreams in the sense of treating them like an object for dissection in the laboratory; more about that in a moment. Nor have I ever had a dream that told me specifically what I needed to do or relieved me from being the choice-maker in this complex existence called life. On the other hand, I have had plenty of dreams that provided rich information, a different perspective, or revealed heretofore hidden motives or impulses that enabled me to make a better, wiser choice than I might have otherwise made. And, in the quest for honesty, dreamwork has not made my life less complicated or happier in the popular sense of the word, though attending my dreams has made my life immensely more meaningful. Finally, every new dream, either my own or another's, still appears initially as strange and incomprehensible as the first dream considered many years ago. Previous strangers across the inner threshold do not make new ones less strange; each arrival requires a fresh effort at hospitality. Dreams have not magically changed my life, yet attending my dreams has been indispensable in changing attitudes toward myself and toward others near and far. Dreams have radically altered my views on religion/spirituality and those experiences we humans have designated divine. No other single practice has had such influence. The strangers who have visited in the night have dramatically altered my daytime world.

I had the strangest dream last night! My dreams are really weird! I had the worst nightmare last night; it still haunts me! Cuing off Shakespeare's famous line in *The Tempest*, "We are such stuff as dreams are made on," indeed *strange is the stuff our dreams are made of!* The familiar exclamations above echo those we have likely made or heard from others. Ironically, *strange* may be the most *familiar* adjective employed to describe our dreams.

The iconic pop star Carly Simon employs the famous Shakespearean words in her song about human love relationships; we can extend her beautiful words and apply them to our relationship with our dreams, with the deep unconscious, personified as the Dreamgiver or the archetypal Self:

> It's the stuff that dreams are made of
> It's the small and steady fire
> It's the stuff that dreams are made of
> It's your heart and soul's desire
> It's the stuff that dreams are made of
> It's the reason we are alive.

Attending our dreams, accessing their recent and ancient wisdom, listening to their images and symbols that seek both to *balance* and to *expand* our view of ourselves and our world can, indeed, be life-giving and life-changing. Dreams originate from and, in turn, nurture that "small and steady fire … our heart and soul's desire." Therefore, it's worth all our effort, time, and probable expense to befriend the *strangers in the night* who always have some gift to offer if/when we can be a receptive host. However, as noted below, that gift may not be wrapped prettily nor initially perceived by the ego as desirable.

We call it dream*work,* and much time, effort, and often money are required to attend our dreams in depth. However, dreams invite our *playful imagination*, as well, which helps modify some of the furrowed brow and grit of teeth when trying to determine why these particular strangers visited on this particular night. Playfully, I like to personify the Self as the Dreamgiver. Personification promotes the possibility of relationship; its danger, of course, is that it can also promote literalism. With that cautionary note, I also like to playfully imagine that the Self has a dream committee, and together they meet early in the evening to review the files of each person in order to craft a particular dream designed to address the current ego-attitude. As explored below, the dream will likely serve a *compensatory* function. On subsequent evenings the Dreamgiver and its committee review the files again and together assess the dreamer's receptivity and response to their previous offerings, and shape another relevant gift as the dreamer sleeps.

If on awakening from deep sleep, we immediately think or say to ourselves, "I know what that dreams means," we are likely deceiving ourselves because what we have seen projected on our inner screen is a piece of unconscious life heretofore unknown or only partially known. The dream is a stranger, or a host of strangers, who have crossed the inner threshold while our ego was on timeout. Those strangers may be imaged as person, animal, situation, object, mood, or drama. Emerging from their hidden domain, they are not immediately recognizable, though the ego may think otherwise, understandably so. When the ego encounters something strange, something other, it immediately tries to reduce it to something already known or to dismiss it as unimportant. We are inclined to say things like, "Oh, I know why I dreamed about those snakes. I watched that show about snakes on the Discovery Channel last night," or "I know why that creepy character showed up in my dreams; he looks like the villain in the book I am reading or like Jack Nicholson in *The Shining* which was on HBO." When the anxious ego tries to make the strange seem familiar too quickly, it dilutes the image. It is safe to assume that every dream is a new stranger seeking hospitality, and there is no way we can know immediately the gift it bears. We can also assume that the stranger wants to reveal itself and desires relationship with the conscious ego. It wants to be brought into what David Whyte calls "the house of belonging."

Speaking of dreams in such a personal way is necessary since every dream is a *subject* desiring relationship rather than an *object* for cold-eyed scrutiny or, as mentioned above, an object for critical analysis. Each dream and each part of the dream is a subject, a subject desiring response from human subjects. Of course, this may be the most difficult of Jung's psychological perspectives to entertain: The *reality of the psyche*, or the unconscious as a living entity rather than a collection of discarded repressions. Or, switching languages, the gods and goddesses that once were thought to inhabit the outer world actually reside in the unconscious from whence their images have been projected onto the outer world and into the heavens (See Essay "Projection and Revelation"). From that inner domain they continue to approach consciousness with the power and felt-presence that our ancestors attributed to outer deities and devils. Dreams are primary manifestations of their visits, crossing the threshold to our house when the ego has gone off duty.

Dreams, like people, don't like to be analyzed. Each time I say or write this, I have a momentary hesitation since I may be undermining my livelihood as a Jungian analyst! Dreams, like people, want to be met first with respect and slow inquiry that allows them to reveal themselves at their own pace. If that kind of climate can be provided, a relational connection can be made, and it is likely that dreams, like people, will reveal more and more of their real selves. When treated like an impersonal object under laboratory scrutiny, people and dreams will retreat. Used in a Jungian context, analysis refers to bringing the light of consciousness to unconscious contents, which frees those contents for integration into the personality. Loosening the tightly wound, restrictive complexes to free their energies is another way to imagine the purpose of Jungian analysis.

Dreams are first and foremost an invitation from the unconscious for relationship with consciousness. Using the familiar language of Jung's analytical psychology, every dream is an invitation for relationship from the Self to the ego. This may be the most important attitude to adopt for working with, playing with, our dreams; all else is commentary. Building the relationship between conscious and unconscious takes center stage in Jungian theory and practice. It was Jung's primary concern that the connection between the two had been ignored, or partially severed, and needed to be restored for individual and collective health. Individual and collective symptoms of dis-ease were evidence of that disconnection and those symptoms could be heard as invitations from the unconscious for a more conscious relationship. The purpose of dreamwork is to strengthen that connective tissue between the ego, the center of consciousness, and the Self, the metaphor for the centering, balancing, reconciling energy of the total psyche, conscious and unconscious. That umbilical-like connection is often referred to as the ego/Self axis. More poetically, dreams are the ways the Self woos or courts the ego. The Self wants, desires, and even needs relationship with consciousness, with the ego, which is consistent with Jung's far-reaching notion that just as the unconscious has an effect on consciousness, so consciousness has an effect on the unconscious. As explored in the Essay "Reimagining *God* and *Religion*," Jung extended this to the divine/human relationship, as well. Whether imaged as the divine or the psychological Self, the Sufi poet, Hafiz, captures the intensity of the pursuit: *I have fallen in love with someone / who is hiding inside you / we should talk about this problem / otherwise I will never leave you alone* (Ladinsky 2002: 174).

If the relational attitude is lost, dreamwork deteriorates into techniques and mechanics, and while the latter may give the ego a sense of mastery, it is unlikely much transformation of personality will happen. Imagining the dream from the viewpoint of the Self, that is from the unconscious, the dream is not a puzzle to solve or a cryptic message to take to an analyst or dream group to decipher. The dream is not a riddle that can be solved by a few simple techniques. Many books and tabloids at the grocery checkout suggest otherwise, of course. Again, from the viewpoint of the Self, the dream is very clear. It is neither confusing nor puzzling. It says what it means and means what it says. It is a very clear expression in its native language, the language of symbol and image, which means that dreams are rarely, if ever, literal. Listening to dreams and relating to dreams requires that we learn and relearn its language, the language of soul. And, to reiterate, it requires our playful imagination even as we call it dreamwork. Referring to a dream, Jung suggests: "Look at it from all sides, take it in your hand, carry it about with you. Let your imagination play round it, and talk about it with other people" (Jung 1933: 150). He goes on to recall how our tribal ancestors shared dreams regularly with their larger community.

Our dreams come from a different world than the one in which we feel most at home, and they are invitations into that other domain. The two domains are very near each other, however. For example, close your eyes and you are in the inner, invisible world; open your eyes and you are in the outer, visible world. The two domains are separated by a very thin membrane called the eyelid, even as the world of matter and spirit, physical and spiritual are separated by a very thin curtain (See Essay "Thin Places and Thin Times"). Dreams come from a darker world, a world of mists and shadow, where the borders and boundaries are blurred, where all things are intertwined and interconnected. The laws that govern the sunlight-conscious world and the moonlight-unconscious world are quite different. Navigating in one requires a sensitivity to the other for, again, they are two sides of the same psychic coin. Again, if we jerk the dream up into the daylight world too quickly by asking what does this mean or trying to figure it out with our good rational faculties, the dream will likely experience a case of the bends, so to speak, and retreat to its home in the unconscious, reform into another image, and return in a subsequent dream.

A very practical exercise to honor the above is to train ourselves on awakening to sit with our dream quietly, perhaps with eyes closed, allowing ourselves to sink back into the misty realm we had just left. Then when the core dream images have been recalled, record them as quickly as possible with details added later. Then, begin to ask two personal questions: First, "Who are you?" Second, "For what purpose have you visited me?" These questions are conversation starters and remind the ego to meet the dream images as subjects seeking relationship. Initially, avoid the *why* question, which often takes us into the left side, more logical side of the brain, which activates cause-and-effect thinking. There will be plenty of time for that later. "For what purpose" opens up a wider conversation, expands possibilities, and implies an expectant attitude. Choosing *for what purpose* rather than *why* is also a helpful practice for other aspects of our lives, as well. Most of the really important things that come our way are too complex (pun intended) to reduce to cause-and-effect. All things, however, are potentially meaningful. Seldom does *why me?* produce a satisfactory answer.

In the same way we cannot know immediately the identity and gift of the stranger at our dream door, nor can we know that for another dreamer. This is true for members of a dream group or a client or analysand. Their dream contents are just as much strangers as our own, though herein lies a great seduction because another person's dream will always look clearer and more revealing than our own. And the more experience one has in working with dreams, the greater the temptation to assume the role of expert interpreter. My experience both in leading and participating in dream groups, primarily through the solid training program provided by the Haden Institute (www.hadeninstitute.com), has taught me that when I am tempted to interpret another's dream is most often when I am unwilling to face the implications of the dream for myself. In other words, pretending to be the expert about another means I am unwilling to face myself. We would do well to remember Jung's rule: "So difficult is it to understand a dream that for a long time I have made it a rule, when someone tells me a dream and asks for my opinion, to say first of all to myself: 'I have no idea what this dreams means'" (Jung 1945c: 283). Ignorance lays the ground for listening to the dream before suggesting to the other person, or the dream itself, what it may mean. Even then, the dreamer is the final expert on his/her dream and must take responsibility for what it may reveal.

Everything that has been said about dreams as relationship thus far can be summed up in a phrase attributed to Jung: *It is not <u>understanding</u> our dreams which brings about transformation, but the intensity with which we engage the images.* We would do well to have this reminder posted over our doorway along with the familiar "Called or not called, the god will be present." With the rather recent publication of *The Red Book*, Jung reveals in word and image what intense engagement means, including some of the costs of working in the unconscious depths and the potential transformation such engagement can facilitate. And while our dream journals will likely not be as beautiful and grand as his, our labors will be equally honored by the unconscious, which desires, and needs, our consciousness, our light to illumine the darkness of mere being (Jung 1965: 326).

The intensity with which we engage the images means how seriously we engage the images as the subjects they are, how much we are willing to invest in the dream relationship, how willing we are to wrestle "Jacob-like" with the stranger who meets us in the night with the potential power to wound us while giving us a new name in the transformational encounter (See Genesis 32:24-31). In his powerful poem "The Man Watching," Rainer Maria Rilke alludes to Jacob's wrestling match with the Angel or, in our words, with the dream stranger in the night. Rilke observes with psychological and theological depth that: *What we choose to fight is so tiny! / What fights us is so great! … / When we win it's with small things / and the triumph itself makes us small.* Truer words about the egocentric ego have never been penned. Then, alluding to the aforementioned wrestling match, Rilke concludes his poem with unparalleled psychological and spiritual wisdom:

> Whoever was beaten by this Angel
> (who often simply declined the fight)
> went away proud and strengthened
> and great from that harsh hand,
> that kneaded him as if to change his shape.
> Winning does not tempt that man.
> This is how he grows: by being defeated, decisively,
> by constantly greater beings. (Bly 1981: 105-06)

Rilke's poem in its entirety is a whole course in analytical psychology long before there was such a discipline. In the parts quoted here, his words capture the intensity, and the ego-attitude, required for relating to our dreams. The relationship between ego and Self that dreamwork entails and enlarges is a mutual relationship with regard to *intimacy* but not with regard to *power*. The archetypal Self is conceived to be the center of the entire psyche, conscious and unconscious, while the ego is the center of consciousness. The Self has a larger view of things, so to speak. Metaphorically, the Self is older and wiser, being the central archetype of the collective unconscious. The Self is universal; the ego is particular to one personality. The imbalance in power and status between the Self and the ego is captured in the difference in Jungian and Freudian psychological frameworks. For Freud, *the ego creates the unconscious* through repression and suppression. For Jung *the unconscious creates the ego*; the ego emerges out of the preexisting archetypal, or collective, unconscious. The difference is most significant, particularly for those with religious or spiritual sensibilities. Honoring the difference in power is crucial when engaging our dreams.

Rilke imagines Jacob being *kneaded* by the larger, more powerful Angel; that is, being shaped or re-formed. Jung employs the same metaphor when he compares the dream to the work of an artist and says: "To grasp its meaning, we must allow it to shape us as it shaped him. Then we also understand the nature of the primordial experience" (Jung 1930: 105). Echoing Rilke's reference to *being defeated, decisively, by constantly greater beings,* Jung remarks that every experience of the Self is a defeat for the ego. Elsewhere, Jung writes:

> In each of us there is another whom we do not know. He speaks to us in dreams and tells us how differently he sees us from the ways we see ourselves (Jung 1933: 153). … The dream is a little hidden door in the innermost and most secret recesses of the soul, opening into that cosmic night which was psyche long before there was any ego-consciousness, and which will remain psyche no matter how far ego-consciousness extends (Jung 1933: 144-45).

Again, the success of dreamwork is not measured by what we have *comprehended* but by how willing we have been to be *apprehended* by that which is greater, by that which is *prior to and long after* our three score and ten; apprehended by the powers and felt presences that approach from within, those same powers once thought to reside in a metaphysical domain or in heaven or hell. From the perspective of analytical psychology, the deities and devils once thought to be removed and remote are now perceived to be very near. That perceived immanence may be one reason Western religions continue to prefer images of external, metaphysical deities and devils. There is perceived safety in distance. Religion requiring adherence to dogma and doctrine is preferable to religion requiring ongoing transformation.

In framing the relationship between unconscious and conscious, or Self and ego, as a mutual relationship in terms of intimacy but not in power, I am intentionally calling attention to the autonomy and power of the unconscious, which too often gets overlooked or ignored by our Western prejudice for reason and conscious thought. As indicated earlier, to grasp Jung's idea of the unconscious as a living, breathing subject remains very difficult for most people; it takes being grasped by the unconscious to be convinced. Again, I am aware of granting more attention to the role of the unconscious in this particular topic, which honors the folk proverb that we should take our dreams seriously because we are not intelligent enough to create them (Hollis 2009: 124). However, the ego must play its side of the relational equation for the relationship to deepen. The ego cannot grant the unconscious all its power by abandoning its vital role in the reciprocal relationship nor deferring to the unconscious the decisions only the ego can make. The theological parallel, and perversion, would be to "turn everything over to God" and abandon the responsibility for one's life. Jung says it this way:

> Experience has shown me that a slight knowledge of dream psychology is apt to lead to an overrating of the unconscious which impairs the power of conscious decision. *The unconscious functions satisfactorily when the conscious mind fulfils its task to the very limit.* A dream may perhaps supply what is then lacking, or it may help us forward where our best efforts have failed (Jung 1945c: 296, Emphasis mine).

In other essays, nature's gift of reflective consciousness to the human species has been explored and honored as our species' best hope for the future. It is that gift, ever evolving, that must be brought to bear in relating to our dreams, in relating to those strangers who cross the inner threshold every night and leave their calling card. It is that gift that must be brought to all daytime relationships, as well, to familiars and strangers alike. Furthermore, our hospitality to the two sets of strangers, invisible and visible, are intimately related. For example, what to do about the strangers who slip over the Southwest border of the United States each night seeking refuge cannot be solved by walls or laws. Only as a significant number of our citizens and political and religious leaders learn to be hospitable to their inner, dream strangers will a satisfactory solution be found. Inner and outer are of one piece, and each calls to the other. This may be the most important wisdom dreamwork can offer the collective.

Of the many lenses through which to peer as we consider our dreams and their apparent gift to ego-consciousness, the lens of *compensation* can be one of the most helpful as Jung thoroughly explores in "On the Nature of Dreams" in Volume 8 of his *Collected Works*. He notes elsewhere that most dreams are not in accord with the conscious ego-attitude; in his experience, so-called parallel dreams are rare (Jung 1944: 44). The ego finds this hard to swallow since all of us look for validation of what we already know about ourselves. Yet, James Hillman reminds us that the dream understands us more deeply than we understand ourselves. Rather than trying to understand the dream, it would be more helpful to implore the dream: "Please help me to understand me. Teach me about me from your larger perspective." Noting the autonomy of the unconscious with its apparent intent to provide balance to the conscious attitude for the overall process of individuation, compensation "means balancing and comparing different data or points of view so as to produce an adjustment or a rectification" (Jung 1945c: 287-88). If the conscious attitude to the life situation is in large degree one-sided, the dream takes the opposite view to promote balance; other dreams may offer a more moderate adjustment. Jung offers the larger, purposeful nature of dreams, personified here as the strangers in the night, when he describes the compensatory role of dreams in the process of individuation:

> This process is, in effect, the spontaneous realization of the whole person. The ego-conscious personality is only a part of the whole person, and its life does not yet represent his total life. ... But since everything living strives for wholeness, the inevitable one-sidedness of our conscious life is continually being corrected and compensated by the *universal human being in us,* whose goal is the ultimate integration of conscious and unconscious, or better, the assimilation of the ego to a wider personality (Jung 1945c: 292, Emphasis mine).

The compensatory function of dreams seeks to aid the ego-personality to live at sea level, neither too high with an *inflated* sense of itself, nor too low with a *deflated* sense of self. Many of us vacillate between the two extremes. The dream may "either repudiate the dreamer in a most painful way, or bolster him up morally. The first is likely to happen to people who have too good opinion of themselves; the second to those whose self-valuation is too low" (Jung 1945c: 296). However, the Dreamgiver, which has a trickster side, may raise the arrogant person to an improbable, absurd status in the dream to make a point, while the all-too-humble person is degraded even more. Working with dreams requires an honesty toward oneself above all else and a careful consideration of all that happens within and without that is descriptive of a religious attitude from an analytical psychological perspective.

In addition to the role compensation plays in dreams, it is operative in the overall individuation process because it is the fundamental dynamic between conscious and unconscious. Murray Stein provides a good summary of the compensatory function:

> The unconscious compensates ego-consciousness over the whole life span and in many ways—by slips of the tongue, forgetfulness, or miraculous revelations; by arranging accidents, disasters, love affairs, and windfalls; by generating inspirational ideas and hairbrained notions that lead to disaster. In the lifelong unfolding that Jung calls individuation, the driving force is the self, and the mechanism by which it emerges in the conscious life of the individual is compensation. This is equally true in the first half of life and in the second (Stein 1998b: 176-177).

Before leaving the dynamic of compensation, Jung notes that it is often objected that the compensation must be ineffective unless the dream is understood. He replies: "This is not so certain, however, for many things can be effective without being understood. But there is no doubt that we can enhance its effect considerably by understanding the dream, and this often is necessary because the voice of the unconscious so easily goes unheard" (Jung 1945c: 294). I include this important comment to balance any impression that understanding our dreams is unimportant. It is vital when placed in the larger context of relating to the dream as a subject.

While all dreams are important, some dreams are more significant than others and announce their significance with strong affect, either in the dream itself or upon waking. In discussing so-called *little* and *big* dreams, Jung notes that little dreams "are the nightly fragments of fantasy coming from the subjective and personal sphere, and their meaning is limited to the affairs of everyday." Significant dreams, on the other hand, "are often remembered for a lifetime, and not infrequently prove to be the richest jewel in the treasure-house of psychic experience" (Jung 1945c: 290). Murray Stein concurs: "Jung was wise to distinguish between little dreams and big dreams. A big dream is one that has potential to become a transformational image … one that channels psychic energy and will into specific attitudes, activities, and goals" (Stein: 1998a: 63).

The sheer volume of dreams can be overwhelming, as anyone who has kept a dream journal can attest; and attending dreams can be all-consuming in terms of time and energy. Over the years, I have adopted a pattern that satisfies my own psychology and honors all dreams while giving greater energy to some; it may be helpful to the reader in working out your own dream relationship. I try to *watch* all dreams and *work* some of them. Watching means to be aware that I am dreaming almost continually and that the unconscious is actively at work manifesting in this and other ways. Like any other intimate relationship, the other partner is there through thick and thin, even if words are not spoken; as partners, we carry out our roles and responsibilities. Watching dreams is synonymous with honoring them as a partner.

Working a dream means to grant more immediate time and attention to the partner by recording the dream, identifying its core images, listing personal associations, researching amplifications from mythic literature, and imagining ways to ritualize any insights that might emerge from the encounter. Again, both watching and working a dream communicate to the unconscious the ego's availability to be a conduit for its life; that is, to be an agent of incarnation. Even more astounding is the mystical sense that the dream is watching us and working us; that we are being watched and being worked by that which is ancient and wiser; again, by that which is *prior to and long after* our relatively brief sojourn.

Not all strangers who meet us in the night are easy to welcome and host. Some are downright scary, with apparent hurtful or evil intent. Others are so disgusting that we would rather not look at them, much less invite them in for tea. Though difficult to embrace, we need to assume that every dream stranger has a right and purpose to be in our dream drama or our dream house, though the dream ego and conscious ego may have serious questions about that. We may breathe a sigh of relief that the dream intruder scratching on our screen, or trying to break into our house, or the vicious animal did not get us this time; and we may conclude that our running away and our escape in dreamtime was a good thing. Likely, however, from the point of view of the Dreamgiver, i.e., the personified unconscious, the image and energy of the intruder or animal, or the natural catastrophe of flood or storm, are absolutely essential to balance the one-sided ego perspective. Running away in the dream may represent further ego resistance, or lack of readiness on the part of the ego to give this particular orphan a home. We are all afraid of our shadows, yet the psychological shadow cannot be so easily dismissed. According to Hafiz, it is always dangerous to assume that our inner idiots *Have all packed their bags / And skipped town or died* (Ladinsky 1996: 51).

James Hollis describes the shadow as whatever is within us we wish not to face. He writes:

> If we wish to learn more about the shadow, we must look to our history, but more to our fears. Where the fears are is the shadow's dwelling, and it renews its course in our life through sundry disguises such as projection onto others, repression of a vital part of ourselves, or as a narrowing of life—the wearing of shoes too small (Hollis 2003: 47).

Paying attention to the dream-ego, the "I" or observer in the dream, is critical in relating to the overall dream. Very often the dream-ego is simply trying to remain safe, or uninvolved, or overly involved and too ambitious for the dream situation. Again, each part of the dream, including the stance of the dream-ego, needs to be considered for its symbolic rather than literal meaning. Also, it is necessary to consider dreams in a series over several nights or weeks, even years, to discern the finely tuned gifts they offer. The analogy with human relationships is again apropos.

Rumi, with his Sufi imagination, likens our life to a guesthouse and provides wise counsel to being hospitable to the strangers in the night, whoever they are or however benign or malignant they first appear. He writes: *Every morning a new arrival / A joy, a depression…an unexpected visitor / Welcome and entertain them all.* Invite them in, Rumi implores, *Be grateful for whoever comes / because each has been sent / as a guide from beyond (*Barks 2006: 366). Our nightly visitors, as well as our daytime guests, are both *mirrors* and *icons* capable of expanding our self-awareness and self-knowledge (See Essay "The Universe as *Mirror* and *Icon*"). The mystic and the psychologically minded share the similar experience of being the surprised host in Rumi's guesthouse. At any moment strangers bearing gifts can cross the inner threshold, enter the living room prepared to reveal their identity and offering. A spirit of hospitality is synonymous with a religious attitude for the psychologically minded.

So, what if the visitors in the night are familiar friends, family, or acquaintances in our daytime world? Relating to dream familiars requires special attention and discernment. Having considered this question over the years and experimented with a variety of responses, some of which caused great difficulty, I have settled on the following approach, admittedly not the only one among Jungian-oriented dreamers: *Consider that each dream—and each part, person, figure in the dream—is first and foremost about the dreamer, and rarely about another person.* This perspective is called a *subjective interpretation* whereby the dream is depicting in symbol and image aspects of the dreamer him/herself. When known persons populate our dreams, we immediately imagine that the dream is about that person, or about our relationship with that person. This would be called an *objective interpretation.* However, most often the Dreamgiver is borrowing those outer others as props to symbolize something of the dreamer's invisible, unconscious drama. This is true whether the outer others carry negative or positive associations.

In my experience, the danger of an objective interpretation is twofold: It can be a convenient defense on the part of the dreamer to avoid looking at parts of his/her unconscious life, either negative or positive. Secondly, it is dangerous to tell another person what your dream said about him/her, as if you have been given some divine omnipotent or omniscient information about their life or journey.

A guide is this: *Assume that every dream in all its parts is about you, the dreamer; when you have integrated the wisdom from familiar dream figures into your conscious attitude/life, incorporate that wisdom in your outer relationship with that person(s).* That may never involve a direct comment to the person who had appeared in your dream. For example, suppose we dream about a person with whom we have a conscious conflict or a person we do not like because he/she is controlling, manipulative, and untrustworthy. The objective interpretation would be something like, *See, I knew he/she was like that because my dream confirms it*. However, since the dream will never tell us something we already know, we would be forced to a subjective interpretation to become aware of a part of ourselves that is also capable of being controlling, manipulative, and untrustworthy. If, then, we can own that part of our shadow and take that new knowledge of ourselves back into the outer relationship with the person, it would likely alter the relationship. Having withdrawn and owned the shadow projection, the conflicted relationship might lose some of its intensity. Or, simply, we may be less judgmental of the person who really is controlling, manipulative, and untrustworthy. In either case, the dream has done its work to bring the intended honesty and balance to us, the dreamer.

Support for such an approach in the dream literature is manifold. As noted earlier Jung writes, "One should never forget that one dreams in the first place, and almost to the exclusion of all else, of oneself." Even more direct, and with biblical humor, he continues: "The 'other' person we dream of is not our friend and neighbor, but the other in us, of whom we prefer to say: 'I thank thee, Lord, that I am not as this publican and sinner" (Jung 1933: 151-52). The exception to the subjective approach would be the so-called big dream that carries a potential collective meaning, a meaning beyond one's personal story that seems to address a cultural or even universal meaning. These often appear in times of cultural or religious transitions such as we are now experiencing when a deep unconscious eruption seems to be mobilizing. The individual psyche serves as a conduit for dream images relevant to the masses. These larger and wider meanings may go unnoticed until later reflection on some major historical event that reconfirms to the individual his/her interconnection to all and to all others.

The dynamics of psychological projection, explored throughout these essays, significantly informs the subjective approach outlined above. The reader is referred particularly to the Essays "Projection and Revelation" and "The Universe as *Mirror* and *Icon*" for a review of the profound dynamics of projection. While we may nod to Jung's wisdom that all the contents of our unconscious are constantly being projected onto our outer surroundings, we may not consider that every dream is also a projection, initiated by the unconscious, and flashed mysteriously upon our inner screen. The same dynamics that enable us to see unconscious aspects of ourselves that have been projected onto the outer world/people govern dream activity, as well. "We have to see parts of ourselves in projected form before we can identify them as our own" applies both to daytime and night-time. And, most mysterious of all, at least from this author's perspective, projection is the primary form of *revelation*, replacing the traditional religious view that revelations come from an external, metaphysical domain and deity. For the psychologically minded who may no longer be able to embrace the monotheistic myth's capacity to speak to the modern mind and ancient soul, this view is one alternative.

A further implication of the subjective approach deepens our inquiry. We face the most challenging questions related to granting hospitality to the strangers who meet us by night or day when we ask ourselves: *How am I treating the stranger in me? How do I show hospitality to that part of me I do not like, that part of me of which I am ashamed, that part of me I do not wish to be?* That is, how do I treat my shadow who lives within me day and night? It is well to do unto others as we would like to be treated. It is quite another issue to do unto ourselves as we wish others would treat us. Psychological growth happens when we accept that the real issues are internal. As that happens, the outer world becomes a friendlier place.

One final reflection: Dream images that are especially numinous, either to the dream-ego or the waking-ego, are likely similar archetypal images that have emerged in the dreams of our ancient ancestors and were deemed to be god-images. Some even made it into sacred texts and were canonized. The religious attitude suggested by Jung allows us to consider dreamwork a sacred work, at least for those of us who desire to so designate (See Essay "Reimagining *God* and *Religion*"). Whether the numinous images are seen by day or by night, the ego is invited/compelled to pay careful attention and to bring consciousness to the encounter. This is what is meant by a religious attitude from an analytical psychological perspective. Jungian analyst John Dourley validates such an attitude when he writes, "We now realize that conscious dialogue in whatever form, but especially in the form of the dream, is functionally a dialogue with divinity" (Dourley 1992: 28). Such an attitude fuels the process of individuation whereby one grows in intimate relationship with unconscious contents and in empathic, compassionate concern for all people and all creation. One's embrace of all strangers, inner and outer, is widened. This is the one best validation that dreamwork and the individuation process are authentic rather than an exercise in individualism or that popular pejorative dismissal, navel-gazing.

Dreams are the best antidote for prejudices toward others who are different—culturally, racially, religiously, sexually, and even morally—because the dreamer becomes aware through the strangers in the night that all aspects of humanity reside in his/her inner house. Those persons in the outer world who evoke our strongest fear or repulsion will show up on our inner doorstep every night until they are welcomed into the house. Thus, in-depth dreamwork will cure homophobia and xenophobia, two of the greatest human fears, as well as the pathology of literalism and fundamentalism. This is one reason that Jungian psychology and dreamwork remain threatening to the more conservative Christian and religious communities. Our dreams emerge from that deep dimension where all life is interconnected and interrelated. Dreamwork enables the dreamer to incarnate in the outer, visible world what exists in the inner, invisible world. This mystical perspective is the subject of the final Essay, "The Universe as *Mirror* and *Icon*."

The final word is one of caution: Dreamwork can be dangerous to one's religious health if that health depends on tightly held dogma or doctrine, or if one's god-image is too small to accommodate the largeness of life that continues to emerge from the unconscious depths. Working with dreams in depth and over a period of years will likely alter one's religious/spiritual outlook. Succinctly, dreamwork may well mess up your religious mind but has the capacity to expand your soul. If you are satisfied with religious faith handed to you from the past, you would do well to avoid working with your dreams. However, if you have a sense that you are a part of an ever-unfolding drama initiated and guided by a larger hand, then dreamwork will be a rich resource. For these reasons, depth dream-work takes some more deeply into the center of institutional religious life where they can be "salt and leaven" for the community. For others, their inner work takes them beyond religious structures. In the words of Jung, one must listen to one's inner snake, one's own wisdom. Some seem destined to be religious explorers who respond to T. S. Eliot's imperative in "Four Quartets:" *Old men ought to be explorers / Here or there does not matter / We must be still and still moving / Into another intensity / For a further union, a deeper communion.*

ESSAY NUMBER TEN

THE UNIVERSE AS *MIRROR* AND *ICON*
A Personal Paradigm

*If you bring forth what is within you, what you bring forth will save you.
If you do not bring forth what is within you, what you do not bring
forth will destroy you.* (Gospel of Thomas)

Over the last 40 years, my immersion in analytical or Jungian psychology, as well as various mystical traditions, has resulted in the following paradigm or guiding statement about the nature of reality and our potential role and participation in its unfolding. Implicit in the summary are numerous theological, philosophical, biological, and psychological perspectives, without being limited to any particular religious tradition or school. Rather than a statement to be believed, it is offered as a possible spiritual discipline to practice; that is, to keep in the forefront of our awareness and to live *as if* it could be true; and, more importantly, to prompt readers to create their personal guiding statement from their own experience.

As stated in the "Introduction," this book represents, among other things, my personal testament rather than an exposition of the Old Testament or the New Testament, which have been treasured by the monotheistic religions. Throughout these essays, priority has been given to religious *experience*, defined psychologically, rather than to religious dogma or doctrine. In many ways, the following personal paradigm contains a summary of the psychological dynamics presented in the previous essays, dynamics that are also common to various mystical traditions. When used as a spiritual discipline, the paradigm could be seen as *grounded mysticism,* which, in my own mind, also characterizes analytical psychology when considered in its depth and breadth and practice. *Grounded mysticism* celebrates the interpenetration and interconnection of all things, and all reality, visible and invisible, conscious and unconscious. When deities and devils are no longer perceived to occupy an external, remote heaven or hell, and are seen (rightly, I propose) as archetypal powers and presences which manifest through the human psyche, our species takes on a new value, as well as a new responsibility to each other and to our global nest. Jung devoted his writing to the mysteries within the human psyche, and between psyches, and between humans and what he called the soul of the earth. Concerning his mystical connection to nature he wrote: "At times I feel as if I am spread out over the landscape and inside things, and am myself living in every tree, in the splashing of the waves, in the clouds and the animals that come and go, in the procession of the seasons. There is nothing…with which I am not linked (Jung 1965:225). The paradigm presented here may promote such a mystical awareness of all aspects of life; that is, *meaning* may become a rather constant companion.

Finally, I am aware that what is being offered in this personal paradigm is impossible to practice continually, nor is that the goal. Rather, it can be viewed as a touchstone to return to time and again to clarify the wonderfully awful mystery of human consciousness, which is both our gift and burden as a species. We did not choose this gift but we are responsible for using it wisely. To do so may well be our most important sacred duty. For the psychologically minded the paradigm constitutes a "religious attitude" toward life, though one does not need to be a self-described religious person to experiment with it. Simply weigh it on the scales of your own experience, on the scales of your own knowing, on the scales of your own authority.

The paradigm, **THE UNIVERSE AS *MIRROR* AND *ICON*** follows:

THE UNIVERSE AS <u>MIRROR</u> *AND* <u>ICON</u>

(A Personal Paradigm)

**The essence (soul) of everything and everyone
In the outer, visible world
Reflects (Mirror) and Reveals (Icon)
Something of our inner, invisible essence (soul)
For which we are ultimately responsible
To recognize,
To own,
And, where necessary, To transform,
To offer back to the outer world
As conscious gift
For the continuing creation.**

Everyone lives by a myth by which to navigate the contours, crevices, and heights that make up human existence. Actually, most live by several myths that may or may not be in agreement; generally speaking, there are at least three. There is a collective myth, which grants a sense of belonging, be it religious, political, cultural, racial, or ethnic. It consists of collective histories, memories, norms, and values that identify us with our group, our human tribe, though that identity may remain largely un-examined, without reflection, i.e., unconscious. There is an ideal myth consisting of values and dreams to which we aspire and would like to incarnate, often given voice by an idealized other(s); that is, by a religious, political, or cultural hero past or present. Then there is the myth by which we actually live, which guides our actual choices and expenditures of time, energy, and money. If our myths diverge or disagree significantly with each other, and if they remain largely unconscious, fragmentation accompanied by various degrees of anxiety will likely be our experience. Finally, our myths—our maps of reality—are living entities. They are either changing or transforming as we move freely along life's path, or else they are becoming more rigid and confining. The choice is always ours. In the words of William Blake, if we do not create our own myth, we will be enslaved to someone else's (Hollis 2009: 127).

While not a fully formed myth, the personal paradigm presented here provides a touchstone for the present and a cornerstone for future development. It is an ideal that begs to be fleshed out, resourced with time, energy, and money, i.e., incarnated. When the foundational monotheistic myth that was supporting Christianity collapsed for me, and I fell off the back porch of the Church, all my mythic models were called into question. "The Universe as *Mirror* and *Icon*" is the culmination of my wilderness wandering between the religious home that once nurtured and sustained and the mythical home that draws me, and us, forward. And though it provides a guide for the present it, too, like all living entities, will necessarily need revisions or perhaps a future replacement.

The centerpiece of this personal paradigm recognizes that our species, along with a conservatively estimated 16 million extant species (Nye 2014: 13), are the *present tense* of a very old process that began approximately 13.8 billion years ago. That beginning is described by science as the Big Bang and by various religions as being the work of a Creator God. Both Big Bang and Creator God are metaphors for a mystery that likely will remain. If the mystery of what preceded the beginning of the universe is ever revealed, it will be by the discoveries of science rather than through more theological speculation or interpretations of ancient texts deemed sacred. But I digress. Moving along, our planetary home occupies some 4.5 billion years of that history with the first signs of biological life appearing about a billion years later. Early versions of our species appeared roughly two million years ago (Nye 2014: 35-37), though our capacity for what we now call self-reflection did not come online until the most recent 250,000 years. We are the new kids on the evolutionary block.

In his book, *Undeniable: Evolution and the Science of Creation*, Bill Nye offers an imaginary time line that captures the long evolutionary unfolding that has carried us to the present day. He imagines walking across our vast country from San Diego on the West Coast to Boston on the East, obviously a very long hike. Every step would represent about 1,000 years of cosmic time. He chronicles the appearance of familiar parts of creation along the way—our Milky Way galaxy, planet Earth, the first signs of biological life, the ancient dinosaurs, etc. Early versions of our species would not appear until about two kilometers from the Atlantic

Ocean, representing about two million years ago. He ends his imaginary sightseeing trek with the startling conclusion: "All that we know of history, all the people and their affairs, everything you've come to know, takes place in less than your last stride" (Nye 2014: 37).

Another example, using vast units of cosmic time, illustrates that our uniqueness as a species—self-reflection—is a rather new acquisition. Imagine that we create a Cosmic Calendar using our familiar 12-month one and using numbers that are, necessarily, approximate. January 1 would represent the metaphorical Big Bang, and each subsequent day would cover approximately 35 million to 40 million years. Over the first eight months, January through August, we would witness a fiery show of the birth and death and rebirth of stars and galaxies and cosmic contents yet to be observed and named. By September of this imaginary calendar, we would finally get a glimpse of our Milky Way galaxy and our Earth home, though yet to be occupied by biological life. Remember, we are patiently waiting for the appearance of the human capacity for self-reflection, that amazing gift of nature to our species that allows reflection on nature and reflection on our human nature. We would have to wait until December 31, the last day of the year, and it would be 11:53 p.m., seven minutes before midnight before we humans would appear with the capacity for self-reflection, which is a prerequisite for what we now call reflective consciousness.

In those last (or first) seven minutes, we would have begun to create language and culture as we moved through the familiar ages known as Stone, Bronze, etc. With the birth of imagination, we would have begun to ask the now age-old questions about our origins, purpose, and destiny. Only in the last few minutes would we have created any images of gods and stories about experiences we now call numinous. Major religions would appear in the last minute before midnight: Hinduism and Buddhism in the final five to seven seconds, and the birth of Christianity in the final four seconds. Only in the last one second of this cosmic timetable would we discover that the Earth was not the center of the universe but revolved around the sun in our own galaxy, which is but one of billions of galaxies with even more billions of stars/suns that are our cosmic neighbors.

And, only in the final one-fourth of the last second would we discover something called the unconscious, thanks largely to Freud and Jung. So, here we are, full of awe and wonder.

Against this gargantuan history, my 12-sentence paradigm attempts to describe my/our potential place and role in it. Each time I rehearse this cosmic, biological, sociological, and psychological sweep, I am left with a complex (pun intended) of emotions: On the one hand, how late our arrival on the scene and how relatively insignificant our species against the cosmic unfolding; on the other hand, how unique and significant has been our relatively brief appearance. A further paradox prevails: Our species, the new kid on the evolutionary block, has achieved the reputation as the most creative, and the most destructive, species ever to inhabit the planetary nest we call home. Therefore, the pursuit of knowledge about ourselves—self-knowledge, psychological knowledge—must be paramount for individuals and collectives. We must learn more and more quickly concerning what makes us tick and what makes us sick, and how to foster our interdependent relationship with nature and with each other. Imagining the universe as mirror and icon can be a lens to promote the self-knowledge so essential both to our survival as a species and our capacity to be more than consumers and creators of larger carbon footprints.

The two previous examples of the long evolutionary span of space and time preceding our arrival illustrate a primary premise of this paradigm: The recognition that the human species—we—are an intimate and integral part of nature herself. We are neither separate from, superior to, nor apart from nature. Nor are we an afterthought or add-on. We are nature *naturing*. Our species, along with an estimated 16 million extant species, are the present tense of a very long evolutionary past. In the poetic words of physicist Brian Swimme, "We are the latest, the most recent, the youngest of this stupendously creative Earth" (Swimme 1984: 31). We are a link in a very long and complex chain of biological life and, as such, we share properties with all other species and objects. Our bodies are made of the same atoms and molecules as stones, water, and air. Even more astounding, Carl Sagan's observation, now repeated by many, reminds us that the "iron in our blood, the calcium in our bones, the carbon in our brains ... were manufactured in red giant stars thousands of light-years away in space and billions of years ago in time. We are, as I like to say, starstuff" (Sagan 1996: 14, footnote). We are similar to all the other 16 million extant species in essence and different only in form and function. John Philip Newell concludes: "We carry the essence of all things within us. And all things carry the essence of our being within them" (Newell 2011: xv).

Though sharing some of the same essence, each of nature's species performs a theoretically unique and necessary function in nature's continuing unfolding (though I am not so sure about crabgrass, squirrels, and voles!). Nature has gifted our species with the capacity for self-reflection, which is a prerequisite for what we now call reflective consciousness, though having the word does not mean we know much about its mysterious ways, as discussed later. For the purposes of our paradigm, self-reflection can be described as the capacity to step outside or beside ourselves to reflect on our nature and to reflect on the nature of nature herself.

Nature's gift of self-reflection grants our species a unique seat or standing place in creation—inside, front row and outside as witness/observer. Exercising our imagination, the human psyche/soul stands on the threshold between those domains we call outer and inner, visible and invisible, or conscious and unconscious. Psyche mediates the flow of energy and psychic contents, back and forth, day and night, constantly. With a variety of psychological functions, articulated by Jung, we are able to *see* both ways, Janus-like, which permits memory and hope. We can remember and resurrect the past and imagine the future. We can see the outside, visible world, and consciousness allows us glimpses into the interior, invisible world. As far as we know, no other species is gifted and burdened with such.

Poets, who are some of our best and most efficient theologians and psychologists, are familiar with the threshold connecting the visible and invisible. From there, they employ round words capable of holding multiple meanings. They and their poems are mirrors and icons. They reflect something of our forgotten essence and reveal depths of the archetypal unconscious heretofore unknown. Mirrors show us something more or less familiar though forgotten or hidden for a time; icons invite a closer, deeper, more meditative look, which opens up glimpses behind the veil separating the visible and invisible. The psychologically minded will recognize that mirrors reflect something of the personal unconscious, contents once conscious but temporarily lost, while icons reveal the contents of the deeper, ever-fecund collective or archetypal unconscious. Both mirrors and icons are agents of revelation.

The Sufi mystic Rumi, perhaps the most popular poet in today's world thanks primarily to the dedicated translation work of Coleman Barks, enjoins us to *Work in the invisible world / At least as hard as you do in the visible*. His simple invitation likely catches us off guard, addicted as we are to the externals of life, especially as Rumi notes, *caught up with fear and hope about your livelihood.* Elsewhere, with psychological urgency before there was such a discipline, Rumi urges us to consciousness, noting: *The breeze at dawn has secrets to tell you / Don't go back to sleep* (Barks 2006: 268). Staying awake is a prerequisite for both psychological and spiritual work. A Brahmin priest, noticing the Buddha, inquired whether he was a god, a spirit, or an angel. The Buddha replied, "None of these; I am awake."

Self-reflection makes possible a wakeful attitude and grants us a unique perspective on all of life. We are able to approach everything and everyone with what could be called a mystical greeting: "While I am not you, neither am I other than you." To the tree, or bird, or elephant: "While I am not you, neither am I other than you." To the person we love or hate: "While I am not you, neither am I other than you." To those of another race, sexual orientation, religious tribe, or political party: "While I am not you, neither am I other than you." I first heard this core idea from James Finley, a Thomas Merton scholar, who was speaking on mysticism a few years ago. The poet Mary Oliver captures this same mystical perspective with her lovely line, *I look upon everything as a brotherhood and sisterhood* (Oliver 1992: 10-11). Both perspectives from Finley and Oliver have proven to be a blessing and a curse: A blessing to approach all lovely things and lovely people with such an intimate awareness; a curse to bring the same awareness to those persons and things I would rather not embrace! The gift and burden of consciousness!

John Philip Newell writes profoundly and poetically about the mysteries of our interrelatedness with the cosmos and with each other. From his Celtic background and heart, he says:

> The deeper we move in the mystery of our soul, the closer we come to hearing the beat of the cosmos; and the more we expand our awareness into the vastness of the universe, the closer we come to knowing the unbounded Presence at the heart of our being and every being. As new science is teaching us, the microcosm and the macrocosm are one. Our lives are part of the cosmos, and the cosmos is part of us (Newell 2011: xi-xii).

Not only are we privileged to see both ways at the psychological threshold, but another mystical possibility awaits our imagination: We are seen by a greater other; we are *beheld* by that which we *behold,* which grants the experience of being known and embraced. In short, being seen by the other confers blessing. Indian philosophy and religion, particularly Hinduism, describe this mystical encounter as *Darshan* or *Darshana* (Sanskrit: "Viewing"). It refers to the beholding of an image of a deity, a revered holy person, or sacred object, all of which inundate Indian life. Rather than being objects of worship as commonly thought, the images, persons, or objects serve as *icons* that, when viewed meditatively, reveal a divine background. The Darshan experience is considered to be reciprocal—that which is viewed bestows blessing on the viewer.

This mystical encounter plays out rather continuously in the Hindu consciousness and spills over to ordinary human relationships as well. A personal experience of this mystery while on pilgrimage to India will be with me forever. A small group of us was attending the Kumbh Mela, the Indian pilgrimage festival that attracts literally millions of pilgrims over a 45-day period and includes ritual baths in the sacred Ganges. Surrounded by thousands of pilgrims watching a colorful parade displaying Indian culture, images of Indian gods and goddesses, and revered holy men, many of whom had traveled from their Himalayan retreats, I suddenly felt a tug on the back of my shirt. Turning, I saw standing there a smiling Indian family--mother/father, two beautiful children, and an older man, likely a grandfather. Having encountered the ever-present beggars throughout the morning, my first thought was, "Here are more of the same." We nodded, spoke briefly. The parents motioned to their children, obviously proud of them and proud to be at this auspicious event as a family. All the while, I was in my Western defensive and dismissive posture and turned back to view the parade, hoping they would leave. Nevertheless, they remained. I could feel their presence. Out of the corner of my eye I could see their lovely, smiling countenance. After what seemed like a long time, they slowly retreated. I stole glances of their departure and still remember the smiling faces of the two children who kept turning to catch a view of this one pale white man in a sea of beautiful brown.

Only after they were gone, and I had recovered some of my senses, did it occur to me what the encounter likely meant for them. They simply wanted to have a human connection and to confer blessing onto this stranger and to receive the same, especially for their children. My paranoia blinded me from seeing them to complete the Darshan exchange. My failure haunted me for days and still does. Ironically, I had recently spoken about the power we have to confer blessing onto others by simply seeing them and honoring our interconnection. Sometimes it is a long way from the head to the heart, and even further to the hands where we actually touch.

Taking a closer look at our paradigm, we remember the profound, revelatory dynamics of psychological projection (See Essay "Projection and Revelation"). The outer, visible world serves as a blank screen onto which are projected (at the initiative of the unconscious) contents of the unconscious so that they can be recognized, withdrawn, owned, and integrated by the ego personality. While the projective processes are happening naturally and rather constantly in all encounters and relationships with people and objects, those that evoke intense affect invite, and demand, immediate attention and response from consciousness. The affective contents reveal some vital matter that needs to be brought into consciousness, *Something of our inner, invisible essence or soul / For which we are ultimately responsible / To recognize / To own.* Furthermore, as one of my colleagues, Paula Reeves, shared many years ago, it is a psychological law that when we ignore or repress what really matters, especially over time, it predictably becomes *what's the matter with us!* This wisdom reflects that found in the apocryphal Gospel of Thomas, which preceded depth psychology by centuries but which conveys its heart: *If you bring forth what is within you, what you bring forth will save you. If you do not bring forth what is within you, what you do not bring forth will destroy you!*

Jung's psychology provides an empirical basis and a scientific language for what our ancestors knew intuitively. Drawing on the work of Mircea Eliade, Karen Armstrong writes, "All ancient religion was based on what has been called the perennial philosophy, because it was present in some form in so many premodern cultures. It sees every single person, object, or experience as a replica of a reality in a sacred world that is more effective and enduring than our own" (Armstrong 2009: 6-7). Analytical psychology and the paradigm presented here offer ways to see old realities in a new light.

From our threshold standing place, we can imagine: *The essence or soul of everything and everyone / In the outer, visible world / Reflects (Mirror) and Reveals (Icon) / Something of our inner, invisible essence or soul.* Some of the unconscious contents seen in projected form (especially those that have been attached to an ideal), which *mirror* one's own hidden creative qualities or potential, can be integrated directly into the conscious personality, though not always quickly or easily. Those qualities may be considered the light side of the unconscious and of life itself, contents sometimes referred to as the *bright shadow*. Even if the unconscious contents are theoretically desirable, they may still be a threat to one's self-image. Jung reminds us that the emergence of unconscious contents, whatever the valence, is very often preceded by a darkening. This may take the form of apprehension, unease, or a mild depression even though no external cause is apparent. Creative endeavors are very often preceded by the kind of depression that pushes one deeper and permits access to unconscious resources otherwise unavailable. Some artists, poets, and writers have grown to expect such experiences; it allows them to wait with pregnant patience.

The darker, destructive aspects of one's unconscious are also seen in projected form. The dark shadow often appears on those persons we deem enemies: Those we fear, hate, despise, or those whose religious or political worldview we find threatening to our own. Those contents also mirror one's own interior strangers, one's inner enemies long denied or ignored. Those unconscious contents also beg to be brought into the personality for they, too, have a place in the psychological house. They, too, *Reflect and Reveal / Something of our inner, invisible essence or soul / For which we are ultimately responsible / To recognize / To own / And, where necessary, To transform / To offer back to the outer world / As conscious gift / For the continuing creation.* The withdrawal and ownership of undesirable psychic contents have a cleansing and transformative effect. Underneath the content, regardless of how undesirable or despicable, resides hidden gold, some quality or energy the personality needs for balance and wholeness when manifested in a conscious, responsible fashion. What appeared as an outer enemy to reject, or even to destroy, can become a gift to the wholeness of the individual and, profoundly, to the world; a piece of shadow will have been reprieved from doing outer damage to another or from poisoning the relational atmosphere. Succinctly, world peace begins in the inner world of individuals.

Referred to in an earlier essay, Rumi, with his Sufi imagination, likens our life to a guesthouse where *Every morning a new arrival / a joy, a depression ... an unexpected visitor / Welcome and entertain them all.* Invite them in, Rumi implores, *Be grateful for whoever comes / because each has been sent / as a guide from beyond* (Barks 2006: 366). Our everyday guests, our everyday encounters, human and psychic, are mirrors and icons capable of expanding our self-awareness and self-knowledge. The mystic and the psychologically minded share the similar experience of being the surprised host in Rumi's guesthouse. At any moment, strangers bearing gifts can cross the inner threshold, enter the living room prepared to reveal their identity and offering. A spirit of hospitality is synonymous with a "religious attitude" for the psychologically minded.

Gandhi has been credited with the phrase, "Be the change you want to see in the world." That popular challenge is a *paraphrase* of something he actually said that is even more relevant to our topic:

> We but mirror the world. All the tendencies present in the outer world are to be found in the world of our body. If we could change ourselves, the tendencies in the world also change. As a man changes his own nature, so does the attitude of the world change towards him. This is the divine mystery supreme. A wonderful thing it is and the source of our happiness. We need not wait to see what others do (Morton 2011).

From our imaginary perch at the intersection of the visible and invisible, looking outward to behold the essence or soul of person, living thing, or object, we see mirrored some aspect of our own being, as well, something that has been temporarily lost to our view now residing in what analytical psychology calls the personal unconscious. That metaphorical psychic storage place houses those contents that once appeared to conscious view but were either ignored, suppressed, or repressed. Those contents retreat, as it were, but never evaporate; they remobilize for another incursion into consciousness.

In addition to mirroring aspects of the personal unconscious, contents once known to consciousness, the soulful outer contents reveal something of the deeper contents of the collective or archetypal un-conscious, sometimes referred to as the objective psyche. Other essays in this book have referenced the objective psyche as a *meta-personal* dimension as contrasted with *metaphysical* dimension, which is a staple of monotheistic religions. Meta-personal means that the contents therein are beyond the command, creation, and control of the ego, yet not beyond the physical world; this dimension is juxtaposed to metaphysical dualism inherent in theism and monotheism. This metaphorical domain of the objective psyche (the collective or archetypal unconscious) contains patterns of potentials that are also being projected onto the outer screen for the purpose of being recognized, owned, and integrated into the conscious personality. The deeper, archetypal contents of the objective psyche have the character of *icons,* which, when beheld with a meditative or contemplative eye, reveal soulful contents pregnant with meaning. The imaginative mirror and icon serve as instruments of revelation to identify and welcome home contents rightfully belonging to the personality.

A poem by Derek Walcott, "Love after Love," personalizes such a homecoming:

> The time will come
> when, with elation,
> you will greet yourself arriving
> at your own door, in your own mirror,
> and each will smile at the other's welcome,
>
> and say, sit here. Eat.
> You will love again the stranger who was your self.
> Give wine. Give bread. Give back your heart
> to itself, to the stranger who has loved you
>
> all your life, whom you ignored
> for another, who knows you by heart.
> Take down the love letters from the bookshelf,
>
> the photographs, the desperate notes,
> peel your own image from the mirror,
> Sit. Feast on your life (Walcott 1986: 328).

The personal meanings gleaned from imagining "The Universe as *Mirror* and *Icon"* can be very satisfying, even life-saving for those who can no longer embrace traditional religion. Beyond the personal meanings, however, we can imagine a broader function and role for our species, which has been gifted by nature with self-reflection. Engaging our mystical imagination in our myth-making task, nature has created our reflective species for the purpose of reflecting on herself, of nature becoming conscious of herself; or to give herself a voice in her relationship with her most creative, and most destructive, species. Being an integral aspect of nature yet able to "stand outside or beside her," our species has been commissioned by nature, to be her human voice, so to speak, and her partner in the continuing creation. With our unique relationship with nature we can see her, converse with her, reflect on her, show compassion for her and, yes, abuse her. Perhaps the contemporary concerns for the environment, and the symptoms of environmental suffering, are the voice of nature desperately asking for a more conscious and more compassionate relationship with her most conflicted species.

Self-reflection allows for sufficient separateness from Mother Nature to have an actual relationship with her. Paradoxically, a sufficient degree of separateness is required for healthy relationships. Without separateness, one remains identified with, contained in, or codependent with the other; whether that other is person, religious institution, political party, nation or, in this case, with the natural mother who birthed our species. The relational goal is interdependence growing out of interconnection rather than the extremes of dependence or alienation. Unfortunately, the latter, alienation, too often describes our modern predicament with nature as well as with each other.

John Claypool, a bright star in the Episcopal family, once offered a helpful image in this regard. His topic was parenting, and he suggested that a worthy goal might be to create a *hyphenated relationship* with one's children. Since we are all children who have parents if we are not parents ourselves, his counsel was applicable to all. A hyphen, he noted, is a special kind of punctuation: It denotes both connection and separation. A hyphenated relationship between parent and child, then, denotes the same. He also acknowledged what we all likely know: Creating such a relationship requires much psychological work, given that we often end up with too much dependence or too much alienation. Sadly, the coinage of "hover-mother" and "absent-father" validates the extremes. It strikes me that the mystical perspective mentioned earlier could be a helpful lens for both parent and child: "While I am not you, neither am I other than you!" That internalized recognition could help dissolve many parental complexes for people of all ages!

These are some of the mythic and mystical implications of the briefer paradigm suggested in these pages. They are suggestive of a *grounded mysticism*. The mystic is one for whom the invisible domain tumbles into the visible quite apart from one's willful intent and apart from an external mediator. The psyche *is* the mediator between the two, between the visible and invisible, between matter and spirit, and between conscious and unconscious. Understood in this way, analytical psychology, which honors the spontaneous, unmediated experience of the archetypal unconscious, has a mystical character. Unlike the pejorative use of the term "mystic," hurled at Jung by his critics for supposedly being wooly-minded and other-worldly, *grounded mysticism* is rooted in the relational care of Earth and her species.

The remarkable poet Rainer Maria Rilke imagines the fruits of living with such a grounded, interconnected, interdependent attitude:

> All will come again into its strength:
> the fields undivided, the waters undammed,
> the trees towering and the walls built low.
> And in the valleys, people as strong
> and varied as the land.
>
> And no churches where God
> is imprisoned and lamented
> like a trapped and wounded animal.
> The houses welcoming all who knock
> and a sense of boundless offering
> in all relations, and in you and me.
>
> No yearning for an afterlife, no looking beyond,
> no belittling death,
> but only longing for what belongs to us
> and serving earth, lest we remain unused
> (Barrows and Macy 1996: 121).

As hinted above, Jung resisted being regarded as a mystic since his critics invariably used the word in a pejorative, dismissive sense as being incompatible with science and invalidating scientific findings. Jung preferred to be recognized as an empiricist, a scientist whose research is based on careful observation of the facts. He thought of himself as a natural scientist. Nevertheless, writes Aniela Jaffe, a close associate of Jung and his autobiographical collaborator, "the clear analogies that exist between mysticism and Jungian psychology cannot be overlooked, and this fact in no way denies its scientific basis" (Jaffe 1989: 1). Speaking to one of those analogies, Jung writes, "Mystics are people who have a particularly vivid experience of the processes of the collective unconscious.

Mystical experience is experience of archetypes" (Jung 1935: 98). Cuing off that description, Gary Lachman in his book *Jung the Mystic*, concludes, "And as Jung himself had *a particularly vivid experience of the processes of the collective unconscious*, he would, by his own definition, be a mystic" (Lachman 2010: 2-3). Looking beyond labels, both Jungian psychology and mysticism deal with the experience of the numinous, those powerful godlike visitations experienced at the so-called threshold where the human psyche stands sentinel with both *mirror* and *icon* in hand.

The mystical imagination knows that the two domains—visible and invisible, inner and outer, conscious and unconscious—are continually tumbling into each other with or without our willing. The Celtic imagination, mystical at its core, was especially attuned to those times and places where the invisible veil between the visible and invisible was worn *thin* and the commerce between the two domains was especially active (See Essay "Thin Times and Thin Places"). There were times when the veil was lifted totally, like on the Celtic New Year, Samhain, when "much trafficking takes place between spirits and mortals ... when the worlds tumble into each other" and more goes on than meets the eye (Cowan 1993: 55).

The Celts, whose roots were believed to be in the East, saw the world in terms of a unified whole as opposed to the Platonic matter vs. spirit, body vs. soul dualism, which characterizes the Western monotheistic worldview. For the Celts, the world and everything in it was part of the essential oneness of the gods and nature. As they encountered the visible world, "they saw a numinous aura that enlightened and warmed everything before them. Every hill was holy ... and could be the dwelling place of a deity" (Rabey 1998: 82). In her book *Drawing Down The Moon*, Margo Adler summarizes the mystical Celtic perspective: "The World is holy. Nature is holy. The body is holy. Sexuality is holy. The mind is holy. The imagination is holy. You are holy. ... Divinity is imminent in all Nature. It is as much within you as without" (Adler 1979:16).

My imagination that *The essence (soul) of everything and everyone / In the outer, visible world / Reflects (Mirror) and Reveals (Icon) / Something of our inner, invisible essence (soul)* was stimulated and fertilized over the years on numerous pilgrimages to ancient Celtic lands, particularly Ireland and Scotland. There, with keen attention, the thin places and thin times can still be experienced; that is, if one has a religious attitude similar to that proposed by analytical psychology. It was Jung's rich imagination and the empirical psychology that flowed from it that preserved the experience of the world as an ensouled thin place while speaking to the modern scientific mind. John O'Donohue, a beautiful Celtic soul, describes the imagination as the great friend of possibility and creativity. He writes, "The imagination works on the threshold that runs between light and dark, visible and invisible, quest and question, possibility and fact" (O'Donohue 1997: 183).

Jung's Essay, "Healing the Split," written late in his life, can be considered a commentary on the Celtic experience of the natural world as numinous. His essay is a lament over what has been lost in the modern world "through the destruction of its numinosities." In contrast to the Celtic experience, wherein both the visible and invisible worlds are holy, Jung offers this alarming critique: "We have stripped all things of their mystery and numinosity; nothing is holy any longer." The results, he writes, are dehumanizing and dangerous:

> Man feels himself isolated in the cosmos. He is no longer involved in nature and has lost his emotional participation in natural events, which hitherto had a symbolic meaning for him. ... His immediate communication with nature is gone forever, and the emotional energy it generated has sunk into the unconscious (Jung 1961: 255). ... The great religions of the world suffer from increasing anemia, because the helpful numina have fled from the woods, rivers, and mountains, and animals, and the God-men have disappeared underground into the unconscious. There we suppose they lead an ignominious existence among the relics of the past, while we are dominated by great *Deesse Raison*, who is our overwhelming illusion (Jung 1961: 261).

Considering our religious ancestors and their beliefs that spirits, gods, and goddesses were everywhere available, the modern mind inquires: *Where did those deities and spirits go? Where did the powerful and personal Greek deities who once inhabited Mount Olympus go, or those revered by the Egyptians or the Danes? Where did the God of the Bible go— that God who manifested in burning bushes, in dreams and visions, in a cloud by day and a fire by night? That God who appeared in a whirlwind, or in a still small voice? That God who spoke through Balaam's donkey, or the one who knocked Saul off his own donkey on his way to Damascus and on his way to becoming the Apostle Paul? What happened to all those very "real" deities so meaningful to our ancestors?*

With a giant leap of the imagination still not appreciated for its genius, Jung proposed that those powerful deities and devils who once populated the outer world disappeared into the unconscious where they are still actively approaching human consciousness day and night. Of course, the unconscious had always been their metaphorical habitat, but it can now be recognized as such by a more differentiated human consciousness. Those powerful, godlike energies continue to cross the invisible threshold in numerous manifestations, including dreams and visions, synchronistic events, so-called slips of the tongue, bodily and psychological symptoms, intuitions and, yes, via psychological projection so central to the paradigm being considered in this essay. The great gift of Jung's psychology might be the preservation of the experience of religious realities while honoring modern, scientific consciousness, thereby ending the unnecessary war between religion and science. For Jung, the universe is of one piece: *The spirit is the invisible aspect of matter, and matter is the visible aspect of spirit.* The human psyche is the mediator of the mysterious relationship, rendering obsolete notions of external mediators conceived as personified deities, religious institutions, priests and/or popes.

As explored in previous essays, the theistic and monotheistic god-images and the religions supported by them have lost their meaning for a growing populace of spiritual seekers, yet the energies and powers they once symbolized remain alive in the unconscious and make their incursions into consciousness in both creative and destructive ways. For many of us, the psychological myth referenced here replaces the theistic and monotheistic myths; it allows some to retain their identity as a religious person and provides those who prefer a nonreligious identity a meaningful alternative.

The 12-sentence paradigm, "The Universe as *Mirror* and *Icon*," may shed light on one further mystery—human consciousness and its creation and expansion. The disciplines of analytical psychology, philosophy, biology, and neurobiology continue to study this amazing human faculty, which is readily recognizable but escapes definition and explanation. In many ways, human consciousness is as elusive as "soul." We are yet to discover the physical basis of human consciousness and its relation to the brain; however, we have explored the revelatory dynamics of psychological projection, which contributes to the creation of consciousness.

It will be noted by the careful reader that in describing nature's unique gift to our species, I employed the phrase *self-reflection*, the capacity to stand outside oneself and to reflect on one's nature, as well as nature herself. That initial gift of self-reflection is often referred to as the gift of self-consciousness, yet in this essay I wanted to reserve the word "consciousness" for a more advanced psychic function, perhaps a further human gift and achievement. As used here, consciousness is more than awareness, though awareness might be a first step or stage. Being well-educated, or even being very sincere, does not equate with consciousness as defined here; neither is consciousness equated with knowledge or the acquisition of information. A person may be very knowledgeable about many things yet still exhibit attitudes and behavior that seem to come from the shallow end of the consciousness pool. Paradoxically, we have greater access to information and knowledge of the outer, physical world than ever before; almost unlimited knowledge is literally at our fingertips—one click away. Yet knowledge of the inner, invisible world, so essential to consciousness, lags dangerously behind.

Perhaps this discrepancy gives us a hint about the meaning of consciousness, at least one meaning. Edward Edinger's insightful book, *The Creation of Consciousness*, subtitled *Jung's Myth for Modern Man*, is a thorough exploration of the topic. With Edinger, we can imagine consciousness as a psychic substance, a substance created when opposites are sufficiently held and honored by the ego to allow an unforeseen third to emerge; the third would be a new increment of consciousness. The primary opposites of psychological life are conscious and unconscious, and it is the interplay and intercourse between them, mediated by the ego, by which new increments of consciousness are birthed (Edinger 1984: 17ff).

Addressing this vital topic in his autobiography, Jung offers a succinct summary of a lifetime of psychological exploration, and a poetic challenge to all psychologically minded readers:

> Man's task is … to become conscious of the contents
> that press upward from the unconscious. Neither should
> he persist in his unconsciousness nor remain identical
> with the unconscious elements of his being, thus

evading his destiny, which is to create more and more consciousness. As far as we can discern, the sole purpose of human existence is to kindle a light in the darkness of mere being. It may even be assumed that just as the unconscious affects us, so the increase in our conscious-ness affects the unconscious (Jung 1965: 326).

This passage distills the work of a lifetime, writes Edinger, "a life which in my opinion is the most conscious life ever lived. If we condense the statement to its essence we arrive at this: *The purpose of human life is the creation of consciousness*" (Edinger 1984: 57). Elsewhere Edinger expresses his conviction that Jung's discovery of his own personal myth will prove to be the first emergence of a new collective myth. Edinger concludes: "In fact it is my conviction that as we gain historical perspective it will become evident that Jung is an epochal man. I mean by this a man whose life inaugurates a new age in cultural history" (Edinger 1984: 12).

The purpose of human life is the creation of consciousness. This is the cornerstone of the emerging myth that Jung envisioned and that has caught the imagination of many others; and, it should be noted, has caught the idealization so apparent in Edinger's analysis. Edinger's remaining idealized projection can be forgiven, however, at least by this writer, who remains indebted to Jung and his interpreters and amplifiers for providing the outlines of a meaningful myth worth creative pursuit.

The passage quoted above concludes with Jung's far-reaching vision of the reciprocity of relationships, both psychological and theological: *It may even be assumed that just as the unconscious affects us, so the increase in our consciousness affects the unconscious* (Jung 1965: 326). When Jung makes the transfer from psychological language to religious/theological language, as he often does, the same reciprocity holds true. As an example, Jung the scientist and empiricist easily makes the transfer when he writes, "Man is the mirror God holds up before him (God), or the sense organ with which he apprehends his being" (Jung 1953: 112 Emphasis Mine). Or, in *Answer to Job*, Jung comments: "Existence is only real when it is conscious to somebody. That is why the Creator needs conscious man even though, from sheer unconsciousness, he would like to prevent him from becoming conscious" (Jung 1952b: 373). And in the same book: "Whoever knows God has an effect on him. The failure of the attempt to corrupt Job has changed Yahweh's nature" (Jung 1952b: 391). Jung had argued that Job, with his intense, insistent interaction with God had enabled God to become more conscious of heretofore divine unconsciousness. These examples of the reciprocity of the divine/human relationship caused, and continue to cause, great consternation among the literally minded religious. To the psychologically minded, however, the proposed dynamics ring true.

The personal paradigm explored in these pages provides a way to imagine how new increments of consciousness are created. With our imaginary standing place at the intersection where visible and invisible, matter and spirit, conscious and unconscious collide and converse, the self-reflecting ego has a remarkable opportunity and responsibility. Each moment as we bring our psychic *mirror* and *icon* to the imaginary crossroads, and participate *responsibly* in the ancient exchanges taking place there, we help to create new increments of consciousness. *Responsibly* means *To recognize / To own / And, where necessary, To transform the psychic content / To offer it back to the outer world / As conscious gift / For the continuing creation.* The paradigm seeks to identify an ongoing psychic process and the essential role the human psyche plays in it. The process may be instantaneous or extended over long periods of time, but with each completed exchange, consciousness is birthed. Consciousness, then, can be understood as an internalized, integrated, and incarnated awareness; or, succinctly, embodied awareness.

The *myth of consciousness* grew out of Carl Jung's deep immersion into the unconscious, his own intimate connection to nature, and his lifelong exploration of religious realities. Taken in its entirety, the myth of consciousness can be seen as a necessary and timely compensation to the prevailing myths that have formed and deformed theistic and monotheistic religions and the institutions, cultures, and politics they have inspired. The goal of analytical psychology could accurately be summarized as the promotion of human consciousness in general and religious consciousness in particular. The same could be said about the goal of a Jungian analysis or the goal of in-depth dreamwork. The expansion of consciousness in general and religious consciousness in particular promotes the process Jung calls individuation, whereby one's empathic embrace extends to all inner and outer friends and strangers alike. Far from individualism, which shrinks one's world, individuation extends one's borders, known and yet-to-be-known.

While the expansion of consciousness and the widening of one's embrace extends over a lifetime, daily choices either promote or frustrate the process of individuation. James Hollis provides very practical, yet profound, wisdom in this regard. He suggests, "Ask yourself of every dilemma, every choice, every relationship, every commitment. ... Does this choice diminish or enlarge me? ... Does this path, this choice, make me larger or smaller?" We usually know the answer intuitively, he notes, but we may be afraid of what we know and even more afraid of what the choice may ask of us (Hollis 2009: 13, 71). Such an approach to our everyday decision-making can be very clarifying; not just for our personal lives, but also for the effect we have on the collective. Growth in consciousness is individual and personal but never private; it impacts the whole world.

While the creation of consciousness may be our psychological purpose and humanity's highest achievement, it can also become an idol to be worshipped rather than a means to a greater end. Consciousness in itself is not the cure for what ails the human soul or our species or our world. Yet it is the best medicine for the human ego, which serves either as a conduit for the deep springs of unconscious life or which frustrates the same. Consciousness dilutes egocentricity, the inflated notion Jung often described as "god-almighty-ness," the illusion that we stand alone and above all else. Consciousness gives birth to compassion, which allows the ego to experience itself as a conduit for a larger life and a bridge to all of life.

Summarizing the larger myth to which this brief paradigm points, Edinger writes poetically:

> The new myth postulates that the created universe
> and its most exquisite flower, man (sic), make up a vast
> enterprise for the creation of consciousness; that each
> individual is a unique experiment in that process; and
> that the sum total of consciousness created by each
> individual in his lifetime is deposited as a permanent
> addition in the collective treasury of the archetypal
> psyche (Edinger 1984: 23).

Finally, reiterating what was said in the first part of this Essay, imagining "The Universe as *Mirror* and *Icon*" is not a statement to be believed. Rather, it is offered as a possible spiritual discipline or practice; that is, to live *as if* it could be true. Experiment with holding it before your eyes as you go through your day and see what happens both internally and externally. Experiment, too, with verbalizing your own paradigm, your own map of reality and your possible place/role in the larger scheme of this awesome universe.

AFTERWORD

I had a dream. I have a dream.

I had a dream that I took to my first Jungian analyst a half-lifetime ago when I was 38. It was an initial dream that often speaks to the major issues and complexes that are seeking consciousness. Initial dreams often lay out the psychological contours of a Jungian analysis, though those contours are initially unseen, even unimaginable to the dreamer. Analysts may carefully, reverently, hold the initial dream(s) of their clients in their consciousness while watching for how and when their meanings may be revealed; neither is the analyst initially privy to the dream's mysterious manifestation and potential meanings. The dream:

> My father has died, and we are standing beside the casket at the gravesite. A disembodied voice announces that there cannot be a burial until an autopsy is performed. I reach for the casket to brush off some ice/snow around the edges while asking, "Is this OK?"
> The voice replies, "Sure."

The size or length of a dream has little to do with its significance. Brief dreams may have enormous existential value and multiple meanings that continue to reveal themselves for many years. Such is the case here. The dream remains alive to this day and will likely continue to be a source of revelation.

In retrospect, the second half of my psychological life has been an autopsy of the death of my *father* in the many meanings of that *complex* identity. My biological father had died a decade before this dream. He was the oldest of 12 siblings, a hard worker and good provider. Emotionally distant except for regular outbursts of anger growing out of his own frustrations, he expressed his love by faithful attendance at my sports endeavors from childhood through college. As a spectator, his loud verbal critiques of the various umpires' decisions were meant to be supportive of his only son; they were also an embarrassment to me—shy, introverted, not wishing to be seen in that way. He was only 52 when he died of lung cancer. He died just before I was emotionally ready to reconnect with him as a young father myself. The early part of my analysis involved grieving that primary relationship, including brushing off the ice and snow, which was symbolic of our emotional relationship. It was also a wake-up call to be more emotionally available to my own three children. As parents, we may repeat how we were parented or go to the other extreme declaring we will be just the opposite, thereby falling in the opposite ditch. Or, with the hard work of consciousness, we can choose something different that fits with our own personality and desires. Parental complexes, both father and mother, frequently occupy the first stages of psychoanalysis and get recycled throughout. The autopsy of the historical and personal father, and my own parenting as a father, continue to this day.

In my professional life as a Presbyterian pastor and Jungian analyst, I have been privileged to serve as a *spiritual and/or psychological father* to many, with a mixture of satisfaction and some inevitable regrets. The helping professions often attract those who need help themselves. That attraction can be doubled-edged. On the one hand, attending to the needs of others can be an escape from tending our own. On the other hand, our mistakes and missteps can force us into therapy and/or analysis. Some of us become analysts because we need so much analysis! The prospective nature of my dream suggested that a continuing examination, a con-tinuing autopsy, of the ever-changing role as pastor and later as a Jungian analyst, would be required.

One further autopsy has motivated and necessitated this writing project, and, in many ways, it remains the most significant at this stage of my life. Unknown and unforeseen by me at the time, yet apparently clear to the unconscious, the dream *foresaw* the death for me of the images *Father God* or *Heavenly Father*, including the inevitable grieving and the necessary autopsy. In an earlier Essay, "Beyond the Back Porch of the Church," I acknowledge the unconscious grief that had symptomized in anger and loss of meaning prior to leaving the sanctuary and the safety of the Church. The ice and snow on the casket were symbolic of the lack of warmth the traditional religious structures and interpretations were providing. They had become cold, frozen, and rigid.

In retrospect, the last half of my life has been directed by the scary and sacred autopsy of the death of the monotheistic myth with its core image of an external, metaphysical, interventionist, divine *Father*. The autopsy report includes the following:

> With the necessary demise and death of antique cosmologies and traditional religious paradigms dependent on external supernatural deities and devils, the modern religious challenge involves two simultaneous sacred endeavors: to eulogize, bury, and grieve the theistic and monotheistic god-images and the religious paradigms dependent on them; and secondly, to bring fresh imagination to the meanings of *god* and *religion* that will satisfy both the modern mind and ancient soul (from Essay "Reimagining *God* and *Religion*").

Autopsies are performed for numerous reasons. In all cases, they are for the benefit of the living rather than for the deceased. They may provide critical information about the cause of death, which may be helpful to the grieving. They may provide research information, which can assist the living in terms of quantity and quality of life. They can provide information about *what was* in order to imagine *what could be*. Physical autopsies are about examining the past in order to be helpful to the present and to anticipate the future.

Religious autopsies may perform a similar function, which brings me back to the aforementioned *I have a dream*. Metaphorically, this dream originates in the future and approaches humanity over the distant horizon. If night-time dreams emerge from the mysterious depths of life, this dream approaches us from the far evolutionary horizon. Ordinarily, we think of the future as an extension of the past coming through the present. Yet, we can also imagine we meet the future as it comes toward us from beyond the horizon, a future inviting human consciousness, and needing human consciousness, to manifest, to materialize. This perspective is an extension of Jung's far-reaching intuition that divinity needs human consciousness to become conscious of itself. To entertain that possibility, one has to get beyond the theistic and monotheistic god-image, which these essays propose has lost its meaning and its evolutionary role. It requires that we bring fresh imagination to the meanings of *god* and *religion* if we are to move beyond our divisive, tribal religions to embrace inclusive, global ones. That is the future of which I dream.

Being reared in a conservative tradition, an old religious adage comes to mind: *You must practice what you preach!* It remains a worthy injunction as an antidote to self-righteousness and religious inflation. However, I do not think we are limited to preach/teach/write only that which we perfectly practice. If that were the case, most sermons would be much shorter, political rhetoric would practically cease, and, as I said in the Introduction, this book would be much shorter! Rather than being limited to that which we practice perfectly, I believe we are asked *to preach/ teach/write to the limit of our vision*. We are asked to attend the images that emerge from the psychological depths and to engage our greatest resource, the human imagination, to birth the images into consciousness. Paraphrasing the mystic Meister Eckhart, *when the soul wishes to express herself, she throws out before her an image, and then enters the image.* We meet soul, then, as we engage the images presented to us night and day that emerge from the mysterious realm Jung called the collective unconscious. We must nurture those images for they are our connection to the past and the seedbed for the future.

As I scan the distant religious horizon, my dream is for religions that will be inclusive, intellectually and scientifically honest, and soul-satisfying. They will be free from imagined external deities and devils. They will build bridges rather than walls, however defined. In the meantime, the unconscious grieving of the death of theism and monotheism will continue with its attendant individual and collective pathos. My psychological conclusion: *As long as our deities and devils are perceived to be beyond the physical world and outside the human psyche, we will continue to do great harm to each other and to our nest.* The fertile marriage of unconscious and conscious has the potential to birth new images of *god* and *religion*.

Hopefully, our species will eventually embrace the psychological conclusion that it is the human imagination that creates god-images and religions, drawing from a meta-personal storehouse of accumulated wisdom. The language to describe these creative mysteries will likely evolve, yet the conclusion seems inevitable. Thus far, theistic and mono-theistic religions have outsourced what is best and worst about our species. The religion of the future will facilitate the retrieval of our capacities for great good and great evil so that we will have some measure of choice about which to incarnate.

Looking back from a place far down the evolutionary road, we may see the religions of the past as necessary stages along a twisting, laby-rinthine path toward the realization that *we are, in fact, what we imaged our former deities and devils to be.* No, we will not see ourselves as gods. Rather, we will accept our full humanity through whom both godly and demonic powers are manifest. Our species will come to recognize and own both our gore and glory, which were projected, necessarily so, onto external deities and devils. We will conclude that, in the wisdom of psyche, it was necessary to see our creative and destructive capacities in projected form until we could own them and manifest both responsibly. Squinting, that is as far as I can see.

However, the realization of the potentials our species once deemed divine will have little resemblance to the illusory super-race or superman syndrome that grew out of the Enlightenment. The antidote to religious or psychological inflation will be the ready reminder of our individual and collective shadow, our capacity for destruction. That dark reminder will light our path forward.

Until we can collectively own that darkness, my immediate concern is whether our species can survive and thrive. To be religiously and psychologically honest, we need to acknowledge that our species may well self-destruct, though the cosmic drama playing long before our arrival would continue. The universe did not come into being solely to meet our species' narcissistic needs, nor does it need our species to continue; that may be a hard religious pill to swallow. We have created massive numbers of instruments of our suicide, which are not-so-safely stored underground, while we spend an inordinate amount of international concern trying to keep more deadly instruments out of the hands of our competitors. Of course, as the world's superpower, America maintains the illusion that we, and we only, are capable of using the instruments of suicide wisely and responsibly, while being the world's chief supplier of armaments. As discussed in an earlier essay, technological information is not synonymous with consciousness. At present, we do not have the collective *psychological technology* necessary for our long-term survival as a species. That was Jung's chief concern; the same concern has fueled this writing.

Paradoxically, for Western culture, which worships at the altars of progress, our future may well depend on coming to terms with our *finitude* rather than trusting in *plenitude.* Our relationship with limits, mortality, and death must replace our worship of abundance, progress, and eternal life; this will be a difficult political and religious sell. Many of our daily concerns are First World worries—my cell phone is not getting good reception; the warning light in my car has come on; my suit or dress is out of style, etc. Collectively, we judge a good day by whether the stock market is up or down. America is a nation of plenty, though with plenty of people in dire straits kept out of sight, even as we try to keep our concerns about our aging, our mortality, our sure and certain death out of sight. Those individual delusions are multiplied in our collective refusal to look at climate change, world hunger, the growing gap between wealth and poverty, and our suicidal relationship with armaments of all shapes and sizes. A further delusion casts these human issues as political rather than religious; we prefer to keep our religious life, and hands, sanitized.

Many years ago, one of my mentors, Quaker John Yungblut, offered wise counsel as he engaged us on retreat and as he engaged his own health concerns, advanced Parkinson's disease. Without blame or self-pity, he said that his current religious task was learning "to hallow my diminishment." It is a phrase whose meaning I will always remember: to *make holy* his decline, his limitations, his mortality, his impending death. He was speaking about his individual situation but he speaks for all of us. No one has gotten out of this life alive, though we all think at some level we will be the exception. How do we hallow this life in all its gore and glory rather than running from it with hollow pursuits? How do we claim our kinship with all rather than competing as if we have unlimited time and resources? What does it mean to be number one if we are no longer around to do a victory dance? As part of my dream, the religions of the future will need to help us live this mortal life fully, passionately, and compassionately rather than promising eternal life and a heavenly reward. Life may well continue in some form since the energy of which we are made never ceases but transforms; however, that possible form lies beyond the reach of our imagination. I have yet to hear a view of heaven that sounds inviting, though I am open to being surprised.

As mentioned in an earlier essay, Jung imagined it would take about 600 years for a new religious myth to emerge. That was a guess, but an educated guess, from one who had descended more deeply into the unconscious, stayed longer, and emerged to write more extensively than anyone so far. He is not to be worshipped, though he might be honored for being fully human, having lived a creative life of passion with compassionate concern for our species. Living our own passion along with compassionate concern for our global community strikes me as a worthy form of worship.

While expressing his concern for our future, Jung remained hopeful, as do I. Half of that hope lies in the power of consciousness itself, the capacity of individuals to be the conduits of the resources of the deep springs of life itself. Small as our individual advancements in conscious-ness may be—akin to placing an infinitesimal grain of sand on the scale of humanity's soul—we would do well to assume that our small offering may tip the scale toward wholeness. The other half of my hope lies in that indescribable, indefinable mystery that, thankfully, lies just beyond my grasp and my knowing, the pursuit of which gives my life meaning.

In the final analysis, writes Jung, our lives count for something only as we are related to that which is greater than we, by whatever image or name we choose to evoke and honor; and if we are not related to such, our life is wasted. Evoking the image of *living spirit*, he concludes:

> The living spirit grows and even outgrows its earlier forms of expression. … This living spirit is eternally renewed and pursues its goal in manifold and in-conceivable ways throughout the history of mankind. Measured against it, the names and forms which men have given it mean very little; they are only the changing leaves and blossoms on the stem of the eternal tree (Jung 1934b: 347).

May it be so!

REFERENCES

Adler, Margot. (1979) *Drawing Down the Moon,* Boston, MA: Beacon Press.

Armstrong, Karen. (2009) *The Case for God*, New York, NY: Anchor Books.

Armstrong, Karen. (2015) *Fields of Blood*, New York, NY: Anchor Books.

Arnold, Matthew. (1965) *The Poems of Matthew Arnold,* Kenneth Allott (ed) London: Longman.

Barrows Anita and Macy Joanna. (Trans). (1996) *Rilke's Book of Hours: Love Poems to God*, New York, NY: Riverhead Books.

Barks, Coleman. (2006) "The Guest House," *A Year with Rumi*, New York, NY: HarperCollins Publishers.

Berry, Wendell. (2010) *Leavings*, Berkeley, CA: Counterpoint.

Bly, Robert. (Trans). (1981) *Selected Poems of Rainer Maria Rilke,* New York, NY: Harper and Row.

Borg, Marcus. (2006) *Jesus: Uncovering the Life, Teachings, and Relevance of a Religious Revolutionary*, San Francisco, CA: Harper.

Bourgeault, Cynthia. (2008) *The Wisdom Jesus,* Boston, MA: Shambhala Publications.

Clark, David and Roberts Andy. (1996) *Twilight of the Celtic Gods,* London: Cassell PLC.

Corbett, Lionel. (2007) *Psyche and the Sacred,* New Orleans, LA: Spring Journal Books.

Cowan, Tom. (1993) *Fire in the Head*, New York, NY: Harper and Collins.

Dillard, Annie. (1982) *Teaching A Stone to Talk*, New York, NY: Harper and Row.

Dols, William L., Jr. (1987) "The Church as Crucible for Transformation," in Murray Stein and Robert Moore (eds) *Jung's Challenge to Contemporary Religion*, Wilmette, IL: Chiron Publications.

Dourley, J. (1981) *The Psyche as Sacrament,* Toronto, Canada: Inner City Books.

Dourley, J. (1985) *The Illness We Are*, Toronto, Canada: Inner City Books.

Dourley, J. (1992) *A Strategy for a Loss of Faith, Jung's Proposal*, Toronto, Canada: Inner City Books.

Dourley, J. (2010) *On Behalf of the Mystical Fool, Jung on the Religious Situation,* New York, NY: Routledge.

Edinger, Edward F. (1984) *The Creation of Consciousness,* Toronto, Canada: Inner City Books.

----- (1996a) The *New God-Image,* Wilmette, IL: Chiron Publications.

----- (1996b) *The Aion Lectures: Exploring the Self in C. G. Jung's Aion,* Toronto, Canada: Inner City Press.

Estes, Clarissa Pinkola, Audiotape #A118: "The Radiant Coat," Boulder, CO: Sounds True.

Fleming, F., Husain S., Littleton C. (1996) *Heroes of the Dawn,* Amsterdam: Time-Life Books.

Hiles Marv and Nancy. (2008) *An Almanac for the Soul,* Sonoma, CA: AJ Printing and Graphics.

Hitchens, Christopher. (2007) *God is Not Great: How Religion Poisons Everything,* New York, NY: Hachette Book Group.

Hollis, James. (2000) *The Archetypal Imagination,* College Station, TX: Texas A&M University Press.

Hollis, James. (2001) *Creating a Life,* Toronto, Canada: Inner City Books.

Hollis, James. (2003) *On This Journey We Call Our Lives,* Toronto, Canada: Inner City Books.

Hollis, James. (2005) *Finding Meaning in the Second Half of Life,* New York, NY: Gotham Books.

Hollis, James. (2009) *What Matters Most: Living a More Considered Life,* New York, NY: Penguin Press.

Howes, Elizabeth Boyden. (1971) *Intersection and Beyond Volume I,* San Francisco, CA: The Guild for Psychological Studies.

Jaffe, Aniela. (1989) *Was C.G. Jung a Mystic?* Einsiedeln, Switzerland: Daimon Verlag.

Johnson, Robert. (2008) *Inner Gold,* Kihei, HI: Koa Books.

Joyce, Timothy. (1998) *Celtic Christianity,* Maryknoll, NY: Orbis Books.

Jung C. G. (1916) "General Aspects of Dream Psychology," *The Structure and Dynamics of the Psyche, Collected Works, Volume 8,* Princeton, NJ: Princeton University Press.

----- (1920) "The Psychological Foundations of Belief in Spirits," *The Structure and Dynamics of the Psyche, Collected Works, Volume 8,* Princeton, NJ: Princeton University Press.

----- (1924) "The Spiritual Problem of Modern Man," *Civilization in Transition, Collected Works, Volume 10,* Princeton, NJ: Princeton University Press.

----- (1927) "Analytical Psychology and Weltanschauung," *The Structure and Dynamics of the Psyche, Collected Works, Volume 8,* Princeton, NJ: Princeton University Press.

----- (1930) "Psychology and Literature," *The Spirit in Man, Art, and Literature. Collected Works, Volume 15,* Princeton, NJ: Princeton University Press.

----- (1931) "Archaic Man," *Civilization in Transition, Collected Works, Volume 10,* Princeton, NJ: Princeton University Press.

----- (1933) "The Meaning of Psychology for Modern Man," *Civilization in Transition, Collected Works, Volume 10,* Princeton, NJ: Princeton University Press.

----- (1934a) "Archetypes of the Collective Unconscious," *The Archetypes of the Collective Unconscious,* Volume 9i, Princeton, NJ: Princeton University Press.

----- (1934b) "Psychotherapists or the Clergy," *Psychology and Religion: West and East, Collected Works, Volume 11,* Princeton, NJ: Princeton University Press.

----- (1934c) Letter to James Kirsch, 29 September 1934, in G. Adler and A. Jaffe (eds) *C. G. Jung Letters, Volume I, 1906-1950,* Princeton, NJ: Princeton University Press.

----- (1935) "The Tavistock Lectures," *The Symbolic Life, Collected Works, Volume 18,* Princeton, NJ: Princeton University Press.

----- (1937) "Psychology and Religion," *Psychology and Religion: West and East, Collected Works, Volume 11,* Princeton, NJ: Princeton University Press.

----- (1939) "The Tibetan Book of the Dead," *Psychology and Religion: West and East, Collected Works, Volume 11,* Princeton, NJ: Princeton University Press.

----- (1941) "Psychotherapy Today," *The Practice of Psychotherapy, Collected Works, Volume 16,* Princeton, NJ: Princeton University Press.

----- (1942) "A Psychological Approach to the Dogma of the Trinity," *Psychology and Religion: West and East, Collected Works, Volume 11,* Princeton, NJ: Princeton University Press.

----- (1943a) "The Psychic Nature of the Alchemical Work," *Psychology and Alchemy, Collected Works, Volume 12,* Princeton, NJ: Princeton University Press.

----- (1943b) "Introduction to the Religious and Psychological Problems of Alchemy," *Psychology and Alchemy, Collected Works, Volume 12,* Princeton, NJ: Princeton University Press.

----- (1944) "Individual Dream Symbolism in Relation to Alchemy," *Psychology and Alchemy, Collected Works, Volume 12*, Princeton, NJ: Princeton University Press.

----- (1945) "The Phenomenology of the Spirit in Fairy Tales," *The Archetypes of the Collective Unconscious, Collected Works, Volume 9i*, Princeton, NJ: Princeton University Press.

----- (1945b) Letter to P. W. Martin, 20 August 1945, in G. Adler and A. Jaffe (eds) *C. G. Jung Letters, Volume I, 1906-1950*, Princeton, NJ: Princeton University Press.

----- (1945c) "On the Nature of Dreams," *The Structure and Dynamics of the Psyche, Collected Works, Volume 8*, Princeton NJ: Princeton University Press.

----- (1946a) "The Fight with the Shadow," *Civilization in Transition, Collected Works, Volume 10*, Princeton, NJ: Princeton University Press.

----- (1946b) "On the Nature of the Psyche," *The Structure and Dynamics of the Psyche, Collected Works, Volume 8*, Princeton, NJ: Princeton University Press.

----- (1948) "The Shadow," *Aion, Collected Works, Volume 9ii*, Princeton, NJ: Princeton University Press.

----- (1952a) "Synchronicity: An Acausal Connecting Principle," *The Structure and Dynamics of the Psyche, Collected Works, Volume 8*, Princeton, NJ: Princeton University Press.

----- (1952b) "Answer to Job," *Psychology and Religion: West and East, Collected Works, Volume 11*, Princeton, NJ: Princeton University Press.

----- (1953) Letter to Pastor Amstutz, 28 March 1953, in G. Adler and A. Jaffe (eds) *C. G. Jung Letters, Volume II*, Princeton, NJ: Princeton University Press.

----- (1954) "Transformation Symbolism in the Mass," *Psychology and Religion: West and East, Collected Works, Volume 11*, Princeton, NJ: Princeton University Press.

----- (1954b) "On Resurrection," *The Symbolic Life, Collected Works, Volume 18*, Princeton, NJ: Princeton University Press.

----- (1955a) Letter to Walter Bernet, 13 June 1955, in G. Adler and A. Jaffe (eds) *C. G. Jung Letters, Volume II, 1951-1961*, Princeton, NJ: Princeton University Press.

----- (1955b) Letter to Helene Kiener, 15 June 1955, in G. Adler and A. Jaffe (eds) *C. G. Jung Letters, Volume II, 1951-1961*, Princeton, NJ: Princeton University Press.

----- (1955c) Letter to Piero Cogo, 21 September 1955, in G. Adler and A. Jaffe (eds) *C. G. Jung Letters, Volume II, 1951-61*, Princeton, NJ: Princeton University Press.

----- (1955d) *Modern Man in Search of a Soul*, San Diego, CA: Harcourt Harvest.

----- (1956) "The Hymn of Creation," *Symbols of Transformation, Collected Works, Volume 5*, Princeton NJ: Princeton University Press.

----- (1957) "Commentary on the Secret of the Golden Flower," *Alchemical Studies, Collected Works, Volume 13*, Princeton, NJ: Princeton University Press.

----- (1958) "Jung and Religious Belief," *The Symbolic Life, Collected Works, Volume 18*, Princeton, NJ: Princeton University Press.

----- (1959a) "Christ, A Symbol of the Self," *Aion, Collected Works, Volume 9ii*, Princeton, NJ: Princeton University Press.

----- (1959b) "Foreword," *Aion, Collected Works, Volume 9ii*, Princeton, NJ: Princeton University Press.

----- (1960) Letter to Pastor Oscar Nisse, 2 July 1960, in G. Adler and A. Jaffe (eds) *C.G. Jung Letters, Volume II, 1951-1961*, Princeton, NJ: Princeton University Press.

----- (1961) "Healing the Split," *The Symbolic Life, Volume 18*, Princeton, NJ: Princeton University Press.

----- (1963) "The Conjunction," *Mysterium Coniunctionis, Collected Works, Volume 14*, Princeton, NJ: Princeton University Press.

----- (1964) *Man and His Symbols*, San Sebastian, Spain: Tonsa.

----- (1965) *Memories, Dreams, Reflections*, A. Jaffe (ed.), New York, NY: Vintage, Random House.

Kalsched, Donald. (1996) *The Inner World of Trauma*, London: Routledge.

Lachman, Gary. (2010) *Jung the Mystic*, New York, NY: Penguin Publishers.

Ladinsky, Daniel. Trans. (1996) "Ten Thousand Idiots," *The Subject Tonight Is Love*, New York: NY: Penguin Books.

Ladinsky, Daniel. Trans. (1999) *The Gift: Poems by Hafiz the Great Sufi Master*, New York, NY: Penguin Books.

Ladinsky, Daniel. Trans. (2002) "Beautiful Creature," *Love Poems from God*, New York, NY: Penguin Books.

Moore, Thomas. (2002) *The Soul's Religion*, New York, NY: Harper/Collins Publishers.

Newell, John P. (2008) *Christ of the Celts: The Healing of Creation*, San Francisco, CA: Jossey-Bass.

Newell, John P. (2011) *A New Harmony*, San Francisco, CA: Jossey-Bass.

Nye, William S. (2014) *Undeniable, Evolution and the Science of Creation*, New York, NY: St. Martin's Press.

O'Donohue, John. (1997) *Anam Cara*, London: Bantam Press.

O'Donohue, John. (2008) *To Bless the Space Between Us*, New York: Doubleday.

Oliver, Mary. (1992) "The Summer Day", *New and Selected Poems*, Boston, MA: Beacon Press.

Oliver, Mary. (2004) "Mindful," *Why I Wake Early*, Boston: Beacon Press.

Otto, R. (1923) *The Idea of the Holy*, London: Oxford University Press.

Pennick, Nigel. (1996) *Celtic Sacred Landscapes*, New York, NY: Thames and Hudson.

Pannikar, Ramon. (2010) *National Catholic Reporter*, October 1, 2010.

Rabey, Steve. (1998) *In the House of Memory*, New York, NY: Dutton.

Sagan, Carl. (1996) *The Demon-Haunted World*, New York, NY: Ballantine Books.

Sanford, John. (1981) *Evil: The Shadow Side of Reality*, New York, NY: Crossroad.

Sellner, Edward C. (1993) *Wisdom of the Celtic Saints*, New York, NY: Ave Maria Press.

Spong, John S. (2001) *A New Christianity for a New World*, New York, NY: HarperCollins Publishers.

Stein, Murray. (1985) *Jung's Treatment of Christianity*, Wilmette, IL: Chiron Publications.

Stein, Murray and Moore, Robert (Eds). (1987) *Jung's Challenge to Contemporary Religion*, Wilmette, IL: Chiron Publications.

Stein, Murray. (1998a) *Transformation, Emergence of the Self*, College Station, TX: Texas A & M University Press.

Stein, Murray. (1998b) *Jung's Map of the Soul*, Peru, IL: Carus Publishing Company.

Swimme, Brian. (1984) *The Universe Is a Green Dragon*, Santa Fe, NM: Bear & Company.

Ulanov, Ann B. (1971) *The Feminine in Jungian Psychology and in Christian Theology*, Evanston, IL: Northwestern University Press.

Wilson, Edward O. (2014) *The Meaning of Human Existence*, New York, NY: Liveright Publishing.

Wink, Walter. (2002) *The Human Being*, Minneapolis: MN: Fortress Press.

Yeats, William B. (ed) (2003) *Irish Fairy and Folk Tales*, New York, NY: The Modern Library.

Yeats, William B. (1902) *The Celtic Twilight: Myth, Fantasy, and Folklore*, Dorset, England: Prism Press.

Zeller, Max. (1975) *The Dream, The Vision of the Night*, Boston: Sigo Press.

CPSIA information can be obtained
at www.ICGtesting.com
Printed in the USA
LVHW030359091118
596536LV00005B/92